Helion & Company Limited
Unit 8 Amherst Business Centre
Budbrooke Road
Warwick
CV34 5WE
England
Tel. 01926 499 619
Email: info@helion.co.uk
Website: www.helion.co.uk
Twitter: @helionbooks
Visit our blog http://blog.helion.co.uk/

Designed and typeset by Farr out Publications, Wokingham, Berkshire
Cover design by Paul Hewitt, Battlefield Design (www.battlefield-design.co.uk)
Printed by Henry Ling Limited, Dorchester, Dorset

ISBN 978-1-913118-64-8

British Library Cataloguing-in-Publication Data
A catalogue record for this book is available from the British Library

We always welcome receiving book proposals from prospective authors.

Cover painting by Group Captain S. M. Hussaini (retired)

CONTENTS

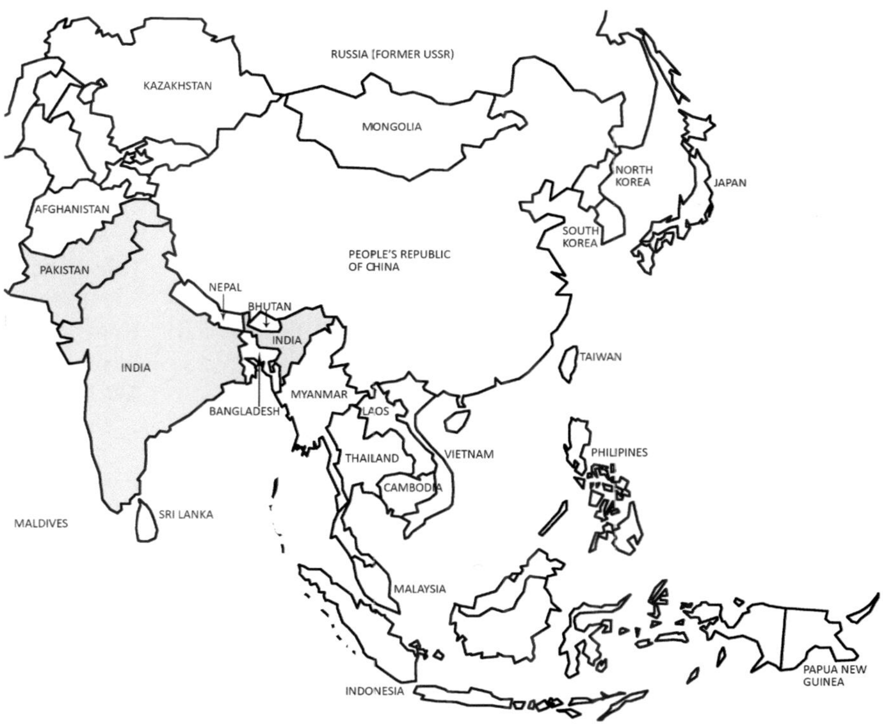

Note: In order to simplify the use of this book, all names, locations and geographic designations are as provided in *The Times World Atlas*, or other traditionally accepted major sources of reference, as of the time of described events.

GLOSSARY OF MILITARY TERMS

Afterburner – A device for augmenting the thrust of a jet engine by burning additional fuel with unburnt oxygen in the hot gases within the tailpipe. The process of regular combustion in the combustion chamber is not affected by afterburning.

Air Interdiction – Air Interdiction involves application of air power against enemy lines of communications well beyond the battlefield, to cut and disrupt the flow of supplies to land forces. Air Interdiction is an indirect form of air support and is aimed at influencing future land battles.

Airfield Strike – These are missions flown to destroy runways and airfield infrastructure, so as to prevent the enemy aircraft from taking off, and to inhibit aircraft maintenance and support operations.

Armed Reconnaissance – This type of mission directly targets trains and vehicular convoys, instead of the lines of communications. Since the targets are in motion, and can emerge at short notice, on-call aircraft reconnoitre the area to pick up the targets. Formation members then take turns to attack, as well as sanitise the area.

ASV – Anti-Surface Vessel warfare

ASW – Anti-Submarine Warfare

Bail out – To jump out of an aircraft by parachute during an emergency.

Barrel Roll – A roll that describes a corkscrew path on the inside of an imaginary barrel. Its three-dimensional flight path helps dissipate forward motion, making it an important tool in air combat both for offensive and defensive purposes.

Battle Formation – A loose formation of four aircraft usually in the shape of a square with sides of about 1-2 miles, depending on the visibility.

Battlefield Air Interdiction – These are missions directed against enemy ground forces and resources within the battlefield that are in a position to directly influence and affect land operations.

Blip – A spot of light on a radar screen indicating the position of a detected object, such as an aircraft.

Bogey – An enemy aircraft, as reported by the radar controller or a fellow wingman.

Break – A turn at the maximum possible rate, without regard to depletion of energy. A break is called by any formation member when an enemy aircraft is sighted within weapon firing range and shooting down is imminent.

CAP – Combat Air Patrol

CAS/Close Air Support – These missions are flown against hostile targets (usually armour) which are in close proximity to friendly forces. This proximity requires close coordination and detailed integration of each mission with the fire and movement of those forces. Close Air Support is aimed at influencing the on-going land battle.

Company – A company is an army sub-unit, commanded by a Major with strength varying from 80-150 personnel in different arms and services. In the organizational hierarchy, companies are normally organic to battalions, but they can be organized to operate as independent sub-units as well.

Concept of Operations – It is a broad outline of a commander's assumptions or intent in regard to an operation or series of operations. The concept of operations is usually embodied in operational plans. The concept is designed to give an overall picture of the operation.

Contact – Visual sighting or radar contact of an aircraft.

DCA/Defensive Counter-Air Operations – Also known simply as 'air defence', these operations are aimed at intercepting attackers. These operations take place in friendly territory, hence the term 'defensive' counter-air. Like Offensive Counter-Air (OCA) operations, DCA operations help achieve some degree of control of the air. The missions entail ground scramble by aircraft on Air Defence Alert, as well as standing Combat Air Patrols (CAPs). When flown over the battle area, these missions are called Forward Edge of the Battle Area patrols (FEBA CAPs).

Drop Tanks – Aircraft fuel tanks mounted externally under the wings or fuselage, which can be jettisoned before air combat or exit at high speed.

Echelon Formation – Aircraft staggered 45° to each other, either close or farther apart.

ECM – Electronic Counter-Measures

ELINT/Electronic Intelligence – Is the collection of enemy's electromagnetic emissions for subsequent analysis, to build up an EOB. Electronic countermeasures are then conducted on the basis of the EOB.

EOB – Electronic Order of Battle.

EOT – Ejected in Own Territory.

Escort – These missions are flown by fighters whose role is to defend the strike aircraft from enemy interceptors. 'Dedicated' escorts perform this role exclusively and are configured only for aerial fighting. 'Armed' escorts, on the other hand, are basically armed for the strike mission; they double up as escorts after jettisoning their bombload, whenever the need arises.

FEBA/Forward Edge of Battle Area – Within the combat zone, FEBA denotes the forwardmost deployment limit of ground combat units. It, however, excludes the area in which the covering or screening troops may be operating.

Fighter Sweep – These missions are flown to destroy patrolling enemy aircraft.

Hard Turn – An energy-conserving turn, tight enough to ward off a threat that is not imminently dangerous.

Infra-Red Missile – A short range missile, which homes on to heat radiation from the target's jet exhaust.

Knots – Nautical miles per hour; a nautical mile (2,000 yards) is 1.15 times a statute mile (1,760 yards).

Mach Number – Ratio of the speed of an aircraft to the speed of sound in the surrounding atmosphere; named after Austrian physicist Ernst Mach. An aircraft flying at the speed of sound would thus be flying at Mach 1. The speed of sound varies from 660 knots at sea level, to 572 knots at 36,090 feet. This altitude band, known as the troposphere, is characterised by decreasing temperature with increasing altitude.

Maritime Air Support – It is provided to directly support maritime operations. Missions include ASW and ASV. Due to their highly specialised nature, these roles are usually performed by naval air arms, but sometimes supplemented by air forces.

Mission – An aerial mission involves one or several formations of aircraft assigned a specific task.

OCA/Offensive Counter-Air Operations – The aim of these operations is to nullify the enemy's ability to conduct a meaningful air campaign, thus helping the friendly air force to establish some degree of control of the air. To achieve this end, several types of missions are flown in enemy territory, hence 'offensive' counter-air. These include Airfield Strike, Fighter Sweep, Escort, and Suppression of Enemy Air Defences (SEAD).

Photo Reconnaissance – These missions involve gathering information by airborne means using the medium of photography, which could be in the visual or infra-red spectrum. As opposed to surveillance, reconnaissance (or recce) is done against specific tactical targets and lasts for limited periods.

Pip – To press the weapon-firing button.

Pipper – Aiming index in an optical gunsight.

Pitch – Aircraft motion about its lateral axis, which causes the nose to lift or drop in relation to the tail.

PRC – People's Republic of China.

Pulse Doppler Radar – It is a radar system that determines the range to a target using pulse-timing techniques and uses the Doppler effect of the returned signal to determine the target object's velocity. Doppler techniques also allow the ground returns to be filtered out, revealing aircraft and vehicles. This gives pulse Doppler radars what is known as 'look-down/shoot-down' capability.

Reticle – A diamond-shaped or other circular pattern placed in the gunsight optics, for purposes of aiming and sighting.

Riposte – It is a 'space oriented' trans-frontier offensive operation conducted by the side on the defensive. A riposte is normally launched by employing strategic reserves in an earlier time frame compared to a counter-offensive. It seeks to capture or threaten a strategic objective in relation to the enemy's offensive, so as to cause it to 'recoil'.

Roll – Aircraft rotation about its longitudinal axis without changing direction or altitude.

SAM – Surface-to-Air Missile

Scissors – An air combat manoeuvre in which two fighters repeatedly criss-cross flight paths in an endeavour to get behind the other's tail.

Scramble – An order by a designated air defence control authority for fighters to swiftly get airborne to intercept an intruder.

SEAD/Suppression of Enemy Air Defences – These are missions flown to neutralise enemy air defence systems, so that friendly strike aircraft have freedom to perform their missions.

Semi-Active Radar Homing Missile – It is a type of missile guidance system in which the missile itself is only a passive detector of a reflected radar signal provided by an external source, usually the parent aircraft. In contrast, an active radar homing missile carries an active radar transceiver.

Sortie – Every aircraft within a formation flies a sortie. Several sorties constitute a mission.

Spin – The flight condition of an aircraft in a spiralling stalled descent.

Split 'S' – An air combat manoeuvre in which the aircraft is inverted and pulled down through a half loop, thus not only reversing the direction of travel but also losing height in the process.

Spoof – Transmit false messages on radio to misguide the enemy aircraft.

Stall – The flight condition when the wings stop producing lift due to airflow disruption at high angles relative to the flight path, causing the aircraft to drop abruptly.

Strategic Air Operations – These operations are conducted against an enemy's war-making potential, and also to undermine their ability to continue fighting; targets include command and control infrastructure, key production facilities, logistics centres, etc.

Tactical Air Support – It involves direct and indirect air support to land operations. Direct air support includes Armed Reconnaissance, Battlefield Air Interdiction and Close Air Support missions. These missions are also collectively termed as Offensive Air Support. Indirect air support includes Air Interdiction missions beyond the battlefield.

Vector – Direction of intruder from interceptor, as reported by the radar controller during conduct of an interception.

Wingman – A companion aircraft, which flies in close proximity of the leader. A wingman is primarily tasked with clearing the tail and general area around, while the leader is engaged in combat.

Yaw – Aircraft motion around the vertical axis, which causes the nose to change direction towards left or right.

Yo-Yo – An air combat manoeuvre, which allows speed to be traded for height or vice versa. In a high-speed yo-yo, the attacking aircraft arrests its high rate of closure by zooming up; after sufficient room is created, it dives down obliquely on its turning opponent. In a low-speed yo-yo, an attacking aircraft dives down to build up speed (and closure rate) before zooming up for an attack. The zooming and diving motion of an attacker is akin to a bouncing yo-yo.

PREFACE

It is always a task of considerable difficulty to attempt a completely balanced historical work, as it is certain to be influenced by the author's outlook regarding the subject. This has been true of all historical accounts, which is why they continue to be reinterpreted by new writers over and over again. All that can be said about this work is that it is indeed interpretive in nature, coloured as it might be by the author's three decades long service as an ardent blue-suited aviator, and a Pakistani one at that. Nonetheless, I have not lost sight of the responsibility that goes with an undertaking of this nature, where veracity and truthfulness must overrun any baser expediency.

Since no dedicated book has been published on the 1971 air war for over four decades – which is rather surprising – it had been left to various articles published in journals and magazines over the years, for a piecemeal study of this short but significant air war. The result has been more of a miscellany than a coherent whole. I have attempted to amalgamate what was already known with new sources of knowledge that contain much more detail. While the work makes no claims to being a major academic treatise, students of war studies, as much as the lay public, could benefit from the candid narration of events and the analytical insights it develops.

The project started many years ago, when our students' study group was tasked to make a presentation on the 1971 Indo-Pak War at the Air War College. With the wealth of information on our hands, we were hard-pressed to present it as we wished, in the limited time allotted to us. The work that had gone in, however, encouraged me to continue further study of this most significant episode in the country's history. Later, in two of my staff appointments, I was luckily also the custodian of the PAF's war records. Curiosity and a quest for sorting fact from fiction, led me to a comprehensive study of these, and several new sources.

While this project is a strictly personal venture, I had complete access, as well as permission to use the war records, and was under no obligation to follow any official diktat. I have had complete freedom to acclaim or critique policies and concepts on their merit, for which

I am grateful to the previous Chief of the Air Staff, Air Chief Marshal Sohail Aman. I am also indebted to two former Chiefs of Air Staff, the erudite Air Chief Marshal Jamal Ahmed Khan and Air Chief Marshal Abbas Khattak, who meticulously scrutinised the draft of this book, and provided me with invaluable guidance.

Besides being an easily readable account of exciting events from the pen of a fighter pilot, this book aims to provide new perspectives and important lessons in earnest, especially for the future air warriors, as well as operations and planning staff.

The book especially seeks to dispel the ludicrous Indian fabrication about Pakistan having initiated the war with 'pre-emptive' strikes by the Pakistan Air Force. Readers are reminded that it was India which brazenly crossed the international borders in East Pakistan, and that Pakistan was justified in hitting back in the west, where it thought its forces were more robust. At a time when Pakistan stood isolated while fighting a bloody insurgency, and was facing a hostile world media, India found it opportune to hang the placard of 'aggressor' around Pakistan's neck. The ensuing military debacle also did no good in preventing people world-wide from looking askance at Pakistan. This work accepts the military loss, but not the calumny of aggression.

I hope that this project spurs others to improve upon it, including rectification of any errors or omissions made by me. Analysis from a more neutral quarter would also be a welcome undertaking, something that I have striven for, but am certain to have left room for improvement.

Any historical work that helps better understanding of past events also leads to keener introspection, which in turn betters the prospects of a saner world for the future. We did lose on the battlefront, but I am sure we did not lose the wisdom to learn our lessons.

Kaiser Tufail
Lahore, 2020

INTRODUCTION

The contents of this book are arranged thematically, in four sections viz, Backdrop, Operations, Review, and an assortment of Appendices for ready reference. The use of endnotes supplements the text, which would otherwise have been swamped with data not to the liking of all but the most avid air enthusiasts.

The Backdrop Section sets the scene, covering the march of events that led to the war, and the plans and preparations for it. The secessionist mood generated by perceived and real injustices in erstwhile East Pakistan is very briefly covered to provide a background to the problem. Thereafter, the elections of 1970, the ensuing power struggle between the two principal contenders, and the resultant civil unrest in the Eastern Wing is discussed. Lastly, the phase of a full-fledged insurgency with complete Indian support, culminating in the latter's underhanded invasion of East Pakistan, is covered. Plans and preparations for the possible response of the Pak Army and the PAF to deal with the difficult situation are deliberated upon, with focus on the war strategies and concepts of operations.

The Operations Section starts with PAF's quest for achieving a favourable air situation through offensive and defensive counter-air missions, which took up the bulk of air effort. These missions facilitated force application, that immense offensive potential of air power known since its very inception. In the context of a tactical air force – which the PAF always was and continues to be – the force application largely centres on tactical air support in all its dimensions. These missions are covered in various Army battle sectors, with considerable explanation of prevalent battlefield situations that warranted intervention from the air. Maritime air support, or the lack of it actually, is covered to highlight the sordid consequences of successive governments' neglect of the Navy over the years.

The Review Section wraps up the operations with an assessment of the air war, as well as the war at large. As honest critiques should be, this one is exacting, without any disconcertment; all the same, credit where due, is easily given. While assessing a war that resulted in major reverses, it has been customarily convenient to cast it in the mould of overall 'military incompetence'. It would, however, be prudent to look at the performance of the smaller services separately, in the context of their limitations. This is not to absolve them of their sins of commission and omission but is just to reiterate that circumstances were not wholly in their control. This aspect can best be elucidated in a book as this, which treats the 1971 air war as a distinct subject.

The Appendices Section has tables and charts which provide an 'at-a-glance' summary of the air war. Definitive lists of overall aircraft losses form an important part of this section.

The readers might note that the final tally of aircraft destroyed in combat, as trumpeted in many renowned aviation magazines and books, is at odds with what is given here. Quite a few of these claims have been found to have little substance and are based on hearsay or have been influenced by patronage or outright propaganda from either side. Unfortunately, since the medium of print is easily taken as gospel, years of reiteration have made it problematic to refute such claims. New inputs, including the other side's story, have made a difference for the better which shows up in this book. In all fairness to the individuals who claimed shooting down an aircraft but have not made it to the 'confirmed' list, no aspersions have been cast while setting the record straight.

There was the ever-present apprehension of meddling with history, and in the process, touching a raw nerve or two if the new data was used imprudently. A practical solution was to maintain focus on the common points that emerged after collation of mission details from both sides. All aerial claims have been corroborated on the basis of stringent verification rules, and unless incontrovertible proof is available, a kill has not been attributed.

The aerial kills have been confirmed on the basis of:

1. Availability of wreckage,
2. Gun-camera film showing catastrophic in-flight failure,
3. Official acknowledgement of a loss, or,
4. Confirmation through KIA and POW records.

This leaves the possibility of an aerial kill being covered up as an accident or an AAA hit, if the pilot managed to eject in friendly territory. There is one such case (and possibly some more), where the IAF has obfuscated the details, but enough circumstantial evidence exists in time and space, to make an odd exception to the devised kill criteria.

Access to each other's stories through the Internet has resulted in some interesting discoveries. This has resulted in a review of the claims, with some sort of a consensus emerging. While the number of

PAF and IAF aircraft losses suffered in actual combat have mostly been accounted for, those lost in combat-related accidents have been mired in some confusion. The readers are assured that on the PAF side, no loss has been concealed; rather, a couple of such accidents have been clearly accepted as attrition losses. In fact, the tail numbers of almost all PAF aircraft lost in the war are listed, and it can be confidently claimed that its authenticity can only be impugned at the risk of some discomfiture.

As far as claims of aerial destruction of armour, artillery pieces and vehicles on the battlefront are concerned, these are hard to substantiate accurately. With gun camera film proving fuzzy at best, it is difficult to ascertain complete destruction or partial immobilisation of the targets. No confirmations have, therefore, been made, and the claims by either side have been left open. The effectiveness of air support to the ground forces has largely been determined by the number of sorties flown, with an *a priori* assumption that both sides faced broadly similar targeting conditions and had similar weapon delivery capabilities.

Of the sources consulted, the PAF's official history book *The Story of the Pakistan Air Force* and the Indian *Official History of the 1971 India-Pakistan War* are the principal ones. Much of the statistics and data in various tables and charts are based on PAF's unpublished official war records. In deference to the classified nature of the records, the complete text had to be duly vetted by the authorities, but happily, no editing was necessary.

Another useful source was the first-hand account of air battles and ground attack missions by the aircrew who were actually involved. These have added an element of excitement to what would otherwise have been a dreary exertion for the reader. Excessive glorification of these individuals has been avoided, which is also one reason for not including their pictures, despite the historical significance of the book. The text gives enough due where warranted. This approach is also in conformity with the concise nature of this work, though it was a challenge to keep it that way, considering the vast data available for consultation.

1
BACKDROP

While charting out a constitutional plan for the Muslims of India, the All-India Muslim League proposed in the Lahore Resolution of 23-24 March 1940 that geographically contiguous units, as in north-western and north-eastern India (which were confusingly also called regions, areas and zones in the same breath), should form independent states, in which the constituent units would be autonomous and sovereign.[1] As is quite evident, the resolution implied two independent states, each having a loose confederal structure for its constituent units (or provinces).

In the event, did the founding fathers renege on the agreed plan of more than one independent Muslim state? It would almost be heretical for Pakistani minds to think that it was anything but a typographical error; however, it seems that some expediency compelled a revision of the original resolution. Thus, while the amended resolution laid the foundations of an independent state, it also sowed the seed of secession in a constituent unit (East Pakistan) by overlooking its 'distinctive culture, language, and a history of being, in effect an outsider in South Asia.'[2]

Quaid-e-Azam Muhammad Ali Jinnah was aware that the Muslim League had a very narrow base of support in Punjab, mostly amongst students. It had not held power in Punjab before Partition and had virtually ceded leadership on Muslim issues to the intercommunal Unionist Party since 1922. It had managed to win just one seat in the provincial assembly in the 1937 elections. In the North-West Frontier Province (NWFP), despite being the largest Muslim majority province (almost 92%), the Muslim League was unable to make inroads in the self-serving politics of the province. It had lost every single election until the June 1947 referendum in favour of joining Pakistan. NWFP indisputably had the strongest 'contrarian streak' in the Muslim majority areas, which manifested itself in rejection of the idea of control from a remote national centre.[3] In Sind, the landlords and the spiritual leaders only came around to supporting the independence movement with some hesitation, though its legislative assembly eventually became the first to approve the Lahore Resolution. Under such shaky and uncertain conditions, it was important to garner support of East Bengal where the League had done well on a Muslim communal platform in the 1937 elections. After all, the Muslim League began in Dacca in 1905, reflecting East Bengal's proud history of Muslim separatism.

For Jinnah the pragmatist, a demand for two independent states would have meant that none might be achievable, given the weak electoral standing of Muslim League at the time of the Lahore Resolution. The resolution was, thus, belatedly amended by a small Legislators' Convention in April 1946 in Delhi; it mentioned a united state of Pakistan. To assuage persisting doubts in the minds of some Bengali Muslim members who insisted on a full session approval, the Muslim League leadership adopted a 'memorandum of minimum demands' on 12 May 1946, stating, 'After the constitutions of Pakistan Federal Government and the provinces are finally framed by the constitution making body, it will be open to any province of the group to decide to opt out of this group, provided wishes of the people of that province are ascertained in a referendum to opt out or not.'

Overruling the clause calling for independent states did indeed help create a united Pakistan, but not to be forgotten was the 'memorandum of minimum demands' of 1946, which had clearly sanctioned secession if a province so desired. It was thus incumbent on the centre to carefully address the aspirations of its Bengali compatriots who had been historically at odds with any central authority. In retrospect, a semi-autonomous formulation between the two provincial units – similar to the way the Peoples' Republic of China (PRC) and the Union of the Soviet Socialist Republics managed their ethnically and linguistically disparate peoples – could have been workable models. How long such an arrangement could continue to ward off any fissiparous tendencies in the unit (or province) is a moot question but would have largely depended on the degree of accommodation the centre was willing to live with.

Language Issue

Soon after gaining independence, the issue of a state language occupied the fledgling government of Pakistan. Believing that a single language was needed for a country to remain united, Urdu was officially declared as the state language of the Dominion of Pakistan on 25 February 1948. It has to be noted that this step overlooked a resolution of the All-India Muslim League (Bengal) which had rejected the idea of making Urdu as the lingua franca of Muslim India during its 1937 Lucknow session.

Omission of Bengali as one of Pakistan's state languages predictably resulted in riots in East Bengal (as it was known until 1956). Following a complete general strike in Dacca on 11 March 1948, the Quaid decided to explain the rationale of one state language during his first and last visit to Dacca after independence. On 21 March 1948, during the civic reception, he stated, 'There can be only one state language if the component parts of this state are to march forward in unison, and in my opinion, that can only be Urdu.' Three days later, the Quaid repeated his stance while addressing students at Dacca University, much to their consternation. The Quaid's declaration caused considerable resentment amongst the Bengalis who were 56 percent of the country's population, as compared to 44 percent of the combined four provinces that formed the western wing. Of the latter, only seven percent spoke Urdu, the rest communicating in their regional languages.

The government of Pakistan based in the then capital of Urdu-speaking Karachi, considered Urdu as a vital element of Islamic heritage and culture. The language, though based on Hindi's Prakrit precursor, had developed under Persian, Arabic and Turkic influence, and even its Perso-Arabic Nastaliq script was somehow fancied as 'Islamic.' In contrast, Bengali, with its Devanagari script that it shared with Hindi, was seen as linked to Hindu culture. To get around this problem, even a *halal* (kosher) version of Bengali in Arabic script was proposed by the government's East Bengal Language Committee, but its official report never saw the light of the day.

Because of the decision regarding Urdu as the state language, a movement demanding Bengali as another state language started in earnest in East Bengal. The movement not only laid the foundations of Bengali nationalism, it heightened the cultural animosity between the two wings of Pakistan. Matters came to a head when language riots led to the death of five students in Dacca on 21 February 1952, a day that is considered as a watershed in the relations between the two wings. The sad event catalysed various Bengali nationalist movements in its wake, including the Six-Point Programme discussed hereafter.

After much squabbling and needless loss of blood, the Constituent Assembly finally voted in support of Bengali as a second state language alongside Urdu on 7 May 1954. The Constitution was accordingly amended in 1956, finally, but much had been lost by way of goodwill between the two wings of the country.

Socio-Cultural Divide

Bengal had a rich culture based on literature, poetry, music, song and dance. The Bengalis were inspired by the Nobel laureate Rabindranath Tagore (1861-1941), a secular poet and writer. To the West Pakistanis however, East Bengalis' adulation of Tagore was somehow inconsistent with an Islamic Pakistan. Tagore's works were banned from government-controlled radio and television because they 'promoted secular Bengali nationalism.'[4] Even the East Bengali nationalist poet, writer and musician, Kazi Nazrul-Islam (1899-1976), failed to find admiration in West Pakistani literary circles. The people of West Pakistan were endeared to Allama Muhammad Iqbal, a poet with a pan-Islamic vision, and an inspiration behind the Pakistan Movement. Any possibility of syncretism of the varied philosophies and ideals was, in large part, obstructed by the language barrier. Attempts at cultural assimilation were tried out through various half-baked methods, but the schism remained wide and unbridgeable.

While the literacy rate of both wings was dismal at the time of partition (remaining so for decades thereafter), the West Pakistanis found themselves better qualified for the civil services. Postings of West Pakistani civil servants to East Pakistan were, thus, a common practice. The Bengalis saw this as a perpetuation of colonial rule in a new form. West Pakistani bureaucrats ordering the Bengalis around were the last thing that could be endured by the latter. The result was an unintended social divide that manifested itself in a 'master-subject' relationship of sorts, rather than as equals.

Despite the seeming social divide, the political front remained less affected as borne by the remarkable fact that in the early to mid-fifties, Pakistan's second, third and fifth Prime Ministers were from East Pakistan.[5] It is another matter that none of them completed their tenures, either due to dissolution of their governments or due to differences with the Governor General.

Perceived Lack of Development

A sizeable share of Pakistan's foreign exchange earnings came through the export of cotton and jute, the latter growing exclusively in East Pakistan. Bengalis complained that the development projects set up in East Pakistan were few and far between, and not at all commensurate with their contribution to the national exchequer. The Awami League, the mouthpiece of the Bengalis, went to the extent of claiming that for 60 percent of the export earnings, East Pakistan's share in development projects was only 25 percent. The contention seems far-fetched if one were to note that several major industrial projects were first initiated in East Pakistan. The world's biggest jute mill was established in Narayanganj, East Pakistan in 1951 by the industrial conglomerate of Adamjee Brothers who contributed a 50 percent share capital, while the rest was sanctioned by the government through the Pakistan Industrial Development Corporation (PIDC). Pakistan's first paper mill was set up in Chandargona, East Pakistan by PIDC in 1953. Many years later, Pakistan's first steel mill was also set up by PIDC in Chittagong in 1969. Clearly, industrial development in East Pakistan was not as dismal as painted out by the Awami League.

A Reactionary Six-Point Programme

The Awami League's Six Point election manifesto was obsessively fixated with devolution of powers from the federation to the provinces, to an unprecedented extent. The federal subjects included only foreign affairs and defence. Two mutually convertible currencies, or as an alternative, a single currency subject to establishment of separate regional Federal Reserve Banks for the two wings of the country were proposed to be established, 'to prevent transfer of resources and flight of capital from one region to the other.' Fiscal policy was to be the responsibility of the federating units, which would provide the requisite revenue resources to the federal government according to a laid down formula. More seditious was the proviso for separate accounts of foreign exchange earnings of each of the federating units, which were to be maintained under control of their respective governments. This stipulation entailed sanctioning the federating units to independently negotiate foreign trade and assistance with other countries. Finally, the government of each of the federating units was to be empowered to maintain a militia or para-military force for 'effective contribution towards national security.'

A latent problem of the Six-Point Programme was that it had unintended consequences for the federating units in the western wing.[6] It implied, for instance that all four federating units (provinces) in the western wing along with the eastern wing, could chart out their own fiscal policy, and could conduct foreign trade and negotiate financial assistance from international donors. There was also the ripe possibility of each of the federating units of the western wing demanding its own Federal Reserve Bank, which would have virtually amounted to independence.

A cursory glance at the Six-Point Programme indicates that the cause of disagreement was essentially the purported flight of capital from East Pakistan to West Pakistan. Most of the points revolved around safeguarding East Pakistan's share of export revenues. It was also clear that a maximalist position had been adopted by the Awami League, which stemmed from absolute confidence that it had the support of the masses and could carry the programme through without any hitch. Relenting on the extreme position was foreseen only if the showing at elections was not as expected, and some compromises had to be made.

Mired in multiple problems and responsibilities, President Yahya paid little heed to the consequences of the Six-Point Programme on Pakistan's unity. On the face of it, the Legal Framework Order (LFO) that circumscribed the 1970 elections process accepted the Six-Point Programme as reasonable and legitimate.[7] On the other hand, it was the LFO, which irked Mujib sorely, particularly a clause that vested powers of authentication of the future Constitution with the President. It implied that Mujib would not have a free hand to implement his Six-Point Programme, even if he obtained a majority in the National Assembly. Apparently, Yahya felt self-assured because he could exercise his powers to veto the Constitution Bill if the need arose. In any case, Yahya trusted his intelligence agencies' prognosis of a split verdict and thought that the stage of a veto may not be reached. In case of a split electoral verdict, Yahya was sure that the points of conflict in the Awami League's radical programme could be resolved through coercive diplomacy when the time came for transfer of power. If Yahya had foreseen that the Awami League could sweep the elections, his plan of action for transfer of power would certainly have been less cavalier. Blaming the Six-Point Programme as subversive after having accepted it as a *bona fide* election manifesto just did not make sense. Disapproving a Constitution Bill passed by the elected representatives on grounds that its Six Points were violative of national integrity was a poor back-up plan, and an extremely provocative one at that. Mujib is claimed to have confided to his senior colleagues, 'My aim is to establish Bangla Desh.[8] I shall tear LFO into pieces as soon as the elections are over. Who could challenge me once the elections are over?'[9]

Elections and the Ensuing Impasse

Elections to the National Assembly were held on 7 December 1970 and to the Provincial Assemblies ten days later. Overall voter turnout was fairly high, with 58 percent of the registered voters casting their votes in the National Assembly elections. The turnout was considerably higher in the West Pakistani provinces – 65 percent, compared to East Pakistan with 55 percent.

Of the 300 seats contested in the National Assembly, Sheikh Mujib-ur-Rahman's Awami League won 160 (all in East Pakistan), while Zulfiqar Ali Bhutto's Pakistan People's Party (PPP) won 81 (all in the West Pakistani provinces of Punjab and Sind). The rest of the 59 seats were won by minor parties and independent candidates without any party affiliation. Clearly, Mujib had swept the elections, and was eager to take the chair of the Prime Minister.

Yahya and his coterie, as well as many West Pakistani politicians, were wary of a government led by the Awami League, whose radical programme was interpreted as thinly veiled separatism. There was also the anxiety about the Awami League allying with the smaller parties and independents to get a two-thirds majority and bulldozing its Six Point Programme in the National Assembly with full constitutional cover.

Two days after the elections, Mujib unequivocally declared:

> The election, for the people of Bangla Desh, was above all a referendum on the vital issue of full regional autonomy on the basis of Six Points… therefore a Constitution securing full regional autonomy on the basis of Six Points formula has to be framed and implemented in all respects.[10]

It was feared that the Awami League could even take the extreme step of an outright declaration of independence in the National Assembly, if it felt that the military was creating hurdles in its agenda. Misgivings also resurfaced regarding Mujib's past involvement (1968) in the Agartala Conspiracy case in which he, along with 34 military officers, was accused of colluding with Indian agents in a scheme to divide Pakistan. A trial for sedition could, however, not go through due to large-scale protests and strikes in East Pakistan, and the charges were eventually dropped as a political expedient.

As if to fortify its position in the face of reservations in West Pakistan, the Awami League held a rally in Dacca on 3 January, where all its recently elected members of the National and Provincial Assemblies took an oath of allegiance to the Six Points. The move clearly signalled that there was no possibility of bargaining, and the Six Points were there to stay, unaltered.

Faced with an utterly convoluted predicament, Yahya decided to visit Dacca on 12 January 1971, for parleys with Mujib and his team, 'to come to a thorough understanding of the Six Points.' Vice Admiral S M Ahsan, the Governor of East Pakistan, who was in attendance, ruefully reminisced later that it was too late to attempt a 'thorough understanding' of the Awami League programme. The discussions, unsurprisingly, were frustrating for Yahya, as Mujib repeatedly insisted on each point by proclaiming that, 'There is nothing objectionable in it. What's wrong with it? It is so simple.'[11] Professor G W Chaudhry, the Minister of Communications who accompanied Yahya to Dacca, thought that Yahya was bitter and frustrated by Mujib's betrayal. 'Mujib has let me down. Those who warned me against him were right. I was wrong in trusting this person,' said Yahya, according to Chaudhry.

A completely flustered Yahya sought counsel from Bhutto at the latter's family residence in Larkana, to which he flew on 17 January. What transpired at *Al Murtaza* is not exactly known, but it appears that Bhutto was able to convince Yahya about the consequences of handing over power to Mujib, in view of the latter's unrepresentative electoral standing in West Pakistan. Bhutto and Yahya also deliberated upon the seditious nature of the Awami League's manifesto, whose actualisation was now imminent. 'We discussed with the President the implications of the Six Points and expressed our serious misgivings about them.'[12] Whatever went on at Larkana during three days of parleys (interspersed with duck shoots), Yahya emerged satisfied after having enlisted his host's support.

Backed by Yahya's brief, and confident of his own astuteness, Bhutto decided to visit Dacca on 27 January. Though piqued by the goings-on between Yahya and Bhutto in Larkana, the Awami League was still amenable to the latter's visit. It was interested in Bhutto's cooperation only to the extent of rendering the President's veto on the Constitution Bill ineffective. There was to be no compromise on the Six Points by the Awami League. Bhutto, on the other hand, was seeking a power-sharing formula on the grounds that his Pakistan People's Party had not received any mandate on the Six Point Programme, and public opinion was against it in West Pakistan. This stance was obviously unacceptable to Mujib, who was not seeking any coalition partners.

With the situation at a total impasse, Bhutto returned from Dacca in a recalcitrant mood.

Under the rapidly deteriorating political situation, Yahya thought it wise not to delay the announcement of the National Assembly session any further. After all, the veto power vested in the President by the LFO was an adequate safeguard against the possibility of the Awami League bulldozing the Six Points through the National Assembly. Yahya had another long discussion with Bhutto on 11 February, but without arriving at any agreement. He decided to go ahead with the logical next step following elections, and on 13 February, it was announced that the National Assembly would meet at Dacca on 3 March. Two days later, Bhutto declared at a press conference in Peshawar about his party's inability to attend the inaugural session of the National Assembly, "in the absence of an understanding, compromise or adjustment of the Six Points.' He even threatened, as reported in *The Dawn* newspaper "a revolution from Khyber to Karachi if the People's Party were left out.'[13]

With people in East Pakistan already seething with resentment at the delay in power transfer, and Bhutto outrightly threatening an uprising in West Pakistan if he did not have his way, matters had come to a head for Yahya. He once again wore his military hat, dismissed the civilian cabinet, and reverted to Martial Law in its classic form.

Vice Admiral S M Ahsan and Lieutenant General Sahibzada Yaqub, the Martial Law Administrator in East Pakistan, were summoned by General Yahya to Rawalpindi for a conference on 22 February. Both were told that Mujib would be given one more opportunity to prove his good intentions. This implied a political dialogue with Mujib, failing which military plans would be operationalised to regain full control in the disorder that was bound to ensue.

While Lieutenant General Yaqub finalised the military plans for internal security, Vice Admiral Ahsan held a round of talks with Mujib. The only outcome of the talks was that Mujib agreed not to insist on application of the Six Points to West Pakistan, but there would be no change to their application to East Pakistan. Nonetheless, it seemed that the Awami League got the drift of military preparations, and was starting to show some flexibility. Lieutenant General Yaqub had, in the meantime, sent a telegram to Yahya, urging him to visit Dacca immediately in the hope of averting a major crisis that he saw looming.

Disregarding Lieutenant General Yaqub's telegram, Yahya announced on 28 February a *sine die* postponement of the National Assembly session, which was originally planned for 3 March. This was done 'to allow more time to the political parties to work out an agreement on the draft Constitution outside the Assembly.' To the Awami League, this act was tantamount to repudiating the popular mandate. Yahya had overlooked the fact that Mujib had immense street power in East Pakistan; more ominously, he had full support of India, which would not let go the distinct possibility of Pakistan's break-up. Regrettably, Yahya had played into India's hands with his ill-considered announcement, and the die had been cast.

Postponement of the National Assembly session resulted in immediate protests, and the start of a civil disobedience movement in East Pakistan. Radio Pakistan Dacca was taken over by the Awami League miscreants and calls for protests were broadcast, triggering a complete shutdown in major cities. Mujib sternly demanded an immediate transfer of power to the elected representatives of the people of Pakistan. Sensing violence, and belatedly heeding to some sane advice, a wavering Yahya made another announcement on 6 March for the inaugural session of the National Assembly to start on 25 March.

Bhutto, who had no chance of forming even a coalition government at the Centre, fast-tracked his machinations in the wake of Yahya's latest announcement. He cleverly floated the idea that, 'If power is to be transferred to the people before a constitutional settlement, then it is only fair that in East Pakistan it should go to the Awami League, and in the West to the Pakistan People's Party, because while the former is the majority party in that wing, we have been returned by the people of this side.' The daily Azad of 15 March 1971 gave a twist to Bhutto's speech with a startling headline that screamed, *udhar tum, idhar hum* (you there, we here). Though the wording of the headline has been incorrectly attributed to Bhutto ever since, a confederal structure, had, in effect, been proposed by him. Bhutto's ambition and impatience came through clearly from his statement. His formula overlooked the fact that the Legal Framework Order had no stipulation for a political party having to win seats in other provinces, or both the wings, to be able to form a government at the Centre. Mujib's disparaging of any such belated ploys was, thus, neither surprising, nor unfounded.

There were a few last-minute amendments to the Six Points suggested by the Awami League Executive Committee, which were conveyed to Lieutenant General Yaqub. The amendments called for a token ratification of some of the contentious provincial subjects by the Central Government before implementation. These amendments were expected to be discussed with General Yahya, if he decided to visit Dacca, which unfortunately, he delayed until it was too late.

Civil Disobedience and Violence

The earlier decision to postpone the National Assembly session scheduled for 3 March had been met with extreme derision and widespread anger in East Pakistan. *Hartals* (general strikes) all over the province were ordered by the Awami League, and Mujib made it clear that the postponement decision would not go unchallenged. Behind the scenes, though, he again pleaded with the Governor, Vice Admiral Ahsan, for a fresh date for the assembly session. Mujib's request was passed on to the Army Chief of Staff (COS), General Hamid, but instead, the top brass took a thoughtless decision to sack the Governor, and Lieutenant General Yaqub was asked to take over that office also, on 1 March.

Press censorship was imposed, followed by a curfew in Dacca. Mujib reacted by closing all doors on further negotiations and launched what he termed a 'non-violent non-cooperation' movement. The Bengali staff of PIA was the first to respond by refusing to handle flights, which brought troop reinforcements from Karachi to Dacca. Charged crowds attacked Government House in which six people were killed in clashes with troops on guard duties. On 2 March, Mujib issued a statement calling on 'all sections of the society, including government servants to rise against the unlawful government and recognise peoples' representatives as the only legitimate authority.' Lieutenant General Yaqub talked to Mujib on the telephone asking him to withdraw the statement, but a hostile Mujib outrightly refused to oblige. The law and order situation continued to worsen. Reports of casualties poured in from all parts of the East Pakistan, with non-Bengalis suffering the worst at the hands of rampaging mobs.

President Yahya initially maintained a nonchalant attitude in the face of constant pleading by Lieutenant General Yaqub for some decision, as the situation deteriorated rapidly. Yahya finally decided to call a meeting of all politicians in Dacca on 10 March, but Mujib reacted furiously by refusing any more 'round-table conferences.' Yahya spoke to Mujib by telephone and tried to talk him out of his obduracy. The result of the conversation became clear only when Yahya called Lieutenant General Yaqub on the night of 4 March and informed him that the planned visit to Dacca had been called off. An exasperated Lieutenant General Yaqub immediately called the President's Principal

A pro-independence protest in Dacca, March 1971. (Albert Grandolini Collection)

Staff Officer (PSO), Lieutenant General Peerzada, in Rawalpindi, and told him that he would be sending in his resignation the following day. Before the resignation reached the president, Lieutenant General Tikka Khan, the Martial Law Administrator of Punjab and Commander IV Corps, had been already been assigned to replace Lieutenant General Yaqub as a three-hatted Commander of Eastern Command, Martial Law Administrator, and Governor East Pakistan.

The 'non-violent' movement that Mujib had promised was getting more and more violent. A particularly bloody day-long battle on 3 March between Awami League terrorists and unarmed non-Bengalis in Pahartali, near Chittagong, resulted in 102 deaths. In Dacca, no one felt secure. Most of the well-off non-Bengalis had sold off their household effects for a pittance and purchased tickets to fly off to Karachi. The poorer ones went into hiding or sought refuge in the cantonment areas that were relatively safe.

On 6 March, the Awami League went into session to take a final decision on the unilateral declaration of independence of Bangladesh. Getting wind of what might follow, President Yahya called Mujib, advising him not to take a hasty decision, and assured him of honouring his (Mujib's) aspirations and commitments to the people. Yahya also promised to visit Dacca soon. The declaration of independence was perhaps averted as a result of the timely call, much to the satisfaction of the Martial Law Headquarters in Dacca. The same day Yahya announced that the National Assembly would meet on 25 March. Mujib responded to the announcement with four preconditions for attending the session:

1. Lifting of Martial Law
2. Return of the Army to barracks
3. Transfer of power to the people's representatives
4. A judicial inquiry into the killing of Bengali people.

General Yahya decided to make one last attempt at finding a political solution to the deadlock, and flew to Dacca on 15 March. Soon after arrival, he asked his military commanders for a situation report. At the end of the briefing, Yahya muttered, 'Don't worry. I will line up Mujib tomorrow … will give him a bit of my mind. Then if he doesn't behave, I'll know the answer.' While the Generals in attendance were dumbstruck, the PAF's Air Officer Commanding (AOC), Air Commodore 'Mitty' Masud sought permission to say something. After Yahya nodded a go-ahead, Mitty opened up, 'Sir, the situation is very delicate. It is essentially a political issue and needs to be resolved politically, otherwise thousands of innocent men, women and children will perish.' Nodding his head in fatherly fashion, Yahya replied, 'Mitty, I know it … I know it.' A few days later, the highly decorated 1965 War hero, Air Commodore M Z Masud was relieved of his duties.

No Way Out

After a rather cold informal meeting the following day, it was evident that the time for accommodation of any sort between Yahya and Mujib had passed. Yahya was smug with his hold on absolute power, while Mujib too seemed to exude complete control due to the massive mandate of the people of East Pakistan.

During the formal talks on 17 and 18 March, neither side was willing to compromise, which came as no surprise. The talks failed miserably, with Yahya and Mujib emerging dejected and irate over the fiasco. The Awami League had insisted that Martial Law be lifted and power transferred immediately to them, while two independent committees of the National Assembly chalked out ways to promulgate a new Constitution agreeable to both the wings. Yahya agreed to the Awami League proposal on condition that Bhutto had no objection to it. This, despite the grave threat to Yahya's regime as it would lose legal sanction with the removal of martial law. As for Bhutto, he was averse to any arrangement that saw him out of power, but, so as not to be seen as a spoiler, he agreed to visit Dacca nonetheless.

On arrival in Dacca on 21 March, Bhutto was briefed by Yahya about the Awami League's proposal for power transfer. Bhutto reacted by drawing Yahya's attention to the impropriety of approving the scheme without full knowledge of the people. He was of the opinion that 'two or more political leaders could not ignore the existence of the entire Assembly vested with constitutional and legislative power.' He also told Yahya that he saw 'seeds of two Pakistans' in the Awami League's proposal.

Behind the scenes, an apprehensive Yahya had conveyed to Lieutenant General Tikka to 'be ready', implying plans and preparations for military action in case the political talks failed.

23 March, regularly celebrated countrywide as the Pakistan

Members of a pro-Pakistan militia demonstratively marching in Dacca. (Albert Grandolini Collection)

The military had planned to conduct Operation 'Searchlight' starting at 01:00 hrs on 26 March, by which time General Yahya would have safely landed in Karachi. Major General Rao Farman Ali, the advisor on civil affairs, was put in charge of operations in Dacca and its environs, while Major General Khadim Hussain Raja, General Officer Commanding (GOC) 14 Division, was given charge of the rest of East Pakistan.

Some of the more important tasks assigned to Farman's subordinate, Brig Jehanzeb Arbab, (Commander 57 Brigade), included the disarming of about 5,000 personnel of East Pakistan Rifles, disarming of 1,000 policemen at the city's Police Lines, neutralisation of Awami League strong points inside Dacca University, and capture of Sheikh Mujib-ur-Rahman (code-named 'Big Bird'). Additionally, combing operations and show of force was to be conducted, wherever required.

Resolution Day, saw tumultuous rioting all over East Pakistan. Pakistani flags were burnt and replaced with those of Bangla Desh, while Quaid-e-Azam's portraits in offices were replaced with those of Mujib-ur-Rahman. Joi Bangla (Long live Bangla Desh) slogans could be heard everywhere. It was quite clear that the writ of Martial Law was weak, and a parallel government, supported by the people, was in control in East Pakistan.

The following day, the Awami League proposed the formation of two Constitution Conventions to draw up separate Constitutions for East and West Pakistan. The National Assembly was to subsequently assimilate these Constitutions into a framework for the 'Confederation of Pakistan.' Yahya and Bhutto met soon after the announcement and concluded that the Awami League had shifted radically from its demand of maximum provincial autonomy, to the outright disintegration of Pakistan. The hint of a tenuous link between the two wings in the Awami League offer was seen by Bhutto as a hindrance to his quest for absolute power – a departure from his earlier position of sharing power under the so-called *udhar tum, idhar hum formula*, which was no less a confederal arrangement. Yahya, on the other hand saw it as the first step towards secession under his watch, and he may have apprehended a severe reaction within the Army, as well as the masses in West Pakistan. Matters had come to such a pass, that use of force to keep the country united seemed to be the only remaining option for Yahya.

Military Crackdown

On 25 March, Yahya and his aides quietly flew back to West Pakistan, followed by Bhutto a day later. As ominous clouds gathered over the horizon, it was clear that the time for politics was over.

The operation in Dacca was over by first light, with all objectives achieved. The 'Big Bird' was in the cage and was whisked off to Karachi three days later. The casualty figures for the Bengalis, especially at the University, remain moot. While the Army sources estimated around one hundred deaths in the University area, Bengalis insisted that these ran into thousands.

The main task of securing the rest of East Pakistan with a single army division was not an easy one. The rebel strongholds in Chittagong, Kushtia and Pabna were particularly formidable and well-defended, and needed to be neutralised promptly before the rebels went on the rampage against the non-Bengalis.

Chittagong had just one battalion with 600-odd troops to fight off an estimated 5,000 rebels. Reinforcements from the brigade headquarters at Comilla, including an infantry battalion and a mortar battery, were blocked by the rebels after blowing up of a bridge *en route*. All attempts to make headway towards Chittagong were thwarted, and eventually, contact was lost with the relief column. The GOC himself undertook a search for the column from a helicopter, braving intermittent fire and several hits, but to no avail. A detachment of commandos was also flown in from Dacca to search for the column, but soon it came under rebel crossfire and took substantial casualties.[14] When the Officer Commanding of 24 FF fell in action, the Brigade Commander (53 Brigade) at Comilla, Brig Iqbal Shafi, himself took charge of the battalion, and was able to break the rebel resistance not long afterwards. The way to Chittagong was cleared, but unfortunately, the troops were too late to prevent a horrid massacre of unarmed non-Bengali men, women and children at Ispahani Jute Mills near the edge of the city.

The important tasks in Chittagong included destruction of radio transmitters that had been spewing virulent anti-Pakistan messages, as well as the neutralisation of East Bengal Regimental Centre and Reserve Police Lines. The latter two locations had a strong presence of trained saboteurs and were reported to have been heavily stocked with weapons.

After two abortive and costly attempts by a commando detachment to blow up the radio transmitters, PAF Sabres were called in to do the job, which was easily accomplished.[15]

The East Bengal Regimental Centre was attacked with a couple of tanks, a heavy mortar battery, as well as unconventional fire support from the destroyer PNS *Jahangir* and two gunboats; *Rajshahi* and *Balaghat*. After a raging battle that lasted for three hours, the target was destroyed and the rebels subdued.

The defenders at the Police Reserve Lines could not face the Pak Army's battalion-sized onslaught, and promptly vacated the area.

A group of Pakistan Army troops planning their next move during early operations against the insurgency. (Albert Grandolini Collection)

While the main operations in Chittagong were over in five days, mopping up continued into the first week of April.

In Kushtia, the task for the Army was to maintain security and establish their own presence with the help of a company detached from its battalion headquarters at Jessore, 55 miles away. On 28 March, the local Superintendent of Police informed the Company Commander that an attack on the town by rebels was imminent. The attack commenced with heavy mortar fire early on the morning of 29 March. Troops of an East Bengal battalion, joined by the Indian Border Security Force, charged on the police armoury occupied by Pak Army troops. In the next few hours, twenty soldiers had fallen. The company headquarters, as well as posts at the telephone exchange and VHF station were also attacked by the Bengali-Indian combine, resulting in heavy casualties. Desperate requests for reinforcements were denied due to other commitments, and air support had to be called off due to poor visibility. Kushtia was abandoned, and 65 surviving soldiers out of 150 were driven out in a convoy to Jessore. *En route*, a deadly ambush cut down all but nine soldiers who managed to escape, only to be rounded up and subjected to a barbaric end. The ill-prepared company had been virtually wiped out in what was the worst disaster faced by the Pakistan Army during Operation 'Searchlight'.

In Pabna, the task was not much different from the one at Kushtia, being mostly show of military presence in the area, by a lightly armed company of troops. Some important vulnerable points like the power house and the telephone exchange were also to be defended against the rebels. A costly mistake was made in wrongly assessing the strength of the rebels in the area. This realisation came too late when the rebels carried out a surprise raid on the telephone exchange, in which 85 troops were martyred. The remnants were evacuated by a relief party from Rajshahi but were met with heavy resistance as they fought their way out. The column reached Rajshahi with just 18 survivors; 112 had been martyred in the operation.

Operation 'Searchlight' was deemed to have helped achieve full control over much of the province by the end of April. While the Bengalis claimed that their casualties ran in hundreds of thousands in less than a month, Pakistan Army sources insist that rebel deaths did not exceed four figures. India had good reason to inflate the numbers to paint Pakistan Army in bad light in the eyes of the international community, an exercise in which it succeeded resoundingly. Expulsion of foreign press prior to the operation did not help matters either and it was only too pleased to parrot India's line on the subject.

Full-blown Insurgency

While Operation 'Searchlight' was underway, two more Army divisions (9 and 16 Divisions), as well as additional paramilitary forces, were flown in from West Pakistan. These forces were lightly armed, and their heavy equipment was left behind. A new Commander of Eastern Command, Lieutenant General A A K 'Tiger' Niazi was also posted in, and he had three new GOCs of the three divisions for conducting counter-insurgency operations.

The Indian government had, meanwhile, declared its full support to the rebels, having perceived a distinct possibility of Pakistan's breakup. The Director of the Indian Institute of Strategic Studies, Krishnaswamy Subrahmanyam, gave heft to that perception when he brazenly suggested at a symposium, to destroy Pakistan: 'What India must realise is the fact that the breakup of Pakistan is in our interest, and opportunity the like of which will never come again.'[16] He called it a 'chance of a century' to destroy India's enemy number one.

India started a crash programme of military preparations, including reorganisation and re-equipment. On the diplomatic front, she went all-out in creating a favourable world opinion, as well as getting the Soviet Union's commitment to help in the impending military action.[17] The presence of Bengali refugees and their plight was also exploited advantageously.

The most consequential action by India was the formation of an organised, well-trained and well-equipped rebel force, to thwart the Pak Army's efforts in fighting the insurgency. The *Mukti Bahini*

Trucks of the Pakistan Army in the Dacca area in August 1971. (Albert Grandolini Collection)

Insurgents of the Mukhti Bahini undergoing training on a machine gun in a camp in India. (Albert Grandolini Collection)

(freedom fighters) force was cobbled up with Bengali defectors from the army and para-military forces, students and able-bodied volunteers. Their task, as recalled in *India's Second Liberation* by Pran Chopra, was: 'Deployment in their own native land with a view to initially immobilizing and tying down the Pakistan military forces for protective tasks in Bengal, subsequently by gradual escalation of guerrilla operations, to sap and corrode the morale of the Pakistan Forces in the eastern sector, and finally, to avail the cadres as ancillaries to the Eastern Field Force in the event of Pakistan initiating hostilities against us.'[18]

With a constantly growing number of training camps in India, as many as 100,000 *Mukti Bahini* had cycled through training courses by the end of November. 300 frogmen had also been trained by India to undertake sabotage operations against shipping and riverine craft.[19]

The Pak Army had a total of 45,000 troops, including 11,000 paramilitary forces and police.[20] It also had additional support of about 50,000 Urdu-speaking Biharis and some sympathetic Bengalis under the support of an umbrella organisation called *Razakars* (volunteers). While the Razakars had been fired by patriotic fervour, they did not have proper training to transform their zeal into anything worthwhile. They could hardly conduct operations independent of the Pak Army.

The Pak Army earnestly started active counter-insurgency operations in April. The main focus was on maintaining the occupation of border posts and controlling major towns. Rebels followed hit-and-run tactics and could not be countered as they disappeared before the Pak Army arrived on the scene. This modus operandi of the *Mukti Bahini* continued incessantly for many months. With time – and ceaseless Indian support – their methods became well-planned, and the rebels became more audacious in their attacks. Bridges, railway lines and electric power stations were the preferred targets. For the Pak Army, fighting an insurgency spread over more than 55,000 square miles was a tall order besides being involved in a prolonged insurgency without any relief resulting in indifference and apathy setting in.

The writing on the wall was clear: the population of East Pakistan was not going to stop short of an independent Bangla Desh, as the West Pakistani power brokers had nothing to offer that could meet their aspirations. Retracting at this stage, when too much blood had been spilt, would have been seen by the Bengalis as an insult to their dignity. Sadly, the time for reconciliation was past.

General Yahya seemed completely afflicted by inaction and inertia over the nine months spanned by the insurgency. His efforts at some sort of reconciliation were confined to superficial measures, including replacement of Lieutenant General Tikka Khan with a civilian Governor to assuage the feelings of the Bengalis who saw Tikka as a tyrant. A former dentist, trade union leader, and elderly politician, Dr A M Malik was sworn in on 3 September. One day later, a general amnesty for 'miscreants' was announced, but there was no mention of the release of Sheikh Mujib-ur-Rahman, which made it appear meaningless to the Bengalis. Yahya's actions were, decidedly, too little, too late.

A Chance of a Century for India

While preparing for a military intervention in East Pakistan, India continued with shrewd diplomatic efforts in parallel. Notably, India signed the euphemistically dubbed Indo-Soviet Treaty of Peace, Friendship and Co-operation on 9 August 1971. Her diplomatic offensive centred around the 'massive humanitarian problem' of refugees who had fled to India because of the civil war in East Pakistan. It also helped assuage any apprehensions of a possible wider conflict, especially with regard to the US and China, whose beleaguered ally, Pakistan, could have clamoured for help. In any case, the US was unwilling, and China unable, to do much to avoid a conflagration.

The Indian military, in the meantime, found enough time to prepare for war on two fronts viz, West Pakistan as well as East Pakistan, the latter being considered as the main theatre. Equipment and manpower shortfalls were speedily addressed, and war plans adequately reviewed.

War preparations on the Pakistani side were seriously constrained by shortfalls in the Army's fighting formations. The move of two infantry divisions from West Pakistan was clearly a short-term response to the deteriorating situation in East Pakistan; it gravely altered the balance of forces in the West – the main theatre of war. Any operational reverses that might occur were to be redressed by denuding the strategic reserves. Unfortunately, this meant that the very foundations of a Pakistani military response had been utterly weakened.

While the insurgency within East Pakistan continued without let, India started artillery shelling on the border outposts in late June. This activity increased in the following months, with as many as 2,000 rounds falling daily.[21] On the one hand, it served the objective of controlled escalation by India, while on the other, it helped the *Mukti Bahini* in occupying many salients and enclaves, as these became indefensible under constant fire. By the time of General Yahya's address to the nation on 12 October, in which he declared that every inch of the sacred soil of Pakistan would be defended, 3,000 square miles of border area were already under Indian control.[22]

India had carefully assessed that Pak Army troops in East Pakistan were tired of fighting an insurgency for over eight months, and their morale was not at its best. The Indian Army had the numbers to overwhelm Pak Army troops three times over and had adequate mobility and logistics support to make a fast run for Dacca. In West Pakistan, India enjoyed numerical superiority, especially in the Desert Sector where it was overpowering. Indian defences were strong in all sectors, and they were confident of stopping any Pakistani foray, were Pakistan to attempt capture of vital territory as a sop for the loss of East Pakistan.

As for the Pakistan Air Force, India saw it mostly in a supporting role for the Pak Army, and if the latter's design could be stymied through deft planning, the aerial battlefront was not seen as a major threat to her designs.

As war clouds appeared over the sub-continent, India found it opportune to act on Subrahmanyam's advice to avail the chance of a century. Sadly, at this stage, there was hardly a way out of the morass that Pakistan found itself in but to fight, however best as was possible.

Plans and Preparations

The prevailing environment, as well as the lopsided disposition of military forces in the two wings of Pakistan, dictated that an offensive in the West be launched by the Pakistan Army for some redemption in the face of major reverses that were foreseen in the East. Any territorial gains accruing from the offensive could, thus, be later traded on favourable terms. Under the prevalent disparity of forces in East Pakistan that had not been redressed for decades, this was the only military option available.

The Pakistani military junta's war strategy was, therefore, to turn the West into the main theatre of war, while producing a stalemate in the East. This was in line with the pre-1965 expedient of 'defence of East lies in the West.' Dividing the forces and deploying them equally in both wings of the country would have made them too weak and vulnerable in either of them. As such, it was felt that a smaller holding force in East Pakistan would suffice, while the bulk in the West would be able to pose a viable threat to India. Thus, Yahya and his coterie, considered it imperative to offer their people the coveted prize of Kashmir, or other bargainable Indian territory, as compensation for the likely loss of East Pakistan. If the plan ran into any difficulties, Yahya unwisely hoped that his friends in the international community would succeed in their efforts to bail him out.

For India, the main theatre was in the East, where her forces were to drive at maximum speed, to achieve the military objective of breaking up Pakistan, and forcing the Pakistan Army to surrender. In the Western theatre, India did not desire a general war with Pakistan, but if the fighting spread to this region, her strategy was to fight a holding operation, while exercising offensive options when feasible, or where compelled due to vulnerabilities of her vital areas.

Pakistan Army's Articulation of the Strategy

With a pre-emptive operation ruled out by the government due to the likelihood of extreme international censure, a prompt riposte to any transgression by India in East Pakistan was the only military option available. Inaction in the face of Indian aggression would, of course, have been a recipe for civil war in West Pakistan, with a gutless military junta seen by the public as complicit in the break-up of the country.

A riposte was considered a suitable manifestation of the GHQ's dictum, 'defence of the East lies in the West.' Afflicted by uncertainties and unique complications as most military options are, this one too had more than one issue to be resolved. In view of the cleverly devised Indian military scheme of 'creeping gradualism' as opposed to a swift and sudden assault by armour and artillery, it was difficult to define when an aggression in East Pakistan had actually taken place. Any wrong reading of the situation could have had grave consequences. On the one hand, a premature response could have been interpreted as a punishable provocation by the international community. On the other hand, any delay in reading the changed situation on the Eastern front could gravely defer the Pak Army's riposte in the West, much to the satisfaction of the Indian Army, which could then deal with it more robustly, augmented by troops freed from its Eastern Theatre.

Central to any plan for the Pak Army's main offensive was the unachievable requirement of having a superior relative strength ratio (at least the Clausewitzian 2:1 superiority) over the enemy at the decisive point of application of forces.[23] This meant that, either a long-drawn destruction oriented battle had to take place between the equally strong strategic formations of the two adversaries, or else, the enemy reserves had to be lured to another sector by creating a battlefield situation that was seen to be the more threatening one by the enemy.

For the Pak Army's II Corps to remain potent for the formidable undertaking, it was imperative that a slugging match between the main strategic formations be avoided at the outset. Instead, the other strategic formation, Army Reserve North (ARN), could act by proxy to dislocate the Indian strategic reserves. For such a scheme

The quantitatively most important acquisition for the PAF after the 1965 War with India was the purchase of 90 Shenyang F-6 fighters from the People's Republic of China. (Albert Grandolini Collection)

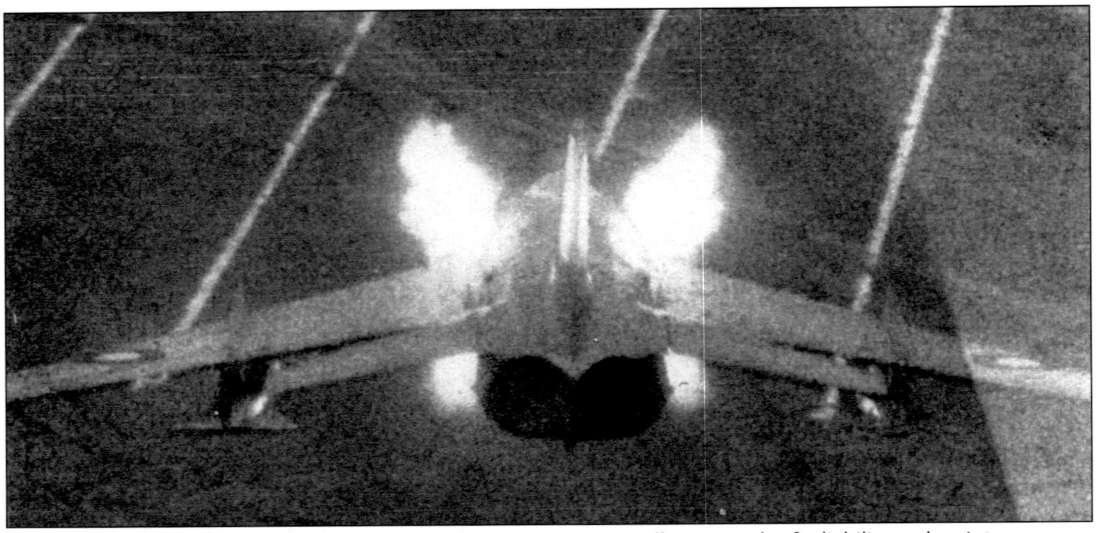

Representing a further improvement of the Soviet MiG-19S – especially in regards of reliability and maintenance, the F-6 packed a powerful punch in form of three 30mm internal guns. Taken during gunnery training and showing a PAF F-6 from behind, this photograph also illustrates the massive gun-blast from the two guns installed in the wing-roots. (Albert Grandolini Collection)

to be actualised, however, ARN had to launch a substantial counter-offensive in the Shakargarh Sector to first vacate any enemy incursion which was a certainty, in view of Indian compulsions stemming from border geography. Only thereafter, could ambitious attempts be made, like severing the vital Kathua-Samba road link to Kashmir, or capturing the equally crucial Madhopur Headworks. If one of the complicated moves succeeded, it was bound to create some kind of a 'pull' on the Indian strategic reserves as they rushed to help with the crisis in the north, thus allowing Lieutenant General Tikka to launch his II Corps.

In East Pakistan, defending a 1,800-mile long border with the aim of 'preserving its territorial integrity' was a most difficult task that GHQ had given to the Eastern Command. Three ill-equipped divisions and some odd battalions of the para-military forces against three Indian Corps, and a large body of *Mukti Bahini* irregulars were too few for the undertaking. Lieutenant General Niazi, Commander of Eastern Command had, however, insisted that his border deployment was actually a 'forward posture in defence' and that it was quite in line with the mission given to him by GHQ. He intended to fight for delaying actions so as to trade space for time, eventually falling back to well provisioned 'fortresses' or strongpoint's in important border towns. The same force was expected to remain viable and continue falling back to defend Dacca Sector (or the 'bowl' as it was commonly known).

The PAF's Concept of Operations

The PAF had accorded the highest priority to supporting the Pak Army's main offensive in West Pakistan, and all other tasks were considered peripheral to this important objective. The PAF was cognizant of the fact that the success of the offensive lay in the provision of the full range of tactical air support, as well as interdiction beyond the battlefield. This required control of the air to keep the IAF off the Pak Army's back, to which end, the PAF had a two-fold plan that included offensive and defensive measures. Strikes were planned against those IAF airfields (runways, essentially) that were likely to generate the bulk of air effort in the sector of the Pak Army's main offensive. Additionally, top cover was to be provided over the Army's thrust as it got underway, by flying trans-frontier fighter patrols; the air cover was to remain in place until the Army had consolidated its gains, dug in, and secured itself fully.

Interdiction of enemy supplies directly serving Indian forces opposing the Pak Army was to commence after the main offensive had been launched, thus preserving an element of surprise regarding its timing and location.

Till such time as the Pak Army's main offensive was launched, the PAF was to ensure its own viability by vigorously patrolling the airspace in the vicinity of its own air bases. During this period, some of the forward IAF bases were to be targeted to maintain pressure and to show an offensive resolve. It was hoped that this round-the-clock campaign would, to some extent, dilute the IAF effort against the Pak Army on the battlefield, as well as the PAF's own bases and installations.

The PAF had also resolved to provide whatever tactical air support that was possible for the Pak Army's holding operations along the entire border. Interdiction beyond the battlefield in sectors other than that of the main offensive was, however, not a high priority. This was a compulsion dictated by the need to preserve air assets that were limited to start with.

As well as acquiring F-6s, Pakistan also received a number of H-5 bombers – the Chinese licenced version of the venerable Ilyushin Il-28 of Soviet origin. They were operated alongside the US-made B-57s for a while under the local designation B-56 but due to general dissatisfaction with their capabilities were quickly returned to China in exchange for additional F-6s. The type saw no action in Pakistani service in 1971. (Albert Grandolini Collection)

One of the early F-6s acquired by the PAF shown in a right-hand turn, nicely displaying the underside of the aircraft and all three 30mm cannon. (Albert Grandolini Collection)

As far as the PAF's support to the Pak Navy was concerned, it was no more than a formality inserted in the concept of operations. The PAF did not have specialised aircraft to carry out maritime reconnaissance, nor did it have anti-shipping weapons to destroy surface vessels from stand-off ranges. Even if the enemy ships were somehow chanced upon, close-range visual attacks were a risky prospect in the face of intense retaliatory anti-aircraft fire. Lack of training for these specialised missions also mitigated against such attacks. The PAF was hard pressed in cobbling up a solution at this late stage, and the matter of naval support, in all earnestness, remained neglected.

In East Pakistan, the PAF's sole F-86 squadron had been conducting counter-insurgency operations since March 1971. In the face of the expected Indian intervention – duly backed up by 12 combat squadrons arrayed all around East Pakistan – the PAF could add little to the concept of operations, other than guessing the staying power of its forlorn squadron.

The PAF's Commander-in-Chief

The PAF was led by Air Marshal Abdur Rahim Khan, an officer with a bearing as impressive as his credentials. Soon after his commission in 1944, Rahim saw action in World War II when he flew Vultee Vengeance dive bombers in the RIAF's No 7 Squadron while stationed in Burma. Interestingly, Air Marshal Rahim Khan's IAF counterpart in 1971 was the former Squadron Commander of No 7 Squadron, Air Chief Marshal P C Lal.

Later in the PAF, Rahim flew Hawker Tempests and Hawker Furies in No 9 Squadron. Rahim started to move on the fast track in the PAF when, in 1951, he was selected to command No 11 Squadron, the PAF's first jet fighter unit equipped with the challenging Supermarine Attacker.

Rahim went on to command PAF Station Mauripur (later named Masroor), which was the PAF's largest Station in terms of assets as well as physical area. He did his staff course at RAF Staff College in Andover, and later, his defence studies course at Imperial Defence College in London. Well qualified in air power and war studies, he went on to command the PAF Staff College in Karachi. His staff jobs at Air Headquarters included those of ACAS (Ops) and ACAS (Admin). As ACAS (Ops), he was at the forefront of planning and conducting air operations during the 1965 Indo-Pak War. The C-in-C, Air Marshal Nur Khan, who had been appointed just 45 days prior to that war, was completely out of touch with the PAF, having been on deputation to PIA for a long period of six years. Rahim not only assisted his boss competently but gained useful experience in the conduct of operations that he was to put to good use in 1971.

Although he had impressive credentials and 'a strong presence and personality,' Air Marshal Rahim Khan was 'not given to articulation,' and could hardly sway an audience with his oratory.[24] On one occasion in November 1971, while delivering an important C-in-C's talk at the National Defence College, he disappointed the student officers with a rather insipid enunciation of his plans for the impending hostilities.[25] Students, ever judgemental about guest speakers, cast hurried aspersions on Rahim's abilities, something the PAF could have done without on the eve of a looming war.

Rahim's autocratic nature has been commented upon in *The Story of Pakistan Air Force – A Saga of Courage and Honour*, which merits attention. In the ostensibly ghost-written official history, the author (Air Commodore M Z Masud), states that Rahim, 'was inclined to be unduly quick tempered over arguable issues and this retarded the flow of new ideas and concepts between him and his subordinates, a process vital to progress.' While this aspect of his personality may have been somewhat of a bane for the subordinates during peace time, in war it could be seen as adherence to the principle of unity of

The most important offensive platform in the PAF's inventory was the Martin B-57 Canberra. This example was photographed while taking-off from Masroor AB outside Karachi. (Albert Grandolini Collection)

The PAF still had 65 North American F-86F Sabre fighter jets in operation as of 1971. While most were made compatible with US-made AIM-9B Sidewinder missiles, their primary task in the coming war was to be ground attack. (Albert Grandolini Collection)

command by a decisive and strict commander.

Air Marshal Rahim's choice of his ACAS (Ops) – the seniormost operations appointment then – was Air Commodore Mansoor Shah, who was, unconventionally, a transport pilot. Rahim thought it was inconsequential whether he had a transport pilot as his ACAS (Ops) during war, or a full-blooded fighter pilot (who could also have been an experienced combat veteran of the 1965 War). Given his overbearing nature, it is more likely that Rahim felt he could do without an 'expert' fighter pilot, who would have been ever so inclined to nit-pick on operational matters under consideration. Whatever the exact reason for Rahim's choice of his key assistant, the two apparently got along well, which was no less important for the working of a cohesive Operations team.

Besides the ACAS (Ops), the PAF's Deputy Chief of Air Staff (DCAS), Air Vice Marshal Eric Gordon Hall, was also a transport pilot – albeit, a good one at that, and a gallantry award holder from the 1965 War. Though the deputy (now the VCAS) had limited powers and mostly oversaw the PAF's non-operational matters, he was the senior-most Principal Staff Officer and was part of the policy-making Air Board. During war, when the C-in-C was busy conducting operations in Command Operations Centre (COC), frequent high level meetings with other services, as well as various senior ministerial staff had to be attended, or even presided over. For such situations, representation by an alternate authority having complete command over operational matters was desirable, something that a DCAS with a transport background was less qualified for. In the setup then prevailing, even the ACAS (Ops), with a similar transport background, could not have filled in.

Another important role of a deputy during war would be to periodically relieve the C-in-C in an intense and incessant round-the-clock activity. Only a similarly qualified officer could fill in as a reliever. Apparently, Air Marshal Rahim treated this matter nonchalantly, and felt comfortable as the sole person in the driving seat.

Two incidents that occurred prior to the 1971 War – which are sure to have rankled Air Marshal Rahim and exacerbated his wrath – need to be seen in context of their subsequent impact on the mindset of the C-in-C and his Air Staff.

Following the military operation against the rebels that started in East Pakistan on 26 March 1971, a group of 20 Mobile Observers of the PAF, (who had been ambushed and arrested by the *Mukti Bahini* earlier), were brutally massacred in Mymensingh Jail. The blood curdling incident (described in the chapter 'Fearless Last Stand') could not have been left unheeded by any military person in authority.

Some months later on 20 August, a Bengali flying instructor attempted to hijack a T-33 jet trainer to India, while on a routine training flight from Masroor Base. The novice student tried to wrest control of the aircraft to prevent the hijack by his instructor, but in the process, the aircraft crashed short of the Indo-Pak border in coastal Sind. The incident invoked the ire of everyone in the country, and it is likely that angst and retribution dwelt in the back of Rahim's mind as well. His mood was clearly reflected in the hard line that he took in discussions about the courses of action open, in the rapidly deteriorating politico-military situation.

The PAF's Inventory of Combat Aircraft

After the 1965 War, the PAF had to overcome the grave effects of military sanctions imposed by USA. All fighters, bombers, trainers and transport aircraft were of US origin, and with the spares supply suddenly stopped, the operational capability of PAF started to nosedive. The C-in-C of that time, Air Marshal Nur Khan, sensed the criticality of the situation and started an immediate search for suitable aircraft from new sources.

For Pakistan, the prevalent geopolitical realities restricted most of the available options. Pakistan's CENTO membership hardly endeared her to the Soviets. The Indians had already made inroads to Moscow, and the first shipment of six MiG-21s had made their operational debut during the 1965 War. The Soviets saw India not only as a socialist ideologue that could be helped militarily, but as its influential proxy and mouthpiece in the Non-Aligned Movement. The prospect of Soviets and Pakistanis developing any kind of patron-client linkage, thus, came to be a non-starter.

China, in the throes of the Cultural Revolution, had not shown much interest in developing newer aircraft technologies for the time being. Content with the copy of Soviet-supplied MiG-19s, China mass-produced this single-role fighter (renamed F-6) in the thousands. When Pakistan approached China for military help immediately after the 1965 War, she was only too glad to offer the F-6 to the new friend, the initial batch of 60 being free of charge. Several more batches were procured at a very affordable price. At the outbreak of the 1971 War, the PAF had 90 F-6s on the inventory. Though limited in range, speed and weapons payload, the PAF assigned it the day interceptor role, modifying it for carriage of two AIM-9B Sidewinders, alongside its 30mm guns. It could also perform a useful close air support task, armed with S-5 57mm rockets.

Another quick-fix solution was found in the shape of 90 ex-Luftwaffe Canadair Sabre Mk-6 (called F-86E in the PAF), which was a more powerful Canadian version of the North American Aviation F-86F. The deal was sealed in 1966 with the help of Iran, who had agreed to be the bogus buyer of West Germany's used fighters; this subterfuge was to bypass any US Congressional objections, which India was bound to stir up, had the deal been open and direct. It was expedient too, for the US administration to look the other way, as Pakistan was still a CENTO (and SEATO) partner, having provided useful aerial spying services against the Soviet Union. At the outbreak of the 1971 War, 74 of these F-86Es remained on the inventory.

A total of 24 modern Dassault Mirage IIIE/D/R (including three dual-seat 'D' and three reconnaissance 'R' sub-types) procured from France in 1968, were the newest and most advanced addition to the PAF combat inventory.[26] Besides performing a wide variety of missions, the Mirages could generate a higher daily sortie rate compared to the aging F-86s, F-104s and B-57s. They could navigate accurately to relatively deeper targets, and after the attack, egress at high speed. They could carry out straight line, hit-and-run intercepts against raiders as adeptly as the F-104s, though the radar performance of both fighters was equally suspect against low-flying targets in ground clutter. Surface attack weaponry of the Mirage was not yet commensurate with the more capable platform that it was. PAF had to rely on the old vintage Mk-117 (750 lbs) high explosive bombs delivered from critical dive angles. Specialist anti-runway weapons like the Durandal had not been produced by the French as yet. Air-to-air weapons included first generation AIM-9B Sidewinder missiles, and the semi-active radar-guided Matra R-530 missile. The latter missile was found to be impractical in combat situations due to its stringent launch parameters and very short range, particularly at low level, where most of the interceptions were expected.

It goes to the credit of Air Marshal Nur Khan for having inducted more than 200 aircraft in the PAF, within three years of the 1965 War. This 60 percent boost in aircraft numbers within a very short period put pressure on the pilots' training programme; however, the PAF was up to the challenge, and the pilots had full command over their new steeds in no time.

Alongside these latest acquisitions, the PAF had the aging F-86F and F-104A/B fighters, and B-57B/C bombers which were already second-hand aircraft previously belonging to the USAF or air forces of partner nations, and had been transferred to Pakistan under the US Military Assistance Programme. Sixty-five F-86F remained from the original package of 120, received in 1957-58. A nominal batch of eight F-104s remained out of the original 12 received in 1961, and two more received in 1964-65. Ten additional Royal Jordanian Air Force F-104s belatedly flew in to help the PAF in the last days of the war. Eighteen B-57 bombers remained out of 25 that were delivered in 1959-60.[27] Ten-odd T-33 jet trainers modified for bomb carriage were also inducted for war fighting as light attack aircraft. Even the few C-130B transports and T-6G piston engine trainers were modified for weapon delivery, as every bit counted. Spares for all these old aircraft were hard to find in the clandestine arms bazaars, as the US embargo continued. Despite such difficulties, the PAF managed to keep these out-dated aircraft fully operational.

All put together, the PAF had 290 combat aircraft in its inventory

Table 1: PAF Combat Aircraft Inventory

Aircraft Type	Number of Available Aircraft
B-57B/C	17
F-6	90
F-86E	74
F-86F	65
F-104A/B	8
Mirage IIIE/R/D	23
RB-57B	1
T-33A/RT-33A	12
Total	290

Table 2: IAF Combat Aircraft Inventory

Aircraft Type	Number of Available Aircraft
Canberra	80
Gnat	128
HF-24	32
Hunter F.Mk-56	112
MiG-21FL	136
Mystère IVA	32
Su-7BMK	104
Vampire FB.Mk-52	16
Total	640

Table 3: Indian Naval Aviation Aircraft Inventory

Aircraft Type	Number of Available Aircraft
Alizé	15
Sea Hawk F.Mk-6	18
Total	33

The second most-important acquisition for the PAF in the late 1960s was a total of 90 Canadian-built Sabre F.Mk 6 (also CL-13Bs): this was probably the most powerful variant of the original Sabre design. (Albert Grandolini Collection)

A major morale booster and a step forward in regards of technology was the acquisition of 24 Mirage IIIEP/DP/RP interceptors, starting in 1968. This pair was photographed at the tarmac of the Sargodha AB shortly after their delivery. (Albert Grandolini Collection)

By 1971, No. 9 Squadron, PAF, was down to only eight operational F-104As – one of which is visible on the right side of this photograph, next to one of the brand-new Mirage IIIEPs. (Albert Grandolini Collection)

on the eve of war, of which only 215 could be fielded, the remainder being under various stages of second- and third-line maintenance.[28] The enthusiastic technicians were expected to recover quite a few of the 33 under-repair F-86s during the course of the war. In effect, these F-86E/F – worth two squadrons' strength – could be considered as a small fleet of 'reserve' aircraft if the war became prolonged. A substantial number of 42 F-6s under overhaul in China, however, had to be counted out completely.

Deployment of Aircraft and their Tasks

Lacking depth, the country's geography dictated that the PAF had to field its aircraft at bases that were within easy reach of enemy strike aircraft. This compulsion was of little consequence as the PAF's fighters were not very long-legged and had to be based forward in any case. The deepest bases were Mianwali and Peshawar, 130nm and 115nm respectively, from the nearest border. The shallowest operational base in the north was Murid, a mere 65nm from the nearest border, while in the south, Talhar (near Badin) lay at a dangerously close distance of 32nm from the border. The average depth of bases was 90nm, translating to about eleven minutes flying time at combat speeds, which was not considered enough to carry out an interception by a ground-scrambled aircraft. Combat Air Patrols (CAPs), were, thus *de rigueur* for any chance of a successful interception.

An important operational consideration for the deployment of aircraft in the ground attack role rested on their useful radii of action, with a safe fuel margin for recovery.

From a maintenance standpoint, aircraft of similar types had to be based close to each other, for prompt availability of spares and other technical support. The deployment of aircraft at a particular base was also governed by the number of hardened pens available for sheltering the aircraft.

Mianwali was the only second-tier base, which meant that any intruder had to run the gauntlet of patrolling fighters from the forward bases of Murid, Sargodha or Risalewala. These first-tier bases lay starkly exposed, however, and could be easily surprised by low flying raiders. The relative safety offered by Mianwali led the planning staff to position a half-squadron detachment of B-57s, along with five Mirage IIIEs, which were considered important deep strike elements, to be kept out of harm's way when not up in the air. The B-57s were well-placed to perform night airfield strikes against Amritsar, Pathankot, Halwara,

The most important reconnaissance platform of the PAF by 1971 became three Mirage IIIRPs. They were equipped with Omera reconnaissance cameras (instead of the Cyrano II airborne intercept radar) in a slightly re-designed nose, but otherwise retained their combat capability. (Albert Grandolini Collection)

Ambala, Agra, Sirsa and Bikaner. In order to ensure the safety of these vital assets, a half-squadron detachment of F-6s was also deployed in Mianwali.

In Peshawar and Murid, a squadron each of F-86F was deployed for performing day air defence, day airfield strikes against Awantipura, Srinagar and Pathankot, and tactical air support in Chamb and Shakargarh Sectors.

The joint civil-military airfield at Chaklala (in Rawalpindi) remained active for the PAF's light communication aircraft and T-6G to carry out light attack operations. Its transport fleet of C-130s was, however, dispersed to different rear bases for safety.

Centrally located in the Northern Sector, Sargodha Base was expected to be the hub of most air activity, and a variety of fighter aircraft with different capabilities were positioned there. A squadron of the multi-role Mirage IIIs was deployed for several tasks including day and night air defence, photo-reconnaissance, and day airfield strikes against Amritsar and Pathankot. At a later stage, when the Army's main offensive was to be launched, the squadron was to suppress more airfields that threatened the sector. A squadron of F-86E, along with one full squadron and a half-squadron detachment of F-6, were deployed for day air defence, and tactical air support in Chamb and Shakargarh Sectors.

The PAF's relatively small fleet of C-130Bs was not only to play its role of transportation, but also chipped in as bombers during the 1971 War. (Albert Grandolini Collection)

Out of about 20 T-33As and RT-33As still in service, the PAF assembled the 12 of them as a secondary asset for ground-support duties. This photograph shows a RT-33, one of which flew some sorties in erstwhile East Pakistan to reconnoitre the position of insurgents during the 1971 War. (Albert Grandolini Collection)

Chander (near Hafizabad), located 42nm from the border, was deemed too vulnerable to surprise raids, and was activated for emergency recoveries only. No aircraft were deployed there.

At Risalewala, a squadron of F-6 was deployed mainly for day air defence. The location of Risalewala was somewhat more up front than Sargodha and was considered to be the first line of defence for the PAF's prime air base, besides providing much needed redundancy.

At Rafiqui, a squadron of F-86E was deployed for performing day

Table 4: PAF, Order of Battle, December 1971

C-in-C & CAS: Air Marshal A Rahim Khan
DCAS: Air Vice Marshal Eric G Hall
ACAS (Operations): Air Cdre S Mansoor Shah

SASO-ADHQ: Air Cdre M Zackria Butt
Director Operations: Group Captain Zulfiqar A Khan
Director Plans: Group Captain Jamal A Khan

Base	Wing	Squadron	Aircraft	Commanding Officer
Peshawar				**Gp Capt M Sadruddin**
		No 26 Sqn	16 F-86F	Wg Cdr S A Changazi
Murid				**Gp Capt A Rashid Sheikh**
		No 15 Sqn	16 F-86F	Wg Cdr S Nazir Jilani
Chaklala				**Gp Capt M A Qayyum**
	No 35 Wing			Wg Cdr A Masood Khan
		No 6 Sqn	6 C-130B	Wg Cdr S Nisar Yunus
Mianwali				**Gp Capt Sultan M Dutta**
		No 5 Sqn	5 Mirage IIIEP	Detachment
		No 7 Sqn	10 B-57	Wg Cdr M Yunis
		No 25 Sqn	8 F-6	Detachment
Sargodha				**Air Cdre Ghulam Haider**
	No 33 Wing			Gp Capt S Sajad Haider
		No 5 Sqn	18 Mirage IIIEP/RP/DP	Wg Cdr Hakimullah
		No 11 Sqn	16 F-6	Wg Cdr Sikandar M Khan
		No 18 Sqn	16 F-86E	Wg Cdr A I Bokhari
		No 25 Sqn	8 F-6	Wg Cdr Sa'ad A Hatmi
Risalewala				**Gp Capt Waheed Butt**
		No 23 Sqn	16 F-6	Wg Cdr S M H. Hashmi
Rafiqui				**Gp Capt S Zaheer Husain**
		No 17 Sqn	16 F-86E	Wg Cdr G Mujtaba Qureshi
Masroor				**Air Cdre Nazir Latif**
	No 32 Wing			Gp Capt Wiqar Azim
		No 2 Sqn	10 T-33A	Wg Cdr A A Randhawa
		No 7 Sqn	7 B-57B/C, 1 RB-57B	Wg Cdr Mahmood Akhtar (Dett)
		No 9 Sqn	7 F-104A/B	Wg Cdr Arif Iqbal
		No 19 Sqn	10 F-86E, 12 F-86F	Wg Cdr Sheikh M Saleem
Talhar		No 19 Sqn	4 F-86E	Detachment
Dacca				**Air Cdre Inam-ul-Haque**
		No 14 Sqn	16 F-86F, 1 T-33A, 1 RT-33A	Wg Cdr M Afzal Chaudhry

AIR DEFENCE ORDER OF BATTLE

SOC North (Sakesar): Gp Capt N Rehmat Khan
SOC South (Korangi Creek): Gp Capt M Anwar Shamim

Location	Radar Unit	Commanding Officer
Sakesar	**Master GCI**	**Gp Capt N Rehmat Khan**
Chuhr Kana	400 Sqn	Sqn Ldr Rab Nawaz Choudhry
Muridke	403 Sqn	Sqn Ldr Farooq Haider Khan
Tatepur	410 Sqn	Sqn Ldr Fateh Sher Khan
Cherat	411 Sqn	Sqn Ldr Jalil Akhtar
Kirana	4091 Flt	Sqn Ldr Sami-ullah
Rafiqui	4092 Flt	Sqn Ldr Nasimullah Khan
Kallar Kahar	4093 Flt	Sqn Ldr M U Kirmani
Badin	**Master GCI**	**Gp Capt Ayaz A Khan**
Malir	406 Sqn	Sqn Ldr Javed Sultan Butt
Pir Patho	4082 Flt	Sqn Ldr Waheed Ahmed
Mirpur (E Pak)	407 Sqn	Sqn Ldr Abdul Moiz Shahzada
Dacca	4071 Flt	Sqn Ldr Muhammad Nazir

The PAF's supersonic trio seen in clean configuration: the F-6 (foreground left) was limited to Mach 1.3, while the Mirage IIIEP (right) and F-104A (background left) were Mach 2 capable. (Albert Grandolini Collection)

air defence, and tactical air support in Sulaimanki Sector. Rafiqui was also expected to provide a sizeable air support effort for Pak Army's main offensive in the area east of Bhawalnagar.

Masroor, located on the northern shores of Arabian Sea, was the only base that could provide air defence in the Southern Sector, alongside the important tasks of tactical as well as maritime air support. Situated fairly in-depth from the land border side, the base was confronted with the dilemma of having no seaward early warning. A heavily beefed-up F-86E/F squadron was the mainstay of day air defence, and tactical air support in the Chor Sector. A half strength F-104 squadron was deployed to provide day and night air defence.[29] A half-squadron detachment of B-57s was deployed to perform night airfield strikes against Jaisalmer, Jodhpur, Uttarlai, Bhuj and Jamnagar, as well as night interdiction in the battle areas. Half a squadron of T-33s was also mustered for attacks against Uttarlai airfield, and air support in Chor Sector.

The closely located base at Drigh Road was a back-up to Masroor in case its runway was blocked, and could house a detachment of up to half a squadron; no aircraft were deployed before the war.[30]

The forward located base of Talhar was made operational with four F-86E, primarily tasked for safeguarding the Master GCI Station at nearby Badin. It also served the purpose of an emergency recovery base.

Surrounded on three sides by hostile territory – at places as close as 40nm – Dacca Base (Tezgaon) in East Pakistan housed a single F-86E squadron; it had the impossible task of providing day air defence over battle areas, as well as tactical air support all over the Eastern Wing. The squadron also had the unusual task of carrying out counter-insurgency missions against *Mukti Bahini* rebels.

Planned Flying Effort

The PAF had planned an optimal aircraft Utilisation Rate (UR) of 2.2 sorties per aircraft per day, for an envisaged war of 14 days.[31] This UR was based on an average of three daily sorties per aircraft for the first three days of the war, and two daily sorties per aircraft for the remaining eleven days. Thereafter, it was expected that the UR would steadily drop as fuel, ammunition and spares stocks started to diminish. It remained an open question, however, as to the duration for which the PAF could continue as a viable fighting force.

Based on an average serviceability rate of 75 percent, 161 aircraft out of the 215 aircraft available at the flight lines were expected to be airworthy at the outbreak of war. At the planned UR of 2.2 per aircraft, this would have produced 4,960 sorties over 14 days.

The Serviceability Rate of 75 percent was a tried and tested peace-time figure, though the serviceability during actual combat operations could vary by about 5 percent either side. Nonetheless, it served as a utile benchmark for war planning.

2
BARING THE FANGS

Planners in the PAF clearly knew that to achieve a favourable situation over the battlefield, air defence alone would not suffice, and the enemy air force would have to be countered through offensive means as well. Runways and air defence radars of consequence were considered the choice targets, and the PAF felt that sufficient disruption, if not outright neutralisation, could be effected. It was well-known that aircraft hidden away in concrete pens would be impervious to damage from air attack, while the well-camouflaged fuel storage facilities, ammunition dumps and command centres would also be problematic targeting choices.

Initial Operations

The PAF's offensive counter-air campaign also had to be carefully orchestrated, as the limited resources could not be frittered away too early in the war, yet pressure had to be maintained throughout. It was decided to attack deeper bases only at night – when the potency of the interceptors' targeting ability was the least effective – while the shallower ones could be attacked round the clock. Moreover, those 4-5 enemy airfields that could support an effort against the Pak Army's main offensive would be attacked in full force, as and when the operation unfolded. Prudent adjustment of attack intensity over time, as well as correct assessment of the desired point of application of force – the 'when' and 'where' – were, thus, the keys to success of the campaign. The PAF was hopeful of achieving a favourable air situation for a limited period, in a restricted area, to be able to provide meaningful air support to the Pak Army.

There have been disparaging commentaries about the PAF's purported 'pre-emptive' strikes on the evening of 3 December. An impression is conveyed as if it was beyond the PAF's professional acumen to pull off a feat of that order, totally disregarding the fact that it was none other than the PAF which had boldly struck IAF airfields pre-emptively on 6 September 1965 (albeit, with mixed results). The IAF may not have been grounded as a result, but its confidence and esteem surely went crashing, right at the outset of the 1965 War.

As has been stated earlier, in 1971 a fundamental difference was that all aircraft were parked inside hardened shelters. Closing down a few runways near to the border, even for short durations was, therefore, considered a not-too-risky option, and well worth the effort. The PAF had wisely decided not to attempt anything foolhardy against deeper targets during daylight hours, which would result in considerable losses, and a consequent blow to their morale early on in the war. Seen in this light, the PAF's first dusk strikes were nothing more than the start of a disruptive counter-air campaign at best, aimed at overburdening the IAF in its flying effort generation capabilities.

To mock these initial strikes as a failed pre-emptive effort is also unwarranted. India was not expected to launch any large-scale offensive on the Western front, beyond general holding operations, and improving defensive posture in some vulnerable areas; the question of pre-emption, thus, did not arise. If at all there was something to be pre-empted, it was the Indian invasion that started surreptitiously at Jessore in East Pakistan on the night of 21/22 November. Alas, this option – and the only one with some military merit – was a non-starter, due to the fear of intense international condemnation of an isolated Pakistan run by a much-derided military dictator.

An interesting rationale for the initial strikes has been elaborated in the book, *The Gold Bird* by Air Commodore Mansoor Shah, who was the ACAS (Ops) during the war.[1] Shah claims that these strikes were meant to provoke the IAF into retaliating against PAF bases, which were the only well-defended target sets in the country. He goes on to state that it was important to keep the IAF's attention focused on the bases or else, it might have switched to countrywide interdiction of lines of communications, where the PAF was defenceless. This line of reasoning posits that the IAF was not inclined to undertake airfield strikes, at least during daytime, unless provoked. The high attrition suffered by the IAF during daylight airfield strikes, and subsequent scaling down of these operations, would only suggest that the IAF had not thought out its counter air strategy carefully. Reading too much into the PAF's 'provocation' trap would only result in a one-dimensional view, and a wholly self-serving inference. Also, the fact that the IAF had simultaneously started its interdiction campaign targeting the lines of communications right from 4 December onwards, undermines Shah's conjecture about where the IAF's priorities lay.

First Strikes

The airfields of Amritsar and Pathankot are located just two minutes flying time from the Pakistani border – which is insufficient even for interceptors already airborne – to prevent any raiders from attacking. Even after the attack, there is not enough time for a fruitful chase before the raiders are safely across. A high-speed exit, especially under cover of fast fading light, almost ensures a clean getaway. Similarly, the airfields at Srinagar and nearby Awantipura nestled in the vales of Kashmir, offer low flying raiders the prospect of ingressing and egressing unobserved by radar, under cover of the hills.

While the ease of attacking the above-mentioned airfields made them tempting targets anyway, they were also crucial due to their ability to support Indian ground forces in the vitally important Chamb and Shakargarh Sectors. The PAF, therefore, decided to subject these airfields to a concerted, round-the-clock campaign starting at dusk on 3 December.

Whereas the hilly terrain in Kashmir provided the necessary shielding against early radar pick up, the plains of Punjab offered no hindrance to the clear line of sight of IAF radars. Two most menacing early warning radars were the Type-35 located at Amritsar and Faridkot. These were, therefore, also singled out for neutralisation in the first wave. F-104s, which were earmarked for air defence of the Southern Sector while based at Masroor, were being held back at Sargodha for two days especially for these anti-radar strikes.

As excitement built up for the first strikes, the President and Chief Martial Law Administrator, General Yahya Khan decided to visit the PAF's Command Operations Centre to monitor the action first-hand. As the President was leaving the Presidency, a most uncanny incident occurred, which could well have been out of a Hitchcock thriller. It is related by the President's ADC, Flight Lieutenant Arshad Sami Khan in his memoirs, *Three Presidents and an Aide*:[2]

> At the appointed hour, General Hameed came in driving a Toyota military jeep with his ADC sitting next to him. Before I could lead him into the visitor's room General Yahya walked out to the porch. Greeting General Hameed, he pointed to the blue winter sky and said "Nice weather for flying, Ham." As we got into the jeep, both ADCs in the rear, General Hameed at the wheel, and the President in front passenger seat and began to move, an unusually large vulture, more like an American condor, appeared from almost thin air and landed a few metres ahead of us. It blocked the narrow road leading to the inner gate of the Presidency. General Hameed slowly moved up the jeep but the vulture refused to budge. Hameed blew the horn but that only made the bird stare back with great defiance. The President jumped out and tried to scare it away with the General's baton (we were all in uniform). Amazingly, the vulture simply hopped a few steps sideways but remained in the centre of the road dividing the two lawns of the compound. Seeing the goings on, a nearby gardener ran up and began to shoo the bird with a large sickle, that finally made the bird clear the road with an ominous gait and we moved on.

Apparently unruffled by the vulture's ill-omened antics, the President arrived at the COC, and was briefed about the raid plan by an enthusiastic Air Marshal A Rahim Khan. After a crisp fifteen-minute briefing – which could not have been more than a mere formality – the President gave the go ahead at 16:30hrs (PST). The decision was instantly communicated to the pilots who were eagerly waiting at the flight lines. The first raid took off twenty minutes later.

No 26 Squadron opened up with strikes against Srinagar, and the nearby non-operational back-up airfield at Awantipura, with a TOT of 17:09hrs. Each strike package consisted of four F-86Fs armed with two 500lb general purpose bombs, and two escorts with guns only. Both missions were considered successful, with all bombs being delivered

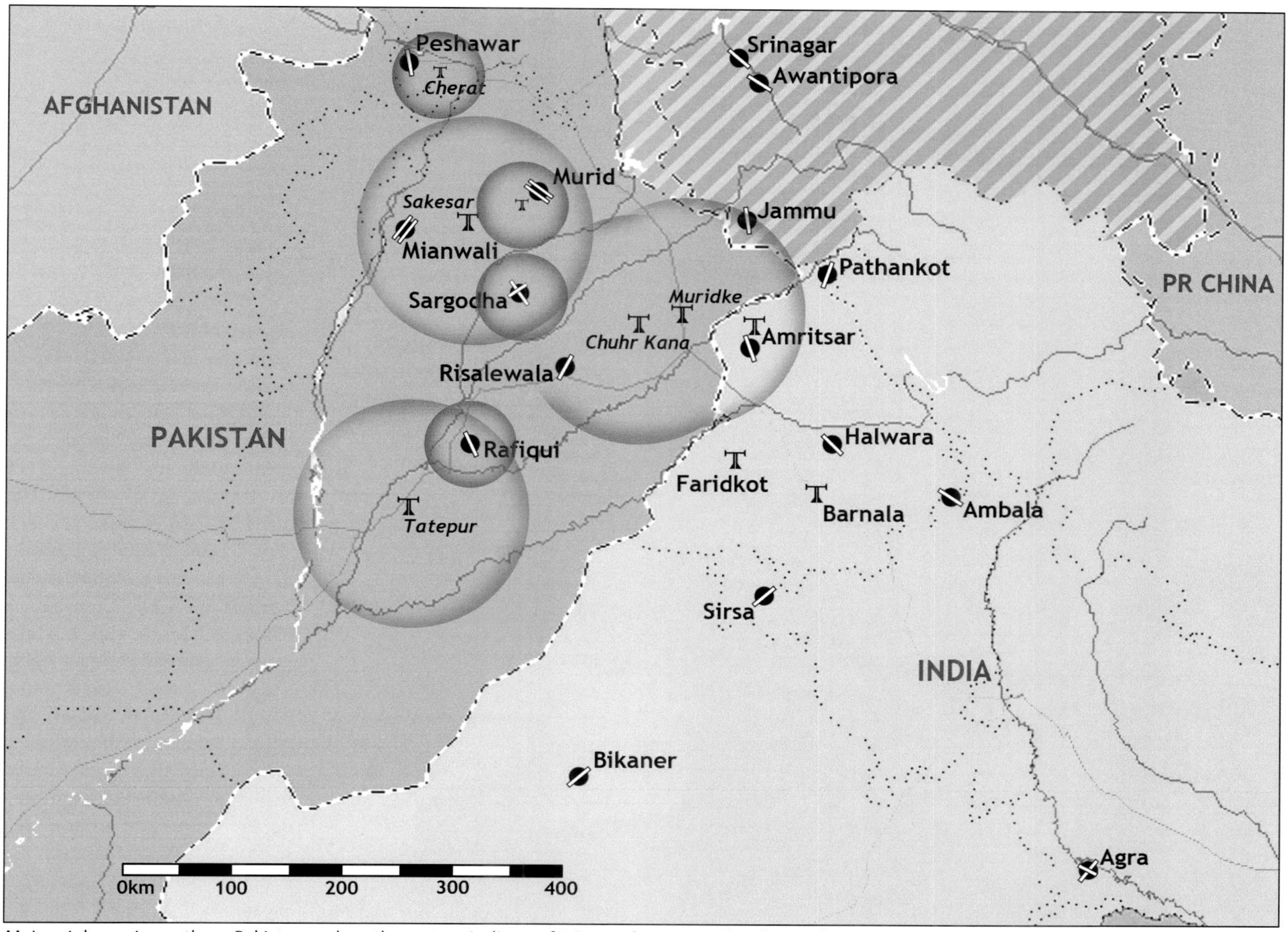

Major air bases in northern Pakistan and north-western India as of 3 December 1971. Also denoted are major radar stations on both sides: large circles on the Pakistani side denote the maximum high-altitude radar coverage; small circles the maximum low-altitude coverage (note that the actual radar range varied with weather conditions and depended on the local terrain). (Map by Tom Cooper)

The F-86Fs of No. 26 'Black Spiders' Squadron, PAF, flew the first air strike of the 1971 India-Pakistan War by attacking the Srinagar AB. This post-war photograph shows one of that unit's Sabres. (Albert Grandolini Collection)

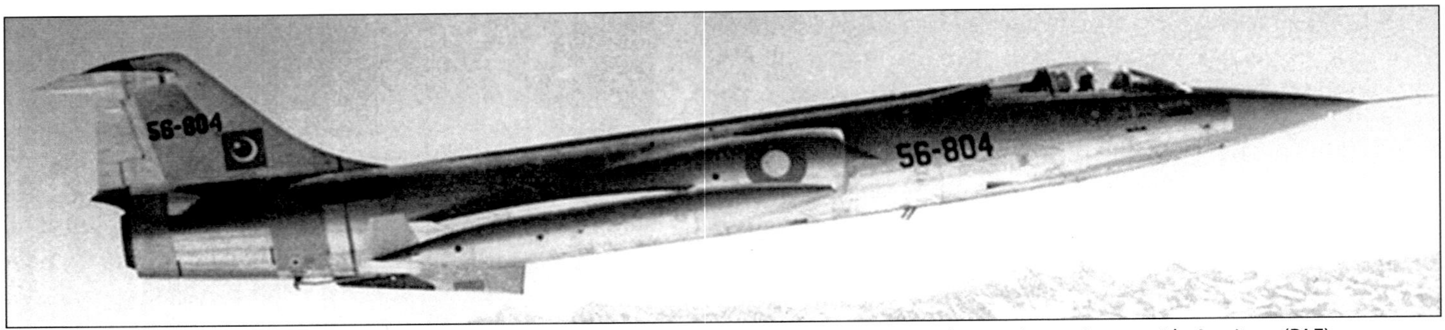

Lacking more advanced technology, the PAF deployed its F-104As into a strafing attack on the crucial IAF radar station outside Amritsar. (PAF)

Ground crew loading US-made Mk-117 bombs on the tandem hardpoint under the centreline of a PAF Mirage IIIEP: four such jets flew the first air strike on Amritsar AB, late in the afternoon of 3 December 1971. (PAF)

on the operating surfaces, and the escorts also getting to carry out strafing runs.

The second set of strikes were designed to neutralise Amritsar and Faridkot radars, so that subsequent strike missions to Amritsar and Pathankot airfields could ingress discretely. A pair of F-104s each carried out a strafing attack on the two radars at 17:10hrs. The antenna of Faridkot radar was claimed to have been hit. During the attack, Wing Commander Arif Iqbal spotted a Krishak light aircraft on the adjacent landing ground, and found it tempting enough to make a risky second pass. The Krishak is acknowledged by the IAF as having been damaged, though Arif claimed to have set it on fire. Amritsar radar was also attacked, with both pilots claiming to have hit the antenna; some damage to the communication equipment is acknowledged by the IAF. The lead F-104 (tail no 56-804) was equipped with a locally developed radar homing device, which was the only one of its type in the PAF. Trials had shown it to be a promising gadget, and as expected, had been instrumental in locating the well-camouflaged Amritsar radar. Damage to the radar was, however, short-lived as it became fully operational sometime during the night, which warranted a repeat mission the next morning.

Amritsar airfield was the next target, which was allotted to the speedy Mirages, with a TOT of 17:16hrs. Four Mirage IIIE, quite at ease without escorts, arrived unnoticed over Amritsar airfield which, incredibly, had its runway lights on. Three of the Mirages delivered two 750lb general purpose bombs each, while the fourth had hung bombs and had to call off dry. All aircraft exited without being intercepted. 'They made four to five craters from the beginning of the runway to about 600 meters,' is how the IAF CAS, Air Chief Marshal P C Lal, notes the attack in his book *My Years with the IAF*.[3]

Pathankot was singled out for two successive raids by Mirages and F-86s. The first raid consisted of four unescorted Mirage IIIE which were to attack Pathankot at 17:17hrs. The formation leader, however, did not have the good fortune of catching the runway with its lights on, and nobody could execute a proper attack in the evening haze and low light. The bombs fell in the general vicinity of the airfield. The second raid on Pathankot followed at 17:23hrs and consisted of four F-86F along with four similar escorts, all from No 15 Squadron based at Murid. Three of the attackers were able to deliver two 500lb general purpose bombs each, while the fourth was unable to release his load. Finding the Anti-Aircraft Artillery (AAA) fire not too menacing, the escorts also dove down for strafing attacks in the airfield area.

Considering that one quarter of the 32 planned bombing and strafing sorties were unsuccessful, any pretence about significant success of the first strikes was rather misplaced. The shallow dive angles dictated by AAA avoidance tactics had also worked against deeper bomb penetration, and whatever cratering that occurred was repaired overnight. The saving grace of the whole operation was that the enemy was unable to interfere in any way, and all aircraft were recovered safely. The results of the opening strikes were, however, not completely dismal, and there were ample indications of operational

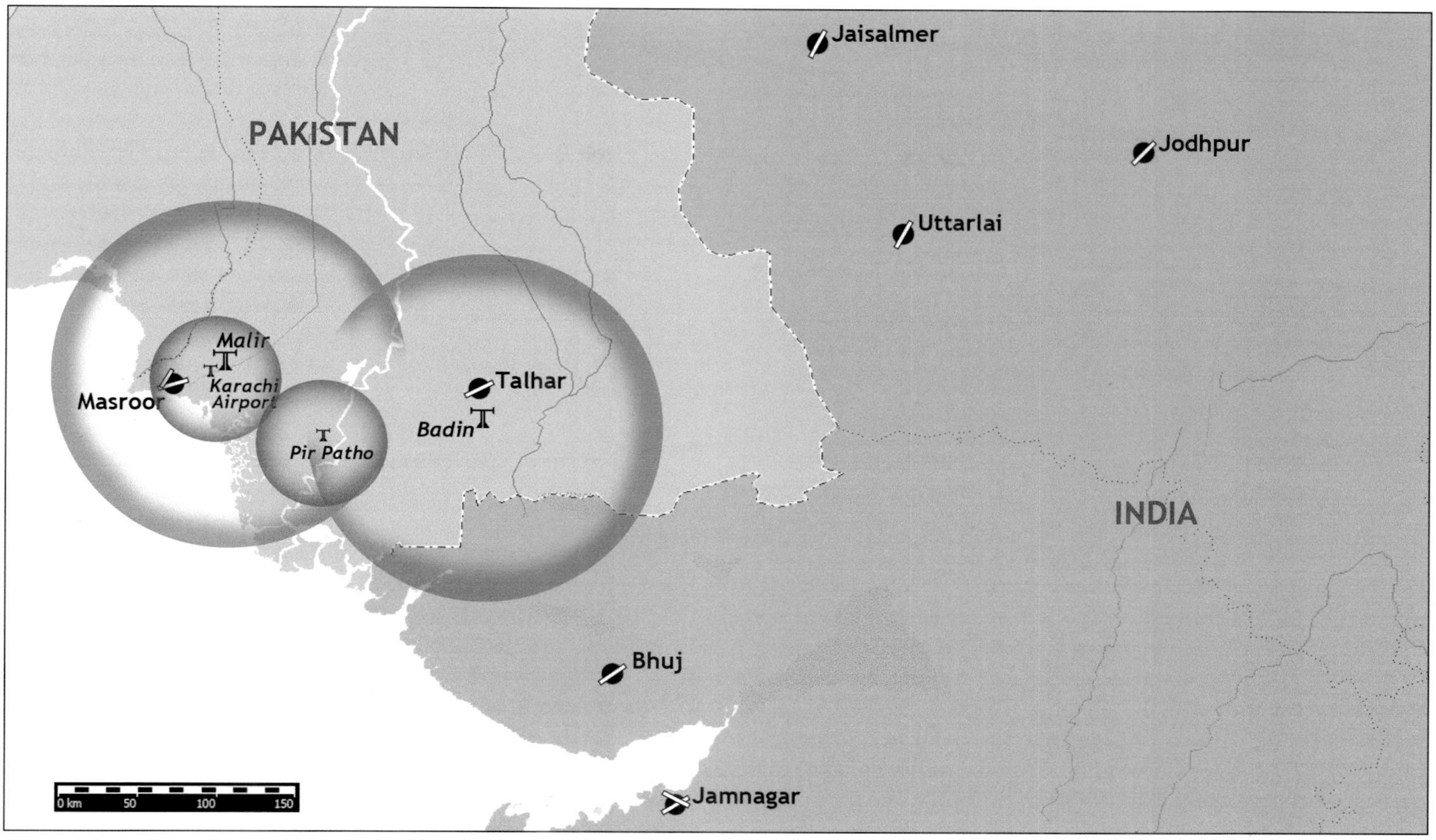

Major air bases in southern Pakistan and western India as of 3 December 1971. Also shown are major radar stations on both sides: large circles on the Pakistani side denote the maximum high-altitude radar coverage; small circles the maximum low-altitude coverage (note that the actual radar range varied with weather conditions and depended on the local terrain). (Map by Tom Cooper)

activities being sufficiently disrupted at these forward airfields. This only reinforced the earlier surmise of the planners that, if administered round the clock, such treatment could go some way in alleviating the IAF's air support effort, at least in the Shakargarh Sector, where the Indian Army had opened up mightily with its main offensive.

Night Offensive

From the night of 3 December onwards, B-57s came to be the mainstay of the night airfield bombing campaign. No 7 Squadron was split up between Mianwali and Masroor, with ten and eight aircraft respectively. The Mianwali detachment was commanded by OC, No 7 Squadron, Wing Commander Muhammad Yunis, while the Masroor detachment was commanded by Wing Commander Mahmood Akhtar, a 1965 War bomber veteran and a former OC of No 31 Bomber Wing.[4] T-33s of No 2 Squadron, under command of Wing Commander Asghar Randhawa, also chipped in usefully in the night campaign. Even the C-130s were mustered to fly a few audacious bombing missions.

Close on the heels of the dusk strikes by the fighters, the B-57s struck eleven IAF airfields: seven in the north, viz Agra, Ambala, Amritsar, Bikaner, Halwara, Pathankot, and Sirsa, and four in the south, viz Jaisalmer, Jamnagar, Jodhpur and Uttarlai. T-33s singled out the latter airfield for their plucky bombing runs on the first night.

Wing Commander Mahmood Akhtar and his navigator Flight Lieutenant A B Subhani spearheaded the B-57 night bombing campaign, when they struck Uttarlai on the night of 3 December at 19:00hrs. The Base Commander of Uttarlai, Air Commodore V K Murthy vividly recalls the B-57 strike.

> On 3 December 71 at dusk, after declaring Guns Free, I was returning to my bunker when I saw Canberra aircraft overhead and wondered who the devil it was coming at this time and without informing the base. The aircraft made a direct approach and flew along the runway at 1,000 feet dropping bombs at will. There were a total of eight craters starting from the dumbbell to the end of the runway, making the airfield totally ineffective. The impact of the bombs made deep craters on either side of the centre line – five on the right and three on the left. To patch up the craters, it took the MES Rapid Repair Force about 7 days.[5]

The raid on Agra airfield on the very first night was significant as it was the deepest target attacked by any PAF aircraft. Two Mianwali-based B-57s staged through Rafiqui, and managed to reach Agra 375nm away, without being intercepted *en route*. The effort was only a partial success as the first B-57 failed to produce any results due to dud bombs. The second B-57 flown by Flight Lieutenant Mazhar Bukhari with Flight Lieutenant Nasim Khan as navigator was able to carry out the attack successfully at 21:05hrs, though it barely survived an AAA barrage from friendly forces on recovery at Rafiqui.

Evidence of the success of some other B-57 strikes flown on the night of 3/4 December can be gleaned from Air Chief Marshal P C Lal's book, in which he makes a mention of the outcome at some of the IAF airfields.

The B-57 strike to Halwara on the night of 3 December at 23:07hrs was flown by Squadron Leader Abdul Basit with Squadron Leader G A Khan as his navigator. 'The B-57 dropped eight bombs, three of which landed on the runway making two major craters,' recollects Lal.[6] The Indian *Official History of the 1971 India-Pakistan War* also corroborates Lal's assessment thus: 'The craters at Halwara were more extensive and were repaired only by the next morning.'[7] Though Lal claims in his book that one of the three missiles fired hit the B-57, the fact is that the aircraft landed safely, without suffering any damage.

The B-57 fleet continued the PAF's offensive on the forward air bases of the IAF into the night from 3 to 4 December 1971. By this time, most of the fleet had its upper surfaces painted in olive green (for details, see the colour section). (Albert Grandolini Collection)

Apparently, Lal has been unable to sift from the spurious static noise when he wrongly claims, 'the PAF Chief admitted this loss.'

In the Sirsa strike on 4 December at 03:18hrs, the B-57 pilot Squadron Leader Yusuf Alvi and his navigator Flight Lieutenant Muhammad Ali, claimed to have seen two bombs explode on the runway. 'Part of the runway was hit … It was enough though to make the runway unserviceable for the night … the bombs had time-delayed fuses and kept on exploding at intervals till dawn delaying clearance and repair work,' confirms Lal.[8]

A report on the outcome of another B-57 attack on Sirsa on the night of 4 December at 20:10hrs came from a most unlikely source. Flight Lieutenant Harish Sinhji, a Sirsa-based MiG-21 pilot, who had become a POW a day after the attack, gave a rather agreeable account of the results of the B-57 bombing to his interrogators:

> After one of PAF's night bombing strikes on our airfield, we were all grounded for six hours. The runway had been cratered at many places. The following morning, our OC, Wing Commander V B Sawardekar, took us all to the runway to show us the Pakistani pilot's bombing accuracy. Pointing to the craters on our runway, he said that this is the kind of accuracy the IAF pilots should achieve against Pakistani targets.[9]

The crew of the B-57, Flight Lieutenant Iftikhar Naqvi and his navigator Squadron Leader M Irfan, had reason to be happy when they received personal compliments from the PAF C-in-C, who was in on Sinhji's report.

The outcome of the attack on Agra on the night of 5 December at 01:00hrs by Squadron Leader Yusuf Alvi with Flight Lieutenant Muhammad Ali as his navigator, is described thus: 'The runway was put out of commission temporarily, and some of the Canberra missions had to be cancelled,' according to the *Official History of the 1971 India-Pakistan War*.[10]

In an apparent chance hit during an attack on Pathankot on the night of 6 December, 'a missile preparation shed was hit but the fire was put out before any damage occurred to the main storage area. Also an aircraft servicing hangar was hit and a Vampire aircraft parked inside was partially destroyed,' notes the official Indian history.[11] Since two sorties were flown against Pathankot during that night, it is difficult to credit any particular set of aircrew.[12]

On the following nights, several other airfields were added to the earlier targets, and included Adampur, Jammu, Srinagar, and Bhuj. All in all, fifteen IAF airfields came to be targeted incessantly over the next twelve nights.

One of the enigmas of the war in the south was the status of Bhuj airfield, against which the PAF flew as many as 14 bombing sorties. Official Indian sources do not list this airfield as having housed any combat aircraft during the war, nor was it used as a stage-through base. Due to its proximity to the Kutch Sector, it was used as a transport base for prompt and regular supply of troops to prevent a repeat of the 1965 Rann of Kutch flop. The raids on Bhuj were a costly undertaking for the PAF in terms of air effort expended, and the couple of lives lost; nonetheless, an unlikely endorsement of the quality of bombing comes from Air Chief Marshal P C Lal, who notes that, 'the PAF bombed it fairly accurately.' Apparently, Lal is referring to the results of three raids flown shortly after midnight of 8/9 December, in which all three sets of aircrew claimed that their bombs had struck the runway.[13]

If the preceding comments are any indicator of how the PAF's night bombing campaign fared at large, one can be sure that the PAF was causing more than just insomnia at IAF bases.

Disappointingly however, out of the 130 sorties flown by B-57s, T-33s and C-130s, 40 percent were reported by the aircrew – in all candour – to be unsuccessful, either due to armament malfunctions, or because the targets could not be located, and bombs were dropped in the general target vicinity on 'dead reckoning'. The effects of the 186 tons of ordnance dropped in the 77 successful night sorties are best known to IAF, as the PAF had no means of carrying out any damage assessment. Going by the few available reports, one can imagine that flight line activities must have been hampered considerably, and repairs to the operating surfaces and other damaged infrastructure would have used up precious manpower and resources. Night bombings would have kept the supervisors and crews awake, giving them no respite, and inducing intense fatigue. Disruption of operational and maintenance activities, as well as exhaustion of base personnel including key decision-makers would, in a most parsimonious assessment, figure out as fair achievements of the night bombing campaign.

Three B-57s, along with their crew, were lost to AAA during raids on the night of 5/6 December. In the north, Flight Lieutenant Javed Iqbal (P) and Flight G M Malik (N) met a tragic end after being shot down at Amritsar. Though they had managed to eject, both were badly beaten up by the mob that had swarmed at the place of landing, and were fatally injured as a consequence.[14] In the south, Squadron Leader Ishfaq Qureshi (P) and Flight Lieutenant Zulfiqar Ahmad (N) went down at Bhuj while Squadron Leader Khusro (P) and Squadron Leader Peter Christy (N) went down at Jamnagar.[15] Apparently, the benefit of attacking an airfield in moonlit conditions – a 17-day old waning moon, about 85 percent of its full illumination – worked both ways, and helped the AAA gunners in sighting and tracking the attacking bombers.

Wing Commander Mahmood Akhtar, the B-57 detachment commander at Masroor was also the field coordinator of all bomber operations, liaising with the COC at Rawalpindi. In his view, 'despite difficulties in maintaining and operating an aging weapon system, the detachment continued flying with gusto and dedication.' He cites enthusiastic plans for bombing Bombay Harbour in retaliation for raids on Karachi Harbour. The mission was to be flown – rather precariously – after being staged through Talhar on the pattern of the long-range strikes to Agra that took off from Mianwali and were staged through Rafiqui. These were flown with especially modified B-57s configured with four F-86 200-gallon drop tanks each. Akhtar was extremely disappointed at the cancellation of the Bombay raid at the last minute, for reasons best known to the COC. His other disappointment was on the wasted effort during the unsuccessful night missions, and in particular, he blames a wrongly-marked location of Jaisalmer airfield on the aeronautical charts, that cost the PAF nine wasted sorties.

Table 5: PAF Night Attacks on IAF Air Bases

Aircraft Type	Number of Successful Sorties	Ordnance Deployed
B-57	62	40 sorties: 9 x 500lbs
		20 sorties: 4 x 1000lbs
		2 sorties: 7 x 1000lbs
T-33	13	2 x 500lbs
C-130	2	1 sortie: 45 x 500lbs
		1 sortie: 35 x 500lbs
Total tonnage		410,000 lbs (186 tonnes)

The Day Offensive Continues

The daylight counter air campaign that had started the previous evening continued on the morning of 4 December at 06:35hrs with a pair of F-104s led by Squadron Leader Amjad Hussain successfully attacking Barnala radar. 'The radar at Barnala was off the air for nearly 12 hours,' reports the Indian official history.[16]

The radar at Amritsar, which had come back on a few hours after being attacked the previous evening, warranted a revisit. Squadron Leader Rashid Bhatti, along with Squadron Leader Amanullah, took off on the morning of 4 December at 06:50hrs, and was able to spot the radar antenna despite the winter haze. As Bhatti was diving for the attack, Amanullah yelled that there was a Gnat behind him, and gave a call to exit. Bhatti jettisoned his drop tanks, lit up the afterburner and sped away. In the meantime, Amanullah, who found the Gnat in his gunsight, fired a Sidewinder; however, being in too much of a haste to join up with his leader, he was unable to confirm the result of his shooting. His gun camera film was also too hazy for ratification of the kill.

Another mission had to be flown against the Amritsar radar, so at midday, Squadron Leader Amjad Hussain and Squadron Leader Rashid Bhatti, took off again. Short of reaching the radar, a sharp-eyed Bhatti spotted a pair of Su-7s orbiting overhead. Amjad found himself favourably placed to get behind one of the Su-7s, but the other one was able to manoeuvre behind Amjad. Sensing trouble, Bhatti warned Amjad, who promptly disengaged and sped away, pretty much as Bhatti had done in the previous mission. With the Su-7 intent on chasing Amjad, Bhatti found it opportune to let go a Sidewinder which, he claims, rammed the Su-7's huge afterburning exhaust with a big flash.[17] Bhatti's attempts at going for the second Su-7 were foiled when he was confronted with an asymmetric flight condition due to a drop tank failing to jettison. Both F-104s landed back with the mission unaccomplished yet again, though the pilots were not altogether cheerless after the scrap with the Su-7s.

The Amritsar radar-busting project came to a halt at midday on 5 December, when the specially-equipped F-104 flown by Squadron Leader Amjad Hussain was shot down by AAA, while carrying out a strafing pass over the radar. Amjad ejected and was hauled up as a POW.

The 12-odd sorties flown for 'suppression of enemy air defences', did not yield the desired results. The F-104s were, therefore, promptly moved to Masroor in the south, where the F-86s were eagerly waiting to be relieved from their largely blind night patrols.

The PAF's day airfield strike missions, in the meantime, continued apace. Besides the four airfields struck on the first evening of war, additional airfields of Jammu in the north and Uttarlai, Jamnagar and Jaisalmer in the south, were included in the day campaign.

Of the 146 day-sorties, including 35 escorts, flown against nine IAF airfields, damage caused to the runways was generally minor, and was usually repaired within a few hours. Some of the missions that caused noteworthy damage have been mentioned in the Indian *Official History of the 1971 India-Pakistan War*, and are worth studying.

On the morning of 5 December at 06:37hrs, Wing Commander Abdul Aziz led a flight of four F-86Fs from No 26 Squadron for a raid on Srinagar airfield. The formation claimed four bombs on the runway, and four on the adjacent fair-weather strip, where a helicopter was seen to be hovering. The Indian official history acknowledges that, 'the runway was slightly damaged, but was soon repaired. One Alouette helicopter flying near the airfield was shot down and both pilots were seriously injured.'[18]

On the evening of 6 December at 16:50hrs, a flight of three Mirages led by Squadron Leader Arif Manzoor successfully attacked Amritsar airfield. At about the same time, six F-86Fs (including two escorts) from No 26 Squadron led by the OC, Wing Commander Sharbat Changazi, attacked Srinagar airfield. 'The runways at both airfields were slightly damaged but were quickly repaired,' according to the Indian official history.[19]

On the morning of 9 December at 08:30hrs, Wing Commander Changazi led a large formation of four F-86F along with a similar number of escorts, for an attack on Srinagar airfield. The bombing caused, 'six small craters on the runway; they were repaired by night-fall.'[20] No matter that the size of the holes failed to make an impression on the Indian historian, the PAF had managed to keep the airfield out of operation for the whole day.

On the morning of 10 December at 10:45hrs, a formation of six Mirage IIIE (including two escorts) led by Squadron Leader Rao Akhtar, attacked Pathankot airfield. While the bombs were delivered accurately, Akhtar also got a chance to strafe at two Hunters lined up for take-off. The stream of bullets passed in between the Hunters which somehow survived the volley. 'The Mirages made three craters on the runway at Pathankot but miraculously, two Hunters about to take-off were not hit,' notes the Indian history.[21] A more forthright account is given by Squadron Leader Keith Lewis, a MiG-21 detachment commander at Pathankot, who was an eyewitness to the raid:

> Regarding the attack itself, the runway was badly cratered, slightly off centre, about a 1,000 yards up, and so was the parallel taxi track. A very detailed inspection of the runway and taxi-track followed, and to the credit of the PAF Mirage formation, it must be stated for the record that they had taken out both the runway and the parallel taxi-track.

Lewis also states that 'both the Hunter Mk 56 aircraft of No 27 Squadron were started up and taxied back to their dispersal area.'[22]

On the afternoon of 15 December at 12:30hrs, four F-86Fs led by

The HF-24 was the last work of the German aircraft designer Kurt Tank, famous from the times of the Second World War, when he used to work for Focke Wulf. Much anticipated by the IAF, the type entered operational service, only following protracted development, in the late 1960s: by 1971, only two units were equipped with the Marut. (Albert Grandolni Collection)

A Mirage IIIEP unleashing a salvo of Mk 117 (750lb) bombs. Up to four of these could be mounted on each of the two RPK-10 drop tanks carried on inboard underwing stations. (PAF)

Wing Commander Changazi attacked Srinagar airfield yet another time. The Indian history notes: 'At Srinagar one Vampire was hit on the ground inside a blast pen.'[23]

In the south, PAF also flew 12-odd day sorties against Uttarlai, Jaisalmer and Jamnagar, utilising the F-104 in strafing attacks. Only one such mission was successful on the morning of 11 December, when Wing Commander Arif Iqbal and Squadron Leader Amanullah came upon a pair of HF-24s lined up for take-off at Uttarlai, and these were duly strafed. Amanullah was able to destroy his target completely, while Arif Iqbal's claim was later learnt to have been a 'damage.'

On the afternoon of 12 December, a similar strafing mission to Jamnagar turned luckless when a pair of F-104s was intercepted by two MiG-21FLs as they were positioning for attack on the airfield. The wingman, Flight Lieutenant Tariq Habib recalls that during the positioning turn, Wing Commander Mervyn Middlecoat, was easily picked off by the pursuing MiGs. Unable to outmanoeuvre or outrun the nimble MiG-21, Middlecoat was shot down in a gun attack off the coast in the Gulf of Kutch.[24] Middlecoat ejected over the marshes not too far from the small coastal town of Sika, but no trace of him was ever found; there have, however, been some claims of the sighting of floating debris.

An Epic Dogfight over Srinagar

The morning of 14 December saw yet another bombing raid on Srinagar airfield led by the squadron's commander, Wing Commander Sharbat Changazi. Other formation members were Flight Lieutenants H K Dotani, Amjad Endrabi and Maroof Mir, whose Sabres were armed with two 500lb bombs each. Escorting the four-ship package were Flight Lieutenants Salim Baig and Rahim Yousefzai. Altogether it was a formidable force, and given the familiarity with Srinagar, it seemed like it would be a routine mission.

After a 25-minute flight through the picturesque hills and vales of western Kashmir, Changazi's commanding voice broke the radio silence, 'Leader pulling up, contact with the target.' The time was 07:30hrs. Dotani, Endrabi and Mir followed at short intervals, none missing the easily visible airfield complex. Popping up to 5,000 feet above ground, they dived one by one to release their bombs on the runway. Baig and Yusefzai loosened into an orbit overhead the airfield, looking out for any interceptors through the relentless AAA barrage.

Flying Officer Nirmal Jit Singh Sekhon of No 18 Squadron was rolling for take-off as No 2 in a two-Gnat formation, just as the first bombs were falling on the runway. Said to have been delayed due to

Developed as a light-weight, point-defence interceptor, the diminutive Folland Gnat F.Mk 1 earned itself the reputation of a 'Sabre Slayer' during the 1965 India-Pakistan War. However, Flying Officer Nirmal Jit Singh Sekhon had no serious chance in a dogfight against four F-86Fs over Srinagar on the morning of 14 December 1971. (Albert Grandolini Collection)

dust kicked up by the preceding Gnat, Sekhon lost no time in singling out the first Sabre pair, which was re-forming after the bombing run. Changazi was, however, quick to detect the attacker behind his wingman. 'Gnat behind, all punch tanks,' yelled Changazi. No 3 (Endrabi), who was just pulling out of the attack, was horrified to see the Gnat no more than 1,000 feet away, and firing at Dotani. 'Break left,' called Endrabi, as he himself manoeuvred to get behind the Gnat. Dotani, who had been turning frantically, found his low-powered Sabre teetering at the verge of stall. Unable to hang around any longer with such a precarious energy state, he decided to make a getaway. No 4 (Mir) had completed his bombing run in the meantime, and having no visual contact with the rest, decided to head home as well. The Gnat Leader, Flight Lieutenant Ghumman, had also lost visual with his wingman just after take-off. Said to have failed in re-establishing contact, Ghumman remained out of the fight leaving Sekhon to handle the muddle all by himself.

The fight had turned into a classic tail chase, with a Sabre followed by a Gnat, which in turn was followed by another Sabre. 'I am getting behind one but the other is getting an edge on me,' is how Sekhon had described the situation to his controllers. With two more free fighters watching over, the lone Gnat was practically up against four Sabres. Endrabi had, by now, closed in behind the Gnat's rear quarters, and was firing steadily. He was sure that he would get the Gnat, he excitedly forecast on the radio. His Sabre was incessantly spewing out a stream of 0.5" bullets, but despite good aim and textbook range, remained off the mark. What should have been a quick kill dragged on clumsily, testing everyone's patience and nerves.

The Sabre had enough firepower to riddle a whole formation with bullets, so everyone was dumb-founded when Endrabi's voice crackled on the radio, 'Three is Winchester!' It meant that he had exhausted 1,800 rounds, and his guns had stopped firing. The Gnat was still turning circles, and it seemed that unless help came fast, Endrabi would soon be at the receiving end.

Changazi was carefully monitoring the dogfight while looking out for the elusive Gnat leader, whose fleeting glimpse he had caught a while ago.[25] On hearing that Endrabi was spent, Changazi called him to join up as his wingman. Dislodging himself from the Gnat's tail, Endrabi moved towards his leader. As the two were forming up, Sekhon took advantage of the slack, straightened out and jettisoned the drop tanks. In the flurry of activity, Sekhon had overlooked a vitally important step, and it was just as well that he shed dead weight for the next round. Nimbler than before, the Gnat could be seen to turn ever more tightly as it started to catch up onto Changazi and Endrabi's pair.

The situation was getting stickier by the minute, and in a couple of turns the Gnat was in a menacing position. The escorts instantly dived down to grapple with Sekhon. While Yusefzai covered up as wingman, Baig easily manoeuvred to get behind the Gnat, much to everyone's relief.

Baig had the privilege of opening his Squadron's account by shooting down a Hunter near Peshawar, ten days earlier. Since then, he had been in the thick of the action in almost every sortie that he went up for. This experience, coupled with his unflappable personality, came in handy as Baig calmly positioned his pipper on the canopy of the Gnat, and opened fire. Less than three seconds later the Gnat started to spew thick black smoke. Baig knew it was all over so he stopped firing, and watched for the next move.

Meanwhile, the Base Commander and some senior pilots who were in the ATC tower to monitor the dogfight, heard Sekhon's frantic call to his leader, 'I think I have been hit. Ghumman, come and get them.' With the mission leader still nowhere to be seen, the baffled ground supervisors tried to help Sekhon with the emergency, but to no avail. Baig, who was following behind, saw the Gnat level its wings and head for the airfield, as if to indicate that for him the fight was over. Suddenly, the Gnat went inverted as it dove down uncontrollably from very low height. In all likelihood, the aircraft's flight control system had failed. Sekhon attempted a last-minute ejection as his canopy was seen to fly off, but the height was too low for the ejection system to function fully. The wreckage of the Gnat was found in a gorge, a few miles from the Base. The Sabre formation made it to Peshawar unscathed after one of the most eventful airfield strike missions of the war.[26]

Appraisal of the Campaign

The PAF flew a total of 288 offensive counter-air sorties, of which 158 were flown during the day and 130 were flown at night. 81 sorties (28 percent of the effort) were unsuccessful as the armament could not be delivered due to several reasons; these included the inability to locate the target, armament delivery malfunction, and interception by enemy fighters. Five aircraft were lost during the missions, two during the day and three at night, amounting to a campaign attrition rate of 1.7 percent which was considered within acceptable limits.

While the PAF had yet to go all-out pending the Army's main offensive, its offensive counter-air campaign disrupted IAF operations to an adequate extent. At 10 percent of the total war effort, the scale of the offensive counter-air operations was optimal for the 'softening up' phase and was well orchestrated at the COC. While the results are nowhere close to those of a textbook campaign, primarily for want of a proper runway denial weapon, the PAF's offensive resolve to take on a much larger enemy was clearly evident. The aircrew had also achieved sufficient proficiency to undertake the all-out phase of the campaign, but for the Army's inability to unfold the much-vaunted offensive.

3
STEMMING THE TIDE

Air Defence in the Northern Sector

With just four low level radars available in the northern air defence sector, there was no possibility of providing uninterrupted coverage along the border, including the battle areas. The large gaps could be easily exploited by tree-top hugging intruders to knock out PAF bases and radar stations before turning their attention to the battlefield. It was surmised by the PAF Air Staff that the few low-level radars could be best utilised for providing cover to the bases, thus at least ensuring the PAF's viability for the all-important task of tactical air support. The only problem with this scheme, and a major one at that, was the rear location of radars which offered barely three minutes early warning; this was considered insufficient even for vectoring nearby standing CAPs. It was hoped that some early warning by Mobile Observer Units (MOUs) would contribute gainfully, by adding to the reaction time.

Group Captain Rahmat Khan, the Sector Commander, Sector Operations Centre (North) located at Sakesar, had a patchwork of reasonably modern sensors at his disposal, but far short of the optimum numbers required for an effective air defence ground environment. High level radar surveillance in the Northern Sector rested with a high-powered FPS-20 radar at Sakesar, while a Condor radar each at Chuhr Kana, Muridke and Tatepur (near Multan), provided medium level cover. Low level cover rested with four AR-1 radars located at Rafiqui, Cherat, Kallar Kahar and Kirana. The hill-top positions of the radars at the latter three locations were seen as a significant plus, due to an extension in the radar pick up range by as much as 50 percent. Major towns like Islamabad, Rawalpindi, Sialkot, Gujranwala, Lahore, Lyallpur and Multan, however, lay outside the low level radar cover.

The locations of air bases at Mianwali, Murid, Peshawar, Risalewala, Rafiqui and Sargodha served the air defence requirements over the battle areas reasonably well and provided sufficient redundancy. Day interceptors in the Northern Sector included 48 F-6, 32 F-86E, 32 F-86F and 23 Mirage IIIE/R/D. Of the latter, 17 Mirage IIIE subtypes also doubled as night interceptors. These had Cyrano II airborne intercept radars, but it was practically useless in the look-down mode, being a simple pulse radar prone to ground clutter. It was, however, presumed that the Cyrano might be of some use in a ground controlled interception at night, if a less clutter prone low-to-high flight profile could be pulled off somehow. Interceptors were equipped with AIM-9B Sidewinder missiles and cannon/guns for the air defence role.

The strategy of defending the bases first and foremost, depended on being able to intercept the intruders before they released their weapons. With the inadequate early warning however, it seemed that the PAF would have to be content with grabbing the 'fleeing burglar's loincloth,' as it were.

Intercepting the Intruders

The morning of 4 December promised action, as the IAF was expected to retaliate forcefully in response to the PAF's strikes against some of the Indian airfields the previous evening and through the night. The

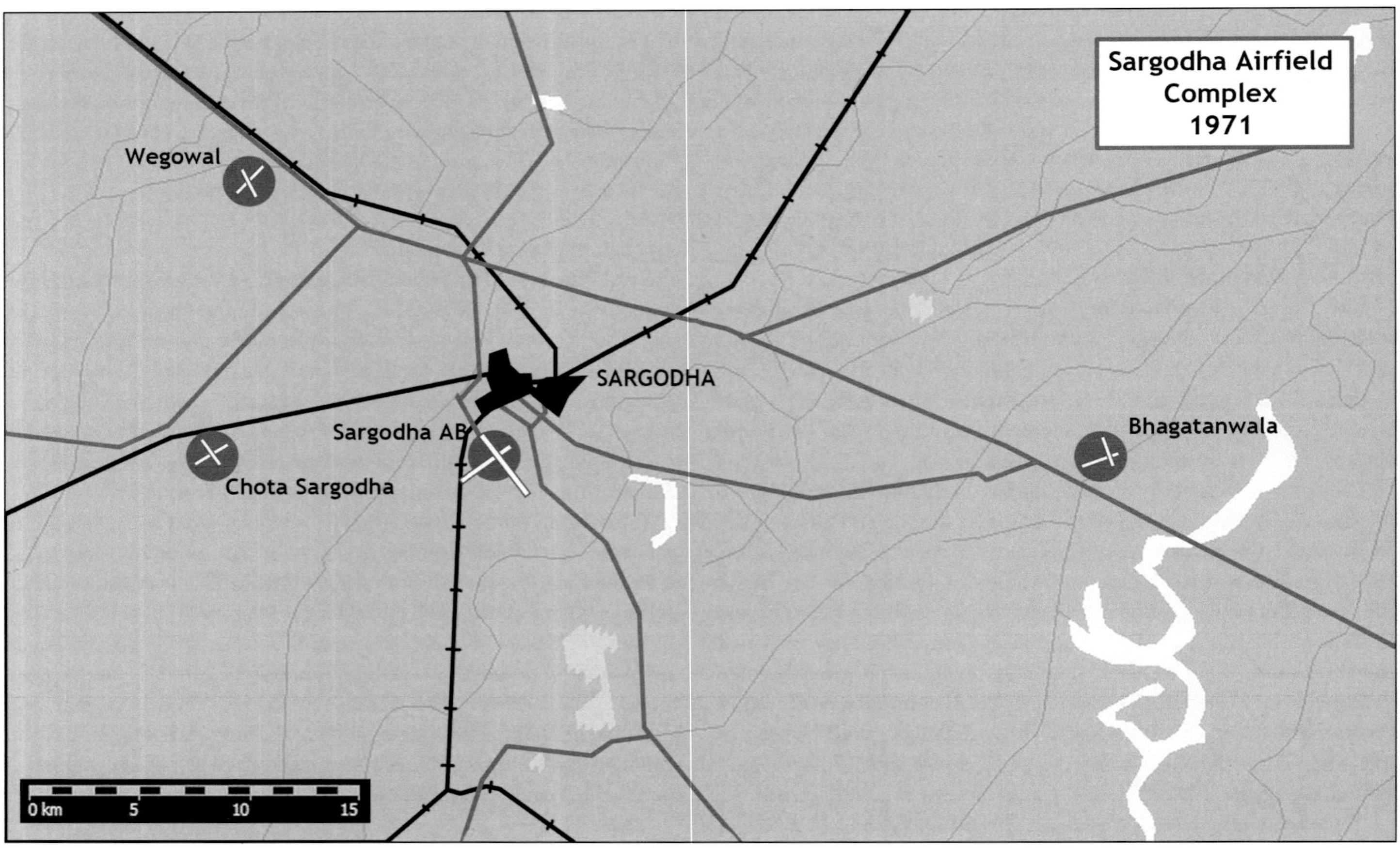

A map of the Sargodha area, with Sargodha AB, as of December 1971. Also shown are three Second World War era airfields that were disused by 1971. Indian intelligence showed these as still being used by PAF. (Map by Tom Cooper)

A Su-7BMK of the IAF as seen in the course of a diving attack and while unleashing 57mm S-5M unguided rockets from underwing UB-16-57 pods. (Albert Grandolini Collection)

A still from a video showing an F-6 of the PAF streaming its breaking parachute on return from a combat sortie during the 1971 War with India. Note the US-made AIM-9B Sidewinder air-to-air missile installed on the outboard underwing pylon (left side of the photograph). (Albert Grandolini Collection)

PAF was ready, with fighters continuously patrolling the skies since first light.

No 23 Squadron's pilots at Risalewala had been methodically scheduled for the day's proceedings. Around 09:30hrs, as F-6s for the day's sixth mission were taxiing out of their pens, an air raid warning was sounded. A mission abort was ordered, and loudspeakers relayed instructions for everyone to take cover. Flight Lieutenant Javed Latif, who was on cockpit standby, started to unstrap from his F-6 for a quick egress from the cockpit. Momentarily glancing out of the pen opening to see what was going on, he was aghast to see a Su-7 diving down straight at his aircraft. 'The scary sight of an intake pointing at me is still etched fresh in my memory,' recalls Latif. As he jumped out of his F-6 to take cover, a salvo of rockets landed smack on the pen.[1] Still scampering towards a trench, Latif was rattled by cannon fire from the second Su-7 as the bullets landed a few yards away. Then the raid was over as suddenly as it had started, and the AAA died down too, as if heralding an all-clear. Dusting himself and recovering his composure, Latif rushed to his pen to help put out the fire that had caught on the hessian camouflage covering. Luckily, his F-6 was unharmed except for a few nicks from slivers of falling plaster. 'I was seething with anger at having been violated thus, and hurried to strap up again to settle the score,' recalls Latif.

Shortly thereafter, a scramble was ordered for the next pair but confusion reigned as the taxi-way had been blocked by the F-6s of the previous aborted mission. This led to yet another abort at a critical time, but the situation was salvaged when Latif, who was standing by for a later mission, took charge and hit the starter button on his own. Just as he was taxiing out, his crew chief came rushing towards the aircraft, signalling for a switch off as another air raid warning had been notified. 'My mind was racing and I had already decided in a split of a second – I was going to take my chances flying, and I was not going to repeat the fiasco of the last pair,' Latif recollects.

Over-ruling the Air Traffic Control's somewhat confused recall message, Latif checked if his No 2 was also taxiing out. Hearing no response, he decided to take-off alone. Changing over to the radar frequency, he heard an eager voice wanting to join up as his wingman. It was Flight Lieutenant Riffat Munir on patrol from the fifth mission, whose leader had aborted due to a technical problem. Moments later Flight Lieutenant Shahid Sarfaraz, the original No 2, also came up on the radio, having taken off in a replacement aircraft. The new partners were only too glad to find themselves as a viable combat entity again. It wasn't long before the ground radar handed the trio over to 'Killer Control,' a cleverly-perched lookout tasked to visually guide the interceptors as to the raiders' position with the help of geographic landmarks. Flight Lieutenant Ahmed Khattak's confident voice called out that two Su-7s were pulling up for an attack from the north-westerly direction, and he pointed out their position over the main water tank. Soon after jettisoning their drop tanks and charging their guns, Shahid picked visual contact with both Su-7s. Darting in at high speed, he opened fire with his three guns, but was unable to score, as the aircraft went into a dicey transonic porpoise. He broke off the attack and aborted the mission. In the meantime, Riffat, who was following Shahid, dived in to attack. Both Su-7s seemed easy prey, so Riffat closed in and pressed the trigger, but the cannon did not fire. Switching to missiles, he tried again but there was no release.

As the attackers approached the airfield, Latif managed to position

A pre-war photograph of one of the IAF's Hawker Hunter F.Mk 56As. Highly popular with its pilots and ground crews, the type formed the backbone of the Indian fighter-bomber fleet from the late 1950s well into the 1970s. (Albert Grandolini Collection)

behind one of them as Riffat cleared the tails. Firing all three of his cannons, Latif waited for some fireworks. Noticing that the aircraft was still flying unharmed, he fired another long burst until all his ammunition was exhausted. Just as he was expecting his quarry to blow up, he felt a huge thud. Thinking that he had been hit by the other Su-7, he broke right and then reversed left, but found no one in the rear quarters. Checking for damage, he found that the left missile was not there and the launcher was shattered. The AAA shells bursting in puffs all around the airfield confirmed his suspicion that he had taken a 'friendly' hit, but luckily the aircraft was fully under control. Pressing on, he started to look for the escaping Su-7s, and within moments, was able to pick one of them trailing a streak of whitish smoke. Convinced that it was the same one he had hit earlier, and assuming it to be crippled, Latif decided to go for the other Su-7. He spotted it straight ahead, flying over the treetops at a distance of two miles. Engaging afterburners, he closed in for a Sidewinder shot but could not get a lock-on tone. To his dismay, he realised that the missile tone was routed through the circuitry of the left missile which had been shot off. Getting below the Su-7, he fired without a tone nonetheless, half expecting it to connect, if it fired at all. Moments later, he heard Riffat's excited voice on the radio, 'Good shooting, leader, you got him!' Not sure if he had really hit him as he had not seen any explosion, Latif was soon relieved to see the Su-7 roll over inverted and hit the ground.[2]

Flight Lieutenant Harvinder Singh of Halwara-based No 222 Squadron went down with his aircraft near Rurala Railway Station. Riffat's chase of the second Su-7 (flown by the mission leader, Squadron Leader B S Raje) had to be cut short as he was getting low on fuel, and his leader was out of ammunition. It was just as well, for Riffat did not know that he had forgotten to turn on the armament switches during the hurried scramble, something he discovered only after the mission. Despite the flurry of aborts and confusion on an eventful morning, No 23 Squadron had finally notched a kill with Latif doggedly in business after surviving rocket and AAA hits.

Murid Base was particularly vulnerable to surprise attack from a north-easterly direction. Intruders from Pathankot could nestle against the Parmandal Range, before swinging in from the Naushahra-Rajauri side in held Kashmir. To counter this susceptibility, F-86Fs from No 15 Squadron were providing constant CAPs since first light on 4 December. At around 10:30hrs, Flight Lieutenant Mujahid Salik and Flying Officer Sarfaraz Toor, who were on patrol, were directed by Kallar Kahar radar to intercept a pair of Hunters heading towards the base. By the time the F-86 pair collected itself for the interception, the Hunters were through with the brisk raid and were egressing. The F-86s spotted one Hunter on the exit heading called out by the radar controller Flight Lieutenant Dildar Qazi, and Mujahid started to settle behind it. Toor, meanwhile, restively looked around for the second one which was being reported in the rear quarters. The F-86s had somehow ended up being sandwiched between the Hunters. Toor was lucky to spot the Hunter trying to catch up behind him, and instantly went into a tight break, blacking out in the process. The Hunter tried to hold a gun tracking solution for about 60 degrees before realising the futility of it all and rolled out to join his wingman. Mujahid, in the meantime, had intently chased his quarry, and managed to gun it down as it came up against a hill crest about 24nm east of Murid. The Hunters had made the cardinal mistake of exiting in line-astern after the attack, rather than quickly reforming in disciplined battle formation for visual cross cover. Flying Officer Sudhir Tyagi, of Pathankot-based No 27 Squadron, had to pay with his life due to his leader's solo flight at a time when he (Tyagi) was falling into Mujahid's clutches and needed support.

Rushing back to his parent base at Peshawar from Karachi, where he was running an official errand, Flight Lieutenant Salim Baig reached his unit at daybreak of 4 December. It wasn't long before an exhausted Baig and his mission leader, Flight Lieutenant Khalid Razzak, found themselves strapped up in their F-86s for air defence alert duty.

After waiting in their cockpits for three excruciating hours, the pair was scrambled and directed to fly in a south-easterly direction at 5,000 feet. Barely ten miles out of the airfield, 'Killer Control' surprised the interceptors with a report about an attack on the base by enemy Hunters. Rushing back at full speed, Baig spotted one Hunter just south of the base, and guided his leader towards it.

While Khalid dived to position behind the Hunter, Baig stayed higher looking for more; he soon saw another Hunter manoeuvring to get behind his leader. Khalid had, by then, commenced firing his guns at the first Hunter. In a snap, Baig rolled over and swooped down to get behind the second one.

The dogfight had rapidly descended to a dangerously low height of about 100 feet, with four fighters flying in a very tight circle at a speed of around 400 knots. 'The first Hunter that was being shot at by Khalid was somewhat out of range,' recalls Baig. 'About a mile behind him was the second Hunter blazing away its four 30mm guns but the bullets were impacting the ground way short of the target, as I could make out from the small puffs of dust.' Baig, being the last one in the tail chase, had started firing a long burst at the second Hunter from about 3,000 feet. He was closing in fast, aiming to quickly finish it off before Khalid fell in harm's way.

A Hunter F.Mk 56 seen while releasing unguided rockets from its underwing launch rails during a pre-war training sortie. The jet could load up to 24 T.10 rockets, installed in four 'banks' of three under each wing. (Albert Grandolini Collection)

In the melee, Baig was continuously warning his leader about the position of the second Hunter which was rapidly closing in. Sensing the critical situation, Baig warned his leader to break off the attack which he did, just in time. 'At the same instant, I saw a puff of thick black smoke appearing from the right wing root of the Hunter that was still in my gunsight,' remembers Baig. A few seconds later, the aircraft rolled over and crashed in a huge ball of fire. Its wreckage was found about five miles south-west of the base near Bara village. Flying Officer K P Muralidharan had been unable to eject and went down with his aircraft.

The Hunters were able to inflict some damage to a maintenance hangar. However, the luckless pair had found a bevy of dummy aircraft on the tarmac too inviting, and had gone in for a second strafing attack; this resulted in grave consequences as it allowed the interceptors to catch up and position themselves for the kill.

While the F-86 pilots were excitedly focused on the kill, the lead Hunter managed to escape. It was later learnt that Squadron Leader Bajpai was able to put down his bullet-riddled aircraft at Jammu airfield, only to wreck it completely after slamming into a truck at the end of the under-construction runway.

Shortly before sunset on the same day, Sakesar radar reported a raid heading towards Mianwali. Squadron Leader Ehsan and Flying Officer Qazi Javed of No 25 Squadron, who were on 'cockpit standby' in the hessian-covered pens, started their F-6s and within minutes, were taxiing out for take-off. Just then, Javed reported seeing two Hunters pull up for an attack. Sensing that they had been caught on the ground at the wrong time, Ehsan decided on a hasty take-off and pushed up the throttles to execute a sharp turn on to the runway. Unfortunately, use of excessive power caused him to veer off into the 'kutcha.' Stuck in the mud, he became an unwitting spectator as the Hunters delivered their attacks.

In the meantime, Javed decided to take-off without his leader. Just as he lined up, he saw the lead Hunter strafing way far to the left of the runway. With half his worries suddenly over, Javed started rolling but danger from the second Hunter remained, as it had all the time to aim carefully and take a hearty shot. Anxious, Javed craned his neck back only to see the Hunter's cannon blazing at him. 'I thought his dive was too shallow, and at the close distance he was, the bullets would overshoot,' Javed recalls his rather masterly prediction. Fortunately, the bullets did land 200 feet ahead and towards the left, so Javed continued his take-off.

Once airborne, keeping the Hunter in sight was a problem in the fast-fading light. Speeding at 900kph (485 knots), Javed remembered that he had not jettisoned his drop tanks. When he did get rid of them at such a high speed, he induced a porpoise but was somehow able to ride it out. Charging in at 1,100kph (595 knots), he had closed in to about a mile and a half, which was just the right range for a Sidewinder shot. He fired his first missile and when he did not see it connect, fired the second one. That too went into the ground. 'All this while the Hunter pilot seemed totally oblivious of what was going on and his leader was nowhere in sight, so I gleefully decided to press on for a gun attack,' says Javed. 'Since things had been happening too fast, I had forgotten to charge my guns after take-off. Having done that, I first fired with my centre gun till all its ammunition was spent.[3] With the Hunter still flying unharmed, I decided to continue firing with the side guns. After a few frustrating bursts, I closed in to about 1,000 feet and fired a real lengthy one. Luckily, the last few bullets of the volley struck the right wing as I noticed a flash. The aircraft pitched up and rolled over to the right. I only learnt of the pilot's ejection later, as I had to break away to avoid overshooting the completely out-of-control Hunter.'

The aircraft fell about 14nm north-east of Mianwali. Flying Officer Vidyadhar S Chati of the Pathankot-based No 27 Squadron, when interrogated about the circumstances of his shooting down, said he suspected he had been brought down by ground fire! Duck shoot it was, over the idyllic Khabbaki Lake, but Chati should have known better where the bullets really came from. Ironically, the pilots of No 27 Squadron who had been declared the 'Top Guns' of the IAF's Western Air Command during a gunnery meet prior to the war, had failed to shoot up the conspicuously exposed F-6s on the runway.

The test of the Mirage's capabilities as an interceptor came on 4 December, when Flight Lieutenant Naeem Atta was scrambled from Mianwali. At around 20:00hrs, the ground controller, Flight Lieutenant Khalid Kashmiri, vectored Atta on to an intruder heading west, towards Mianwali. 'The controller was able to position me three miles astern of the low flying target, but despite a nearly full moon, there was little prospect of visual contact with the target at that distance,' remembers Atta.

As the Salt Range loomed ahead, the target started climbing to avoid the hilly terrain. 'Unexpectedly, this meant that the target was also easing out of ground clutter, and there was a good probability that it would be painted by my aircraft radar,' recalls Atta. Unknown to him, the Cyrano radar was still in standby mode, as Atta had missed a few checks after a hurried take-off. On the radar controller's reminder, Atta rechecked the selection to transmit mode, and was soon able to report a blip on his radar scope at an optimum infra-red missile shooting distance of one-and-a-half miles, exactly tail-on.[4] Following radar lock-on, the Sidewinder missile's seeker head swung to the heat source, and a growl in Atta's earphones confirmed a launch-ready condition; the intruder's fate was sealed.[5] Moments after launching the missile, Atta saw a huge fireball lighting up the night sky.

Next morning, the wreckage of a Canberra was found near Jabbi village located at the south-western edge of the Salt Range, not too far from Khushab town. The aircrew, including the pilot Flight Lieutenant

A Mirage IIIEP configured with 'supersonic' drop tanks on inboard underwing pylons and launch rails for AIM-9B Sidewidner missiles. Note the heavy wear of its camouflage pattern: a result of both intensive operations and local elements. (Albert Grandolini Collection)

A weapons technician of the PAF working on the launch rail for an AIM-9B Sidewinder air-to-air missile: the seeker-head and the canard fins of the latter are clearly visible in the foreground. (Albert Grandolini Collection)

Antenna of the Bendix AN/FPS-20 early warning radar: although big, such a structure was not easy to hit, and even harder to knock out for longer periods of time. (USAF photo)

Lloyd Moses Sasoon and navigator Flight Lieutenant Ram Metharam Advani, belonging to the Agra-based Jet Bomber Conversion Unit, were killed on impact. The ill-fated Canberra had been part of a stream of four bombers, which had staged-through Ambala for an attack on distant Mianwali.

The high-powered FPS-20 radar at Sakesar had received considerable attention on the first day of the war. Shortly after mid-day on 5 December, a pair of Hunters from No 27 Squadron was again able to sneak in and attack the radar with rockets and cannon.

Patrolling nearby, over the picturesque Salt Range, were two F-6s of No 25 Squadron flown by the Squadron Commander, Wing Commander Sa'ad Hatmi, and Flight Lieutenant Shahid Raza. They were promptly vectored by the radar controller, Flight Lieutenant Zarrar Shafique, towards the exiting Hunters but it was a while before Hatmi spotted the pair. As the Hunters sped away over the hilly terrain, Hatmi wisely decided not to waste his missiles given the unfavourable background hotspots. Using his guns instead, he made short work of one of the Hunters which fell near Sodhi village 15nm east of Sakesar. The pilot, Flying Officer Kishan Lal Malkani, was killed when his aircraft impacted the ground.

Next, Flight Lieutenant Shahid Raza, who had all along kept the second Hunter in sight, closed in and opened fire with his guns which found their mark. The pilot, Flight Lieutenant Gurdev Singh Rai, who was the leader of the mission, and had twice visited Sakesar on the previous day, ran out of luck this time. He met his end when his Hunter crashed near the small town of Katha Saghral at the foothills of Salt Range.

The attack by the Hunter pilots was not in vain, as they had managed to pull off two strafing runs each. The FPS-20 surveillance radar and the FPS-6 height finder antennae were badly damaged, while considerable electronic equipment and cables were destroyed. The radar remained out of operation for three days, before spares were rushed in and repairs carried out.

Later that afternoon, a lone intrepid Hunter was able to sneak in for yet another successful attack on the Sakesar radar, adding to the damage and destruction caused by the previous Hunter pair. After the attack, however, a clean getaway for a singleton, right under the noses of patrolling interceptors, was an improbable prospect. As expected, the Hunter was intercepted by two Mirages scrambled from Mianwali. The pair was led by Flight Lieutenant Safdar Mahmood, with Flying Officer Sohail Hameed as his wingman.

Front view of a Mirage IIIEP, with air-brakes partially extended, 500-litre 'supersonic' drop tanks on inboard underwing pylons, and launch rails for AIM-9B Sidewinder air-to-air missiles. The big aerodynamic shape under the cockpit housed the Doppler navigation module. (Albert Grandolini Collection)

Diving down from the hills, the Hunter had built up speed, but not enough to elude the far swifter Mirages. With the help of instructions from the ground controller, Flight Lieutenant Shaukat Jamil, Safdar was able to catch up and settle behind the Hunter, to start his shooting drill. A couple of well-placed bursts of the 30mm cannon got the Hunter smoking. As Safdar held off while watching his quarry in its last throes, Sohail picked up the smouldering aircraft and let off a Sidewinder missile to finish it off.

A PAF F-6 waiting for the next mission. Clearly visible is the is the 760-litre (170 imp gallon) tank drop-installed under the right wing. (Albert Grandolini Collection)

Just before the aircraft impacted the ground, the pilot ejected but it was too late. Squadron Leader Jal Maneksha Mistry of No 20 Squadron was found fatally injured. The wreckage of the Hunter was strewn near the small town of Kattha Saghral.

Chamb was one of the few sectors where Pak Army had made significant advances, and the Indian XV Corps desperately sought the destruction of heavy guns that had been reported in the area. On 6 December, a pair of Su-7s from Adampur-based No 101 Squadron was tasked to locate and destroy the guns. The Su-7s sought out what appeared to be hutments concealing the artillery pieces and were rocketing the place.

Flight Lieutenant Salimuddin Awan and his wingman Flight Lieutenant Riazuddin Shaikh, who were patrolling in their Mirages over the Gujranwala-Sheikhupura area, were vectored by the ground controller, Squadron Leader Farooq Haider, onto the two Su-7s. Salimuddin, who was carrying a Matra R-530 semi-active radar homing missile along with two infra-red Sidewinders, decided to get rid of the bulky – and rather useless weapon – by just blindly firing it off so as to lighten up for the chase.

Spotting the Mirages, the Su-7s jettisoned their drop tanks and rocket pods and started exiting east. With the Su-7s doing full speed, a long chase ensued until Riazuddin found himself close enough to fire a missile, but it went straight into the ground. Salimuddin then moved in, and on hearing the lock-on growl, pressed the missile launch button, not once but twice, to be sure. Two Sidewinder missiles shot off from the rails, and moments later, a watchful Riazuddin called out that one of the Su-7s had been hit. Salimuddin instantly switched to the other Su-7 and fired his 30mm cannon. Just then, Salimuddin noted the outlines of Madhopur Headworks near Pathankot, which was not surprising, as they had been chasing the Su-7s for several minutes inside enemy territory, along the Jammu-Kathua Road. Recollecting themselves, the Mirages turned back and recovered at Sargodha with precariously low fuel. Monitoring of VHF radio by ground radar confirmed a message transmitted by to Adampur that the Su-7 had been 'fired at … the pilot ejected.'

A beautiful study of two of the IAF's early Su-7BMKs: the type was based on the same aerodynamic concept as the MiG-19 and thus the F-6, and the two could be easily misidentified in the heat of combat. (Albert Grandolini Collection)

Wreckage of the Su-7BMK, from the TACDE, IAF, flown by Flight Lieutenant R. G. Kadam, shot down by Wing Commander S. M. H. Hashmi over the Jaranwala area on 8 December 1971.

It was later learnt that the wingman, Flight Lieutenant Vijay Kumar Wahi had succumbed to his ejection injuries. The leader, Squadron Leader Ashok Shinde, was lucky to bring back his Su-7 which had been damaged by bullet hits. High-speed pursuit was a forte of the Mirage, a lesson learnt by the IAF the hard way, and one time too late.

On the afternoon of 8 December, two patrolling F-6s of No 23 Squadron, flown by Wing Commander S M H Hashmi and Flight Lieutenant Afzal Jamal Siddiqui, were vectored on to two Su-7s just as they were exiting after attacking Risalewala airfield. On instructions of the ground controller, Squadron Leader Sami-ullah Khan, Hashmi caught up with one of the pair about ten miles east of the airfield and let off a Sidewinder at the straggler. The missile homed in unerringly, and the Su-7 exploded above the tree-tops; the pilot was not seen to eject. The remains of Flight Lieutenant Ramesh Gulabrao Kadam were later discovered around the wreckage near the small town of Khalsapur.[6]

Hashmi immediately started looking for the other Su-7, and to be sure of his No 2's safety, called out for his position. Afzal replied but the transmission was garbled, which Hashmi interpreted as his No 2 being visual with him and assumed that he was somewhere in the rear quarters. Just then Hashmi picked contact with the second aircraft and did not think twice before launching a missile.

If there was any profile difference between the similar-looking planforms of the Su-7 and F-6, this was surely one time to have had a closer look. His No 2 was nowhere in sight, and his frantic unanswered calls to Afzal seemed to confirm Hashmi's worst fear. Had he mixed up his quarry in the murky winter haze? Afzal, who was chasing the second Su-7 at high speed and had ended up ahead of his leader, was not able to clearly convey his position on a broken radio. Hashmi, an otherwise unflappable Squadron Commander, should have known better, for he had been too eager for a second kill which unfortunately ended up as a horrific fatality for his wingman.[7]

On another occasion, an F-6 was completely outwitted by a Su-7 that it was trying to intercept. Flight Lieutenant S S Malhotra of No 32 Squadron was flying as a singleton on a photo-reconnaissance mission over Risalewala on 13 December. Just after completing the photo run, he spotted a patrolling F-6 and took a pot shot before exiting. It was only later that Malhotra learnt of Flight Lieutenant Ejazuddin's ejection over his home Base.

An Incredible Kill

The morning of 7 December was quite hazy, particularly at lower altitudes where the dust of the Punjab plains mingled with the moist, cold air, giving the sky a murky appearance. While the PAF was conserving its air effort in the early stages of war, the IAF's intensity of air operations was building up at a fast pace.

Flying Officer Man Mohan Singh was ferrying a Gnat from Halwara to beef up a detachment of No 2 Squadron at Amritsar, where these aircraft were deployed to perform air defence duties. As Mohan was nearing home, the controller at Amritsar radar asked him to delay his landing while a pair of Su-7s took off. After holding for a few minutes, Mohan resumed a northerly heading for the base.

Squadron Leader Farooq Haider, a veteran of the '65 War, was sitting as the duty controller in No 403 Radar Squadron which was located in the outskirts of Lahore. Watching the radar scope intently, he had picked up a blip as it approached Tarn Taran, south of Amritsar. With the adversary nearing its home base, Farooq had to act fast. He commenced the interception with steady instructions on the radio:

> Your target now over Tarn Taran, heading 360; do not acknowledge.
>
> Target 20 (degrees) right, five (miles), turn hard left 360, do not climb; do not acknowledge.
>
> Target 12 o'clock, two (miles), go full bore; do not acknowledge.

A pair of Gnat F.Mk 1s of the IAF seen as parked inside their sand-bagged revetment during the 1971 War with Pakistan. (Albert Grandolini Collection)

Okay, target is one mile ahead …

The IAF had been expecting PAF fighters to sneak in below radar cover. Thus, to be doubly sure about any undetected intruders, the IAF used a capability that it was well equipped for: eavesdropping into pilot-controller conversation. Listening in to what was going on, the IAF controller was completely dumbfounded at the development, for he had not yet picked up any blip on his scope. All of a sudden, he frantically shouted on the radio to announce the presence of interceptors in the Gnat's rear quarters! It was no surprise, therefore, that the controller's warning to Mohan sounded eerie, as if a spectre was being reported. With the interceptors' distance rapidly reducing and shooting down of the Gnat almost a certainty, the controller gave a panic 'break' call. Mohan reacted as any fighter pilot would have done in that situation. He yanked back on the control column and threw in a very tight turn to shake off his pursuers.

Farooq noticed that the blip had disappeared from the radar screen shortly after manoeuvring had commenced. Normally, he would have enquired about the fate of the target from the interceptor pilots within moments of the shooting. This time, however, he had to be discrete. 'Maintain radio silence and recover at low altitude,' he called out. Meanwhile, Farooq and his fellow controllers wondered if the vanished blip meant that the aircraft had landed at its base.

India's Official History of Indo-Pak War – 1971, published thirty years later, covers the air operations with a diary of action which includes important events like air raids, aerial victories and losses on both sides. A keen reader would notice acknowledgement of the loss of a Gnat on 7 December 1971 in which, 'the pilot tried to take evasive action when warned of Pak aircraft in the vicinity. He lost control and crashed.'[8] The only inaccuracy with the account is that Pakistani aircraft were nowhere near!

Standing CAPs were a rare commodity due to excessive demands on the PAF's limited assets. Farooq had, therefore, reacted to the emergent situation in a most ingenuous way. He impulsively decided to fake an interception in the knowledge that his calls would be monitored. The thrill of playing a prank was better than getting frustrated at the sight of an enemy blip pacing away unscathed. In the event, Farooq's trick resulted in a bargain of great value, which can be gleaned from the amazing fact that not a gallon of fuel was expended, nor was a single bullet fired. Arguably, it stands as the cheapest kill in the history of air warfare.

A Classic Dogfight

On the last day of the war, two F-86E Sabres led by Flight Lieutenant Maqsood Amir of the PAF's No 18 Squadron took off from Sargodha for a routine patrol over the battle area. The winter haze had not quite cleared up even by mid-day, so Maqsood asked the radar controller for a loiter height of 5,000 feet, instead of the usual 1,000 feet, for better visibility. With his wingman Flight Lieutenant Taloot Mirza in tow, Maqsood set up orbit around Pasrur, which was on the western edge of the battle area.

As expected, the reaction was swift when two MiG-21s of No 45 Squadron scrambled from Amritsar to intercept the Sabre CAP. Sneaking in at low level, the MiGs were out of the PAF's radar cover but their VHF radios were under surveillance.[9] The IAF pilot-controller conversation was a good enough clue for the PAF controller, Squadron Leader Rab Nawaz, to assess exactly what was going on. Carefully monitoring the radio calls of the 'rats' (code-word for MiG-21), he instructed Maqsood to fly at combat speed and keep a good lookout. The moment the MiG leader, Squadron Leader Shankar, called 'contact' with the bogies, Nawaz instantly warned the Sabre pair that the threat was in the vicinity and they had better clear their tails.

As Maqsood threw in a left hand turn to look around, he was astonished to see two MiG-21s diving down at the Sabres from an 8 o'clock high position. The MiGs had blown through the Sabre formation head-on, without having been observed. Subsequently, the MiGs got behind the Sabres through a low-to-high conversion.

Maqsood recalls being struck by the aircrafts' small delta wings and sleek, long fuselages; he also did not miss their desert camouflage, an oddity in the lush Punjab plains. The apparent toy model features of the MiGs, however, made a lethal transformation in front of Maqsood's eyes when he saw a fiery streak shoot off from one of the aircraft!

With an adversary firing from the rear, the drill is to 'break' into it with maximum rate of turn, thus compounding the gun-tracking problem. Incredibly, Maqsood hesitated! Noticing that the MiG's profile appeared somewhat head-on, he reckoned that enough lead was not being allowed. A good gun tracking solution would require the attacker to point ahead; this would consequently show more of the belly and lower wing surface to a defender. Concluding that he was out of harm's way for the moment, Maqsood coolly settled for an energy-conserving hard turn. This would eventually make the MiGs hit a square corner as they would run out of turning room, he imagined.

What Maqsood did not know was that a K-13 missile had been launched, and the flash that he had seen was not of cannon fire.[10] A missile launch would have required him to go for a maddening 'break' leaving little energy for a fight back. Fortuitously, the hard turn had sufficed all the same; it not only defeated the early generation missile but also cramped the attackers for space.

Sensing an overshoot, Shankar eased up for a 'yo-yo' to give himself

A nice study of an early MiG-21FL of the IAF. While the type was much praised for its performance during the 1971 War with Pakistan, it showed numerous shortcomings too. The primary of these was the thick armoured windshield, which greatly decreased the forward visibility out of the cockpit. Note the underwing launch rail for an R-3S missile (Soviet copy of the AIM-9B Sidewinder). (Albert Grandolini Collection)

enough separation, before he swooped down again. A defender endowed with better acceleration could have escaped at this juncture, but knowing his Sabre's limitations, Maqsood had to stay on and fight. Under the circumstances, a smart tactic was needed that could throw off the attackers. Maqsood picked the barrel roll from his repertoire. The comical-sounding manoeuvre was somewhat of a misnomer in the deadly world of air combat. While an essential of any aerobatics display, the barrel roll had turned the tables on an attacker in many a dogfight.

Basically, the roll involves a corkscrew flight path on the inside of an imaginary barrel. Since the aircraft flies in three dimensions during the process, the resultant forward motion is distributed or 'vectored' in the three planes. An unwary pursuer is thus not able to arrest his rapidly increasing rate of closure. This is exactly what happened to the two MiGs that zipped past, as Maqsood went through the complex motions of rolling, pitching and yawing, while 'doing the barrel.'

Recovering to level flight again, Maqsood was in a bit of a quandary whether to fire his six 0.5" Browning guns or the Sidewinder missiles. For the latter he had to wait some seconds, until the MiGs had opened up to an optimum range of several thousand feet. Suddenly, the trailing MiG turned hard to the left, apparently having noticed the Sabre behind. Maqsood did not let go of the opportunity; he placed his gunsight over the target and started firing. The bullets seemed to land square behind the canopy, and after just four seconds of firing, the aircraft started to trail thick black smoke. Maqsood noticed something fly out of the aircraft before it rolled over and dived into the ground in a big ball of fire. Perhaps it was the ejection seat that had shot out of the burning aircraft, but Maqsood was more concerned about his No 2 who was not visible in the rear quarters.

Having stuck around through the arduous manoeuvring as a wingman, Taloot found the other MiG in front too tempting for a pot shot and started chasing it. As expected, not only was the chase futile, but in the process he split up with Maqsood. Luckily, the two re-joined with the assistance of the radar controller, who was interrupting his instructions with a relay of the disconsolate MiG leader's calls. 'Shortie has ejected,' Nawaz heard Shankar tell Amritsar, as he kept his ear to the VHF monitor.

Flight Lieutenant Tejwant Singh had ironically gone down to the Sabre, an aircraft that he had himself trained on in USA, and had befriended some of the PAF pilots during the course.[11] The superior performance of the MiG-21, versus the Sabre was another factor of consequence in the dogfight. In the final analysis, however, it is the man behind the gun that makes the difference, as Maqsood demonstrated in this classic dogfight.[12]

Damage at PAF Bases

The PAF was able to inflict punishment on fleeing raiders only after they had attacked PAF bases and radar installations. For the most part, all raiders went through with weapons delivery. Some of the raids that caused significant damage or destruction are discussed here.

During an attack on Chaklala on 4 December, two Hunters of the Pathankot-based No 20 Squadron damaged a salvaged C-130, along with the ATC building.[13] Next morning, two Hunters, again from No 20 Squadron, destroyed a UN Twin Otter and a US Embassy Beech Queen Air commuter aircraft parked on the tarmac.[14]

On 4 December, two Hunters from No 20 Squadron attacked Murid, and were able to destroy an F-86F and damage another in a strafing attack.[15] Not having learnt a lesson from this attack, the base took the worst beating of the war on the morning of 8 December, when two Hunters from a four-ship formation, yet again from No 20 Squadron, were able to knock out two armed F-86Fs parked in the open. The ensuing inferno caused sympathetic detonations amongst several F-86s parked in hessian-covered pens nearby. Three more F-86s were thus destroyed and two damaged. Many spare drop tanks were also destroyed.[16]

The forward airfield of Chander was successfully attacked at night by Canberras on several occasions. On each of the nights of 3/4, 4/5, 5/6 and 6/7 December, a Canberra cratered the runway regularly – and accurately – till it was rendered unfit for operations. The night raids were overlaid with day attacks by Su-7s. On the morning of 9 December, a pair of Su-7s delivered fragmentation bombs in the airfield area rendering any operational activity, including runway repair, untenable. Luckily, the airfield only figured out as a turn-around facility for emergency recoveries, and its immobilisation did not upset PAF plans in any way.

In an attack at midnight of 3/4 December, a Canberra cratered the fair weather strip adjacent to the main runway at Sargodha. Debris kicked on to the runway took a few hours to be cleared. On the night of 5 December, during an attack by a Canberra, Sargodha runway was cratered, and remained unusable for several hours. A second bomb dropped in the same run landed at an engineering facility, killing two officers who were at work. One of the vintage 3.7" guns of 52 Medium Air Defence Regiment was able to exact instant retribution, so it seemed, when a well-aimed shot hit the intruder. The Canberra struggled to stay aloft for a few minutes, but finally went down near Bhalwal, killing its crew of two.[17]

On the morning of 4 December, a four-ship formation Su-7s of No 32 Squadron operating out of Amritsar, struck Rafiqui Base. The rocket attack resulted in damage to an F-86E parked outside a pen, as also to a transiting B-57 that was being serviced on the tarmac. One dummy aircraft was also destroyed.[18] Early at dawn of 6 December,

A pre-delivery view of a Hunter F.Mk 56A for India. Two jets of this type operated by No 20 squadron caused a major conflagration when hitting a pair of fully armed and refuelled F-86Fs at Murid AB early on 4 December 1971. (Albert Grandolini Collection)

a Canberra was able to make two craters about halfway down the runway, rendering it unusable for the next three-and-a-half days.

A disconcerting daylight attack on the unmanned Skardu airfield by a flight of three Canberras and an An-12, marked the end of the war on 17 December.

A front view of a MiG-21FL (or 'Type 77'): this version made the backbone of the IAF's interceptor fleet of 1971, but also flew ground attacks. This example is shown armed with Soviet-made R-3S air-to-air missiles installed on underwing hardpoints, and a GP-9 pod containing the 23mm GSh-23 gun under the centreline. The latter was available in small numbers and scarcely deployed in combat. Visible in left foreground is the – relatively large – radome, housing the RP-21 airborne radar: the first such system in IAF service. (Albert Grandolini Collection)

Mystery of the 'Soviet AWACS'

During the war, PAF air defence controllers had been hearing coded radio calls relayed to IAF fighters at night. The calls seemed to emanate from a single aircraft flying at high altitude, well inside Indian territory. Word soon spread that the IAF was using a Soviet-loaned AWACS Tu-126 to control its aircraft.

Western aviation experts, ever so eager to pry open Soviet secrets, went along with the intriguing story, which had a twist to it right out of a Frederick Forsyth novel. As an instance, a former RAF Officer and military author, Sir Robert G Thompson, writing in *War in Peace – An Analysis of Warfare Since 1945* (Octopus Publishing Ltd, London, 1981), states:

> The IAF was assisted by Soviet Tupolev Tu-126, (NATO-code name 'Moss'). Every move that the PAF made was immediately known to the IAF, and the AWACS aircraft in conjunction with active electronic counter-measures, threw a blanket over Pakistani radar and communications. The IAF was able to operate between 320 and 480 km (200 and 300 miles) behind the front line with impunity.

Similarly, *The Encyclopedia of World Air Power*, edited by Bill Gunston (The Hamlyn Publishing Group Ltd, London, 1980), while describing the Tupolev Tu-126, states: 'In 1971 a single aircraft was detached with its crew to assist the Indian Air Force in the war with Pakistan.'

The myth of the Soviet AWACS continues to persist even today, though the reality is different, as it turns out. According to IAF sources, it was decided to utilise the services of some experienced MiG-21FL and Su-7 pilots to supplement the Canberra night attacks against PAF airfields. The experts at the Tactics and Air Combat Squadron (a Fighter Weapons School of the IAF, and precursor of present-day TACDE) based at Ambala, were tasked to fly these missions.[19] Attacks were conducted against Chaklala, Chander, Sargodha, Risalewala and Rafiqui for five nights, until the moon phase was no longer helpful. With no worthwhile on-board navigation aids, nor a navigator available for assistance, reaching the target at low level was a problem for the raiders; however, with marginal fuel remaining on return, the recovery was even dicier, leaving no room for error.

Amritsar radar could manage a direction-finding 'fix' on the recovering aircraft but was unable to contact them for steering instructions due to limited radio range at low level. The raiders were extremely wary of climbing due to fear of Mirage interceptors which were likely in tow and waiting for just such an opportunity. The Cyrano II airborne radar of the Mirage could only pick up targets in a clutter-free, look-up mode, as happened on the night of 4 December, when a Canberra eased up over high ground, only to be promptly shot down by a Mirage. 'It was therefore decided to place a fighter at an altitude of 9-10 km to pass messages between the radar and the aircraft returning from the strike mission,' recalls Air Marshal Subhash Bhojwani, who flew some of these radio relay missions.[20] The code word for these missions was 'Sparrow.' This task fell on the shoulders of the Tigers (No 1 Squadron) located at Adampur, and equipped at that time with Type 77 (MiG-21FL) aircraft. They were positioned well away from the border and under positive radar cover, and therefore, safe from PAF interference.

The mystery of the Sparrow aircraft was heightened as the recovery airfields were identified by their cryptic call signs, or even pilots' nicknames. Homing and diversion information was passed using these codes. Often, the controllers used the 'Sparrow' to relay messages to other aircraft, and even to other radar stations. According to Bhojwani, 'Sparrow soon became aware of the complete air situation in a large volume of air space.' It was no wonder that the PAF considered it all to be the handiwork of Soviet AWACS!

Blitz Unchecked

The IAF had a free hand in its interdiction campaign against the railway network, supply depots, and suspected armour concentrations, along with a few attacks against targets of strategic importance. Lack of low level radar cover meant that intruders came in completely unobserved and unmolested by interceptors. Shortage of AAA assets also resulted in these target areas being unguarded, leaving the attackers with little to worry about during weapon delivery. The most worrisome aspect was that unarmed and slow transport aircraft, like the An-12, found it opportune to regularly attack suspected army targets in various sectors. These large aircraft were never detected by the rearward deployed radars, nor were they ever intercepted. While the accuracy of these attacks was never a major concern, bombs exploding in the vicinity of deployed troops were certainly unnerving.

The railway network on the Sialkot-Shahdara Section, Jhelum-Lahore Section, Lahore-Sahiwal Section, Shahdara-Lyallpur Section, Kasur-Arifwala Section, Mandi Sadiqganj-Samasatta Section, and Bahawalpur-Lodhran Section was attacked incessantly. Twenty-five railway stations on these sections were targeted, with Wazirabad and Kasur receiving as many as five visits each. In general, the railway sectors selected for attacks were mostly those, along which the Indians expected transportation of reinforcements for Pakistan Army.

Sixteen trains were also attacked on these sections, while many track segments were damaged. Five of the attacked trains happened to be of 'special military' category. The damage inflicted on these trains was, however, inconsequential. Neither was any Army movement impeded, nor was any vital supplies interdicted.

It was widely rumoured that enemy agents had been placed at sensitive places for passing timely information about movement of the trains to the IAF via clandestine transmitters. It was also apprehended that such agents might have been receiving information about military trains from sources planted in one of several government departments which had advance information about movement of trains. In the event, the widespread rumours about radio transmitters were unfounded. However, given the facility with which clandestine activities could be undertaken in the culturally and socially similar Pakistani Punjab, there are reasons to believe that information about the movement of trains was often available to the enemy. The large number of employees also makes the railway system vulnerable to penetration by enemy intelligence, and the IAF seems to have exploited this weakness well.

Even if one were to avoid reading too much into the purported help from clandestine sources, it can be clearly seen that due to vulnerability of the railway system at large, the IAF felt free to attack it at leisure. Absence of interceptors and AAA only made the IAF interdiction campaign uncomplicated and effortless.

In concert with its interdiction campaign against the railways, the IAF tried its hand at bombing some targets of economic value whose destruction could hamper the war-making potential, albeit over the long term.

On the morning of 6 December a flight of three Hunters from No 20 Squadron attacked Attock Oil Refinery located at the outer reaches of Rawalpindi.[21] Two strafing runs by the Hunters set fire to several fuel tanks. The AAA defences were taken by surprise, but by the time the guns opened up, the damage had been done. The Hunters survived the AAA barrage, and with no interceptors on patrol, they made good their escape.

The next such target was the

Table 5: IAF Night Attacks by An-12

Date	Aircraft Involved/Ordnance	Target
3/4 December	Two An-12, 48 x 500lbs	Changa Manga forest, suspected supply dump
4/5 December	Three An-12, 66 x 500lbs	Changa Manga forest, suspected supply dump
4/5 December	Three An-12, 55 x 1,000lbs, napalm	Changa Manga forest, suspected supply dump
5/6 December	Six An-12, 140 x 500lbs	Poonch Valley, Pak Army concentration
6/7 December	Four An-12, 95 x 500lbs	Fort Abbas, Pak Army concentration
7/8 December	Two An-12, napalm bombs	Sulaimanki Headworks
8/9 December	Four An-12	Sulaimanki Headworks

Table 6: IAF Attacks on Military Trains in Pakistan

Date	Target	Notes
4 December (08:45hrs)	Attack on Havelian-to-Khanewal train, at Walton (Lahore)	No significant damage
6 December (16:10hrs)	Attack on Kot Samaba-to-Tarinda train, at Kot Simaba	One diesel locomotive damaged
7 December (13:08hrs)	Attack on Mardan-to-Sargodha train, at Choa Kariala	Minor injuries to few personnel
9 December (04:55hrs)	Attack on Havelian-to-Khanewal train, at Sahiwal	Two wagons on train and 13 wagons in railyard damaged
9 December (22:50hrs)	Attack on Havelian-to-Khanewal train, at Renala Khurd	No significant damage

From 1968, the PAF acquired a total of 18 Mirage IIIEP fighter-bombers, 3 Mirage IIIRP reconnaissance fighters, and 3 Mirage IIIDP two-seat conversion trainers with combat capability. At the outbreak of the 1971 War, 23 were available. All were camouflaged in gris bleu tres fonce (dark grey) and gris vert fonce (dark green) applied to a standardised camouflage pattern on top surfaces and sides, and sky blue on undersides. Standard equipment for interceptor operations included two DEFA 552 30mm cannon with 250 rounds, one Matra R.530FE air-to-air missile under the centreline (quickly discarded after proving useless early during the 1971 War), and a pair of AIM-9B Sidewinders on outboard underwing pylons. The inset shows the 1,700-litre ferry drop tank. (Artwork by Tom Cooper)

During the 1971 War, the PAF's Mirage IIIEPs flew a total of 38 offensive counter-air sorties. For such purposes, the type was usually armed with its DEFA 552 internal cannons (with a total of 250 rounds, or 125 rounds per cannon), a pair of US-made M117 bombs (750lbs/375kg) under the centreline, a pair of 1,300-litre drop tanks (shown inset) and a pair of AIM-9B Sidewinders. Notable is the application of the serial number on the forward- and rear fuselage, and again on the rudder, where it was prefixed by the year in which the aircraft was ordered: (19)67-116. (Artwork by Tom Cooper)

The Mirage IIIRP was the reconnaissance variant acquired by the PAF. This was equipped with two oblique cameras looking either side of the nose, and one camera positioned to look straight forward. Painted and marked almost exactly like Mirage IIIEP fighter-bombers, Mirage IIIERs could carry exactly the same stores too: this example is shown configured with 1,300-litre drop tanks and AIM-9B Sidewinder air-to-air missiles. The three aircraft available as of 1971 flew a total of 36 combat sorties during the war with India. (Artwork by Tom Cooper)

Starting in late 1965, the PAF decided to acquire Shenyang F-6 fighter-bombers – the Chinese version of the MiG-19S. By the time the 1971 War with India broke out, 90 of these were in service. All were delivered in typical colours for the type in the 1960s: this consisted of two layers of clear lacquer mixed with aluminium powder. The resulting colour became known either as 'bare metal overall', or 'silver-grey'. Their typical armament for air defence operations consisted of a pair of US-made AIM-9B Sidewinders on outboard underwing pylons, and three Nudelman-Richter NR-30 30mm cannon with a total of 201 rounds (73+73 rounds in side cannon, and 55 rounds in nose cannon). (Artwork by Tom Cooper)

For close air support operations, the PAF's F-6s were usually configured in similar fashion as for air defence purposes: in addition to Sidewinders and their internal cannon, they would usually carry two 760-litre drop tanks, and two ORO-57K pods for seven (Chinese-made) 57mm S-5K unguided rockets on inboard underwing pylons. Along with the rockets, the three NR-30 cannons packed tremendous punch: the latter firing milk-bottle-sized shells. As on all of the PAF combat aircraft of the time, national markings were applied in six positions, with a flash on the fin. (Artwork by Tom Cooper)

While the PAF originally received a total of 12 F-104A and F-104B Starfighters from the USA under the Mutual Assistance Program in 1961, only eight were available as of 4 December 1971. All were still operated by No 9 Squadron, PAF, and were still in their metallic silver finish overall. Standard armament consisted of the internal six-barrel 20mm M61 Vulcan cannon with 750 rounds, and a pair of AIM-9B Sidewinders, as shown here. Wingtip-stations were usually reserved for 175-gallon fuel tanks. The high-rate of fire of the Vulcan cannon made it an effective weapon for aerial and ground targets. (Artwork by Tom Cooper)

Starting in 1956, the USA provided a total of 120 F-86F Sabres (mostly F-86F-35s, but also some F-86F-40-NAs) to Pakistan under the Mutual Assistance Program. By 1971, 65 of these were still in service. All still wore their original metallic silver finish and were still armed with six Browning .5" (12.7mm) machine guns with a total of 1,800 rounds (or 300 rounds per gun). While some were equipped to carry AIM-9B Sidewinders, they were mostly assigned to ground attack. For this purpose, they were usually armed with a pair of old AN-M64A1 500lbs (250kg) or M117 bombs installed on inboard underwing pylons. The outboard underwing pylons were usually reserved for 200-gallon drop tanks. (Artwork by Tom Cooper)

When configured for the air defence mission, F-86Fs were usually armed with a pair of AIM-9B Sidewinders on inboard underwing pylons and two lighter 120-gallons drop tanks on outboard underwing pylons. Notably, except for roundels applied in six positions and fin flashes, the PAF's F-86Fs wore their serials applied in quite a different fashion: some, like the example here, had the full US FY serial applied on the rear fuselage (in this case 52-5412), while some had only the 'last four' applied in that position. 'The last three' digits of the serial were nearly always repeated under the front part of the cockpit. (Artwork by Tom Cooper)

In 1966, Iran acquired a total of 90 Canadian-built, Canadair CL.13B (Sabre F.Mk 6), powered by Orenda 14 engines, from West Germany. These were then all forwarded to Pakistan, ostensibly 'for overhauls': the PAF pressed this – the most powerful variant of the original F-86 Sabre – into service with four squadrons, under the designation F-86E. Most retained their standardised camouflage pattern in RAL 7012 Basaltgrau (basalt grey) and RAL 6014 Oliv (olive) on upper surfaces and sides, and RAL 7001 Silvergrau (silver grey) on undersurfaces, as shown here. In addition to bombs, for close air support missions they could be armed with two SNEB launchers for 68mm unguided rockets installed on centre underwing stations in addition to their internal machine guns, and a pair of AIM-9B Sidewinders. Like F-86Fs, they could also carry 200- and 120-gallon drop tanks. (Artwork by Tom Cooper)

Starting in 1955, the USA provided B-57 light bombers to Pakistan under the Mutual Assistance Program. Two were subsequently modified into a unique RB-57B variant that had photo- and electronic-reconnaissance capability. As of 4 December 1971, the PAF had a total of 17 B-57B/Cs and one RB-57B: the former received olive green over their top surfaces, while retaining the original black on the undersides. As usual, national markings were applied in six positions, while serials were applied in light grey. Notable is the installation of up to two US-made Mk.83 bombs (1,000lbs/500kg) on underwing pylons: nine Mk.82 bombs (500lbs/250kg) were carried in the internal bomb bay. (Artwork by Tom Cooper)

The USA provided about a dozen C-130B Hercules transport aircraft to Pakistan Air Force, while five C-130Es were purchased from Iran. A handful of these were operated as bombers during the 1971 War with India, each carrying 45 500lb/250kg Mk.82 bombs. The appearance of these aircraft remains uncertain: while much of the fleet was still wearing its original metallic silver overall livery, photographic evidence shows that several were hastily painted over in grey, with undersides in light blue, or in grey and green (as shown in the insets). National markings were applied in six positions, with service titles on the front fuselage, and fin flashes and large black serials on the fin. Most of the aircraft were also coded with large black letters applied on the forward fuselage, directly below the cockpit. (Artwork by Tom Cooper)

Out of about two dozen venerable T-33A and RT-33A jet conversion trainers still operational as of 1971, ten-odd were modified to carry one AN-M64A1 500lb (250kg) bomb under each wing. Grouped into No 2 Squadron, they were all painted in dark green overall (including undersurfaces), and wore black serials on the rear fuselage (with the 'last three' repeated on the forward fuselage). T-33s performed a total of 39 ground attacks and raids on enemy air bases, 27 of which were undertaken by night. (Artwork by Tom Cooper)

The IAF began acquiring MiG-21s from the USSR in 1963. By 1971, 136 were available, and they bore the brunt of air defence operations, but also flew ground attack missions. Generally, all were left in their bare metal/silver-grey overall, but some received hastily applied camouflage patterns, usually in whatever shades of brown and green were available. The aircraft shown in the main artwork was operated as a fighter-bomber by No 28 Squadron over East Pakistan, while the inset shows one of only a very few examples modified to carry the GSh-23 pack with a twin-barrel 23mm cannon under the centreline. Primary armament was carried on their underwing pylons and consisted either of a pair of R-3S air-to-air missiles, or two FAB-250M54 or FAB-500M54 bombs, or UB-16-57 pods for 57mm S-5K unguided rockets. (Artwork by Tom Cooper)

Between 1957 and 1960, India purchased 160 newly-built Hunter F.Mk 56s, followed by 53 F.Mk 56As in 1965-1969 (and in addition to a large number of T.Mk 66/66D/66E two-seat conversion trainers): 112 were available as of 4 December 1971, and they formed the backbone of the IAF's fighter-bomber fleet. Each packed four powerful ADEN 30mm cannon (with a total of 540 rounds, or 135 per cannon), installed internally, but could also carry up to 36 Hispano-Suisa HS.80 76.2mm or 24 T.10 unguided rockets in 'banks' of three under the wing. Applied following the standard pattern, the camouflage consisted of dark sea grey and dark green on upper surfaces and sides and high-speed silver on undersurfaces. Codes were applied on the aircraft rear, with those of the F.Mk 56s being prefixed with BA, and those of F.Mk 56As with A. (Artwork by Tom Cooper)

India acquired a total of 14 Folland Gnat F.Mk 1s from Great Britain from 1958, and then manufactured around 180 under licence by 1974. The type equipped eight squadrons. On 4 December 1971, 128 were available: they were deployed as point defence interceptors, armed with two ADEN 30mm cannon with a total of 180 rounds (90 per cannon) only. The early variant lacked integral fuel tanks in its wings, and the carriage of two 66-gallon drop tanks was obligatory. As far as is known, all the Gnats of the IAF wore the metallic silver finish overall, with a long anti-glare panel in front of the cockpit, and various dielectric panels in black. This example is shown wearing a kill marking from the 1965 War with Pakistan. (Artwork by Tom Cooper)

India acquired a total of 140 Sukhoi Su-7BMKs starting from 1967, and they equipped a total of six squadrons by 1971. The type was notoriously short on fuel, and always carried at least a pair of drop tanks under the fuselage. Originally delivered in the same silver-grey overall as the MiG-21FLs, many of the IAF's Su-7BMKs were crudely camouflaged during the 1971 War with Pakistan, usually with whatever shades of brown and green were available. Moreover, their big NR-30 guns tended to leave massive traces of cordite on the fuselage. This aircraft (serial number B818) is depicted as armed with two UB-16-57 pods for 57mm S-5K unguided rockets under the wing. (Artwork by Tom Cooper)

Although first-flown in 1964, the HF-24 Marut entered IAF service in 1967: by 1971, 32 were in operation with two squadrons. The HF-24 was equipped with four powerful ADEN 30mm cannons with a total of 540 rounds (135 per cannon), and usually carried two drop tanks under the inboard underwing stations. The two outboard underwing pylons were usually used to carry two French-made Type 116 SNEB pods for 68mm unguided rockets (as shown here), or two 1,000lbs (454kg) general purpose bombs. Additionally, a retractable Type 103 SNEB pack for unguided 68mm rockets could be installed inside the fuselage, right behind the cockpit. (Artwork by Tom Cooper)

The Mystère IVA was procured by the IAF in 1957, and by the time the 1971 War broke out, 32 were still in service. As usual, all were originally painted in clear lacquer, and thus had a highly polished bare metal overall finish. During the 1971 India-Pakistan War, most received makeshift camouflage patterns, applied in whatever colours were available. This example from No 3 Squadron is shown in one such pattern, consisting of beige, olive green and dark green. The aircraft had two internal DEFA 30mm cannons (with 150 rounds per cannon), and usually carried a pair of drop tanks on inboard underwing pylons. Primary attack armament consisted of JL.50 pods for 37mm unguided rockets, or 1,000lbs (454kg) general purpose bombs. Moreover, the Mystère IVA could pack the retractable Matra 101 launcher for 55 Brandt unguided rockets in its belly. (Artwork by Tom Cooper)

The IAF started inducting the Canberra B(I).Mk 58 interdiction bombers (along with photo recce and trainer versions) in 1957. By 1971, about 80 were on strength and most wore the camouflage pattern shown here, including dark sea grey (BS381C/638) and dark green (BS381C/641) on top surfaces and sides, and high-speed silver finish on undersurfaces, together with a full set of maintenance and warning stencils in red and yellow. Wing-tip drop tanks were usually left in bare metal overall. Roundels were applied in six positions and fin flashes at the base of the fin, directly below the serial number. The aircraft were typically configured to carry four 500lbs (250kg) general purpose bombs under the wings, and either nine 500lbs bombs or a pack with four 30mm ADEN cannons (shown here) in the internal bomb bay. (Artwork by Tom Cooper)

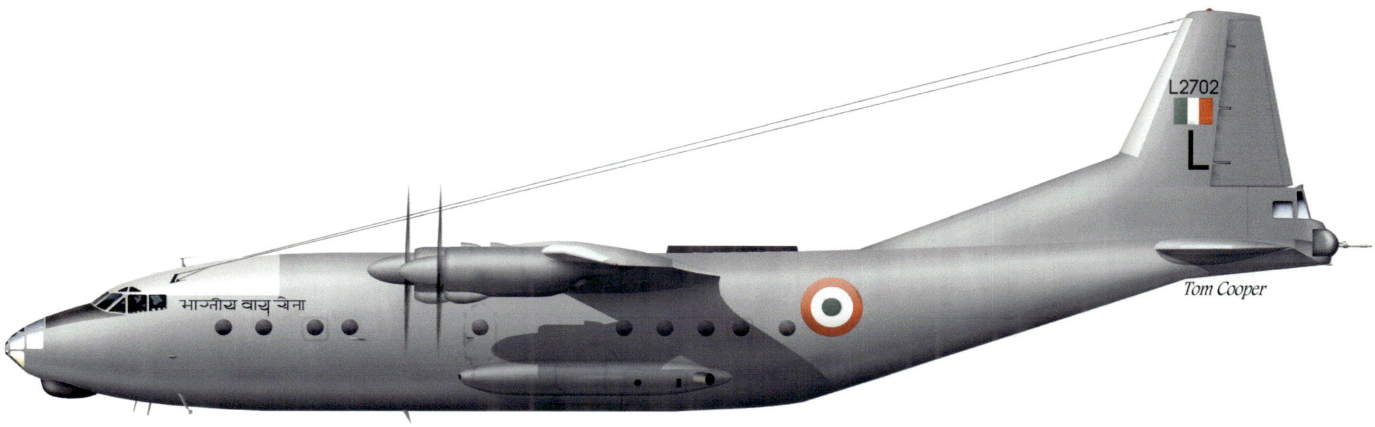

The IAF started acquiring An-12Bs in 1961, and by 1971 had two squadrons equipped with them in service. In addition to transport duties, the type was deployed as a 'makeshift bomber', deploying up to 24 500lbs (250kg) bombs over its loading ramp in the rear fuselage. The entire fleet wore the same livery, consisting of a Soviet colour similar to medium sea grey (BS381C/637) overall: the roof of the cockpit was always painted in white, to decrease the effects of the sun. As usual on IAF aircraft, roundels were applied in six positions, but the fin flash and the serial number were high up the fin. Moreover, An-12s received their full service titles applied in black on the forward fuselage (in Hindi on the left and English on the right side), and large single-letter codes in black on the fin. (Artwork by Tom Cooper)

India acquired 24 newly-built and 12 refurbished second-hand Supermarine Sea Hawk FGA.Mk 6s from 1959. During the 1960s, these were reinforced by up to 30 additional Sea Hawk Mk.100s from the stocks of West German naval aviation. About 18 were operational at the outbreak of the 1971 War with Pakistan, and they formed the key element of the air wing deployed aboard the aircraft carrier INS *Vikrant* (R11). All wore the same livery consisting of extra dark sea grey (BS381C/) on upper surfaces, and Sky S (BS381C/697) on undersurfaces. Each was armed with four 20mm Hispano cannons, with a total of 800 rounds of ammunition. Usually, they would be configured with two 340-litre drop tanks and up to four double 'banks' of two 5in (127mm) unguided rockets reach. Sometimes, up to two 500lb bombs would be carried instead of the rockets. (Artwork by Tom Cooper)

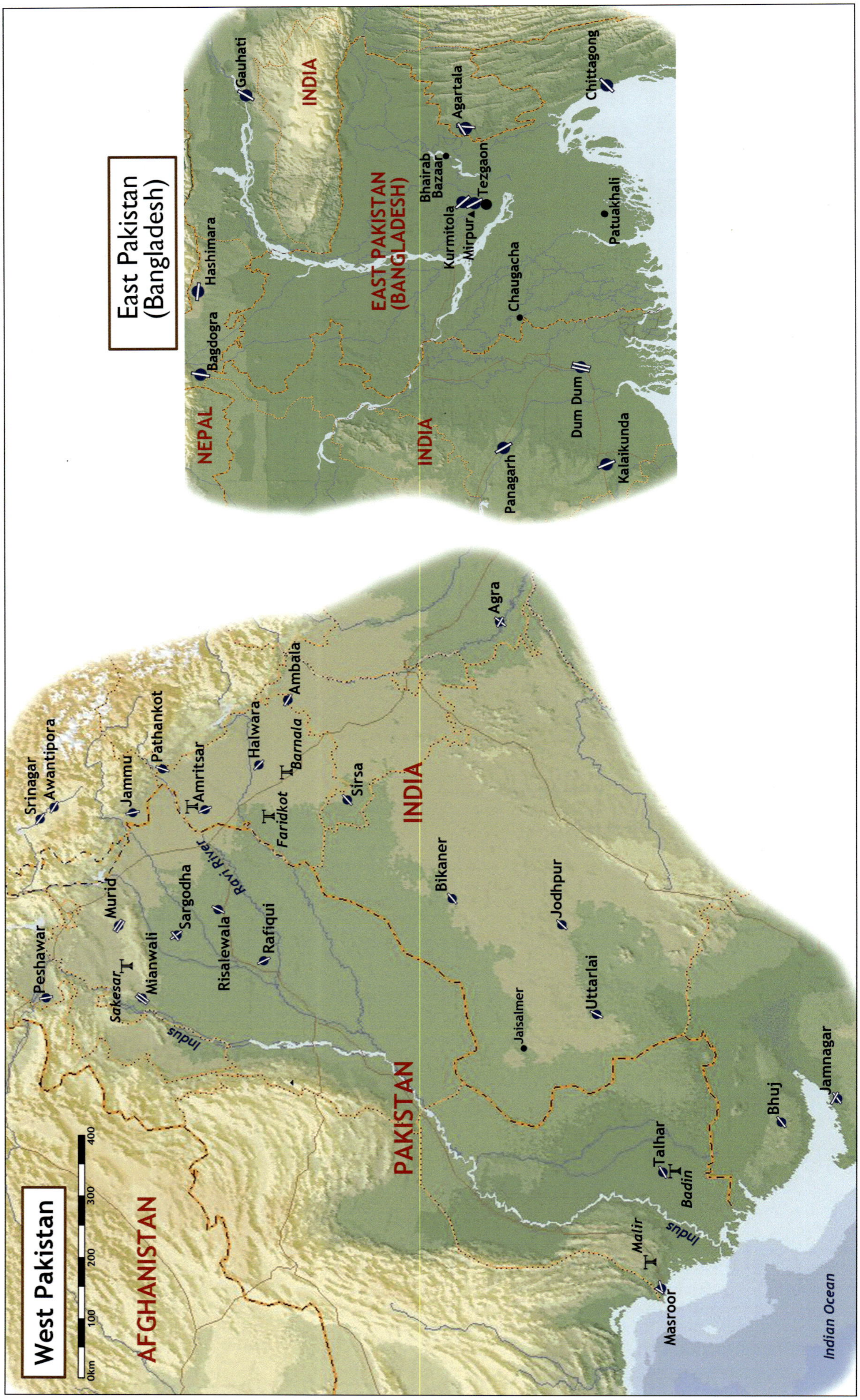

Maps of West Pakistan and East Pakistan (Bangladesh) with major air bases of both the IAF and the PAF. (Map by Tom Cooper)

In an attempt to saturate area-targets such as the railways in eastern Pakistan, the IAF deployed its An-12 transports for nocturnal strikes. These would disgorge up to ninety-five 250kg bombs out of their rear loading ramp. (Albert Grandolini Collection)

power house of Mangla Dam. On the morning of 7 December, a four-ship Hunter formation, again from No 20 Squadron, carried out a rocket attack, but the results were inconclusive due to hung rockets on several aircraft. Another three-ship raid was flown the same afternoon, and some damage was claimed. The dam was defended by AAA, but the attackers were able to catch the defences unawares by ingressing low. Lack of early warning also precluded the possibility of any interception.

The IAF's lackadaisical strategic bombing campaign in the Northern Sector did not go beyond the three-odd missions. Interdiction of the railway system was seen as a far more lucrative exercise due to the complete absence of any sort of defences. Also, interdiction promised rapid results which were of consequence to the on-going land battles, whereas the strategic strikes required a long-term concerted campaign, and were antithetical to an envisaged short war. The IAF strategic bombing effort could, however, be seen as an attempt to further stretch the already thinned Pakistani air defences.

The PAF Survives as a 'Force in Being'

For defence of the Vulnerable Areas and Vulnerable Points (VAs and VPs) in the Northern Sector, the PAF flew a total of 1,451 sorties employing F-6, F-86E/F and Mirage IIIE; these included 1,351 day sorties and 100 night sorties. A total of eleven enemy aircraft were shot down by PAF fighters, all while egressing, after attacking PAF bases or radars. None of the attacking aircraft could be intercepted before weapons release. The saving grace was the Pak Army's AAA, whose gunners bravely manned their guns while bombs fell in their vicinity. Two aircraft were shot down by the guns at Rafiqui, while one was shot down at Sargodha. Despite the scarcity of AAA resources on the battlefield, the Army had whole-heartedly provided cover to all operational PAF bases in the Northern Sector.

The real success of AAA came about over the battlefield where 17 IAF aircraft were shot down in Chamb, Shakargarh, Lahore and Sulaimanki Sectors.

The net result was the infliction of an unacceptable attrition rate, forcing the IAF to stay away from well-defended bases, and turning to interdiction of the railway network. While not having widespread radar coverage to effectively react against the IAF's interdiction campaign, the PAF did manage to keep the IAF from inflicting extensive damage on its bases. It managed to achieve an air situation favourable enough to prosecute the tactical air support campaign in the areas of major land battles, without prohibitive interference.

It was apparent that the IAF had changed its strategy of hitting PAF bases, as it turned out to be disruptive at best, and except for one case when Rafiqui was closed down for a considerable period, PAF operations continued apace. The losses incurred by the IAF during these strikes were morale shattering, though its ability to generate the required flying effort remained unaffected.

Defence of Pakistan's communications infrastructure and energy resources had been put on hold, as the order of priorities seemed to indicate. The looming concern was the do-or-die land battle, which required a totally fixated approach to tactical air support. For this purpose, the PAF managed to remain a 'force in being' while inflicting sufficient damage on the IAF. The role of the Army AAA in helping to maintain a favourable air situation, especially over the battlefield, was indeed commendable.

4 INEFFECTUAL EFFORT

Air Defence in Southern Sector

No 32 Fighter Ground Attack Wing at Masroor was a large composite unit, half of whose assets had been moved to the northern bases. What remained of the fighter units included No 19 Squadron, with a healthy count of 14 F-86E and 12 F-86F. No 9 Squadron moved in from Sargodha on 6 December with seven F-104As, after completing a few strikes against forward radars in Indian Punjab. A detachment of four F-86Es belonging to No 19 Squadron was positioned at the forward base of Talhar (located 100nm east of Masroor) as the first tier of defence against raids emanating from the eastern direction; it also acted as a quick-reaction force for the defence of the high-powered radar at nearby Badin.

On 13 December 1971, the first out of two groups of F-104As of the Royal Jordanian Air Force (RJAF) arrived in Pakistan. Formerly flown by No 9 Squadron, RJAF, which was worked up on Starfighters with help of Pakistani pilots in Jordan in 1969-1970, they were a most-welcome even if much belated reinforcement for the PAF. They had all of their Jordanian insignia removed and replaced by those of Pakistan before going into action. (Albert Grandolini Collection)

A Soviet-made P-35 Saturn radar (ASCC/NATO-codename 'Bar Lock'), as deployed by the PAF at Malir. This was a 3D E/F-band, semi-mobile, early warning radar with a maximum detection range of 350km (217 miles). (USAF photo)

disruptive night airfield strikes with uncertain results. Base Commander Masroor, Air Commodore Nazir Latif, and OC No 32 Fighter Ground Attack Wing, Group Captain Wiqar Azim, had their hands full to juggle the limited assets for the seemingly endless tasks.

Just like his colleagues at Masroor, Group Captain Anwar Shamim, the Sector Commander, Sector Operations Centre (South) located at its war-time site at Korangi, was confronted with a problem of inadequate assets, particularly low level radars and night interceptors.[2] High level radar surveillance cover in the southern air defence sector rested upon a FPS-20 radar at Badin, and a P-35 radar (ex-Dacca) at Malir .[3] Another P-35 radar, which was moved from Malir to Jacobabad mid-way in the war, became operational only when the war ended. A decrepit, fifties-vintage Type-21 radar was located near Khanpur; it was scrapped soon after the war but may well have served a useful purpose of keeping the enemy guessing, as it spewed out queer waveforms at odd hours!

Low level cover was provided by a Civil Aviation ASR-4 approach radar at Karachi Airport, and an AR-1 radar at Pir Patho. The latter location was supposed to cover the south-eastern approaches but was an unfavourable compromise due to constraints of terrain, logistics and security. As a consequence, direct flight tracks from Jamnagar to Masroor remained on the fringes of the radar footprint, and could be easily bypassed by flying a dog-leg and hugging the coast.[4] Practically thus, low-level early warning in the whole Southern Sector rested on the reports by MOUs. Given the inherently tardy chain of reporting, as well as delays in correlation of these reports with own flight plans, the reaction by interceptors was often hopelessly delayed.

A sad reflection of this state of affairs was the shooting down of an F-86E, one of a pair which had just scrambled from Talhar and

A belated, but welcome reinforcement of air defence assets were ten Royal Jordanian Air Force F-104As that arrived in two batches starting on 13 December, and were planned to be used for night air defence.[1] Keen as they were, the RJAF pilots were not immediately cleared to fly operational missions, and could not get a chance to reciprocate the help provided by PAF pilots in the 1967 Arab-Israeli War.

In case of Masroor being knocked out, the runways at Drigh Road Base and Karachi Airport were well-suited for emergency recoveries, though full-scale operations could not be supported at these locations due to scanty logistics support.

Between Masroor and the next northern base of Rafiqui, lay a gap of at least 350nm without fighter cover, through which traversed Pakistan's vital north-south railway link, running as close as 22nm to the border. Elements of Pakistan Army's 18 Division, which were poised for an ill-planned offensive, also lay at the mercy of the IAF as no PAF aircraft were based anywhere close. As in the rest of the country, control of the air was essentially based on air defence missions that relied upon non-existent or suspect early warning, and

The Canberra B(I).Mk 58 was the primary nocturnal strike platform of the IAF as of December 1971. This example (serial IF900), photographed pre-delivery in 1958, belonged to the first batch acquired by India. (Albert Grandolini)

In addition to bomber and training-variants, the IAF also operated two Canberra PR.Mk 67 reconnaissance aircraft (serials P1098 and P1099). Both were delivered in 1971 and are known to have flown about a dozen sorties during the war with Pakistan. (Albert Grandolini Collection)

was too late to intercept an incoming raid of three Hunters on 13 December. One of the Hunters was able to lunge on to the vulnerable F-86E as it was turning out of traffic.[5] Flying Officer Nasim Baig did not survive the Hunter's gun attack, and his aircraft crashed near the airfield perimeter.

On 15 December, Flight Lieutenant Farooq Qari of No 19 Squadron came upon a pair of Hunters that were on an air support mission in Naya Chor area. Qari was able to close into gun firing range despite the Hunters making a fast exit. Though Qari's ciné film showed accurate firing on one of the Hunters, the pair managed to scrape through. Squadron Leader Farokh Jahangir Mehta, who was flying as the leader in a two-seat Hunter with Wing Commander Mian Niranjan Singh, went on to spin a rather fanciful counter-claim of 'using their wits and manoeuvring in such a way that the pursuing Sabre ran into the ground.' Of course, both Qari and Mehta outlived the war; it would be interesting if they could meet to discuss that encounter some day!

An unsavoury surprise came on 17 December, the last day of the war, when two Uttarlai-based MiG-21FLs escorting a flight of four HF-24s on an army support mission, bounced a pair of patrolling F-104s near Naya Chor. After a head-to-head blow through, both pairs turned for each other. Flight Lieutenant Samad Changezi, the F-104 wingman, apparently having spotted the pair earlier, split from the formation and manoeuvred to get behind the lead MiG-21. He took time to close in to gun range as no missiles were being carried on these RJAF F104s – an inexplicable error by the mission planners.[6] In the meantime the MiG-21 wingman, Flight Lieutenant Arun Datta, was able to close in behind Changezi's F-104 and fire a missile, which missed its target. The F-104 leader, Flight Lieutenant Rashid Bhatti, warned Changezi to disengage and exit as he had been fired at, but the warning was disregarded in the heat of combat. That inattention earned Changezi a fatal penalty, when a second K-13 missile slammed into his aircraft with an explosion that left no chance of ejection.[7] A squirming Bhatti tried to chase Datta's MiG-21, but being low on fuel and unsuitably armed, he wisely decided against any more recklessness.

Typically, Canberra night raids were launched from Pune, though some staged through Jamnagar, and Hunter daylight raids from Jamnagar, against Masroor or Karachi Harbour. These were flown in a 'high-low-high' profile, with the high legs flown in Indian territory to conserve fuel. Thus, early warning of a raid was usually available through the high level radars, but as soon as the aircraft descended to low level, prospects of a successful interception reduced drastically. Even the F-104's AN/ASG-14T radar, which promised up to 20nm search range in the look-up mode, was no help at low level, due to the inability of its first-generation simple pulse radar to sift through ground clutter. On a few occasions when the ground radar did manage to put the interceptor behind the target – even though after weapons release – the Canberra's active tail warning radar kicked off an alarm, resulting in evasive manoeuvring and a clean getaway.

The PAF was utterly fortunate that, despite serious air defence shortcomings in the Southern Sector, Masroor runway remained operational throughout the war. Nonetheless, on 4 December, several aircraft being serviced were damaged in a dusk-time strafing attack by three Hunters.[8] Canberras also carried out incessant stream raids during the first three nights, but the main runway was damaged only once, on the night of 4/5 December. As a safety precaution, a flight of four B-57s was moved to Drigh Road Base for the next two days.[9] On the night of 5/6 December, one valuable ELINT/photo-reconnaissance RB-57B was destroyed, and one T-33 damaged by Canberras, in what

Table 7: Results of IAF Canberra Raids on Masroor Base	
Date	**Outcome**
4 December (17:20hrs)	One B-57, one F-86E, one F-86F and one T-6G damaged, one crash-tender destroyed
4 December (20.00-20.17hrs)	Secondary runway cratered at thee spots
5 December (04:20-04:26hrs)	Main runway damaged at one spot; taxiway culvert damaged
5 December (22:10-22:20hrs)	One RB-57B destroyed, one T-33A damaged; secondary runway damaged
6 December (23:05-23:20hrs)	Secondary runway and taxiway damaged

Table 8: IAF Attacks on Military Trains in Southern Pakistan		
Date	**Target**	**Notes**
15 December (07:50hrs)	Train near Dharki	Three wagons caught fire, some military personnel wounded
17 December (14:00hrs)	Attack on Okara-to-Hyderabad train, at Reti	Three wagons caught fire and exploded; 11 railway personnel killed, several wounded

An F-104A of the PAF armed with wing-tip mounted AIM-9B Sidewinders in 1968. By 1971, Pakistani Starfighters were modified to carry these air-to-air missiles on underwing pylons: drop tanks were then installed on the wing-tips instead. (Albert Grandolini Collection)

Not as fast as the Starfighter at low altitude, but able to turn more sharply, the MiG-21FL was a dangerous opponent, as illustrated by their success in the course of the last air combat of the war, fought near Naya Chor on 17 December 1971. (Albert Grandolini Collection)

was most likely a chance hit on a maintenance hangar at Masroor.[10]

The runway at Jacobabad was hit on the morning of 4 December, resulting in a single crater. The ATC towers at Hyderabad and Nawabshah were damaged during morning raids the same day. On the night of 10 December, Nawabshah runway was cratered in two places following an attack by Canberras.

On the evening of 4 December, a pair of IAF fighters struck Badin radar after slipping through unseen. The aerial head and vital components of the FPS-6 height finder radar were destroyed, along with extensive damage to the power house and fuel stores. The radar was recovered, with degraded performance, after a day.

After 6 December, the IAF discontinued airfield strikes in earnest following substantial aircraft losses in the north and switched its focus to interdiction of communications networks and wrecking energy resources. A cannier appraisal by the IAF could have considered the gross weakness of the PAF's air defences in the Southern Sector, and it could have persisted in its counter-air campaign without let or much hindrance. The rewards that the Indian Army's Southern Command could have indirectly reaped on the ground – by not allowing the PAF to be viable over the battlefield in Thar – would have been considerable, as shall be seen in a later chapter.

Due to the lack of low-level radar cover as well as absence of fighters in the Upper Sind area, the PAF found itself completely helpless against the IAF's interdiction campaign which targeted the railway network on Landhi-Khanpur Section, and between Mirpur Khas-Naya Chor Section. Lack of AAA defences over important nodes of the railway network made matters worse. Nine railway stations on these sections were repeatedly targeted, with particular emphasis on the important junctions of Mirpur Khas and Rohri; the latter was attacked as many as five times. Even the An-12 transport aircraft was mustered for a massive barrage of eight tons of bombs against the latter railway station on one occasion. Nineteen trains, including two 'special military type', were also attacked on the above-mentioned sections, while several track segments between Reti and Khanpur were damaged. Besides the general purpose of degrading the country's rail infrastructure on an enduring basis, the IAF's interdiction campaign in the south was more specifically meant to choke off reinforcements of men and material to the struggling 18 Division in Naya Chor. A Pak Army relief brigade, and much-needed ammunition and other supplies were still able to arrive by train in time to staunch the onslaught of the Indian 11 Division; it clearly shows that the IAF's interdiction effort in the south fell short of what was desired. It was also some solace for the PAF, much discomfited as it was, in the given situation.

The IAF continued its strategic air offensive sporadically in the south, against a few select energy resources including oil storage tanks at Keamari Terminal in Karachi, and the natural gas facility at Sui. Commencing with an audacious morning attack on 4 December, a flight of four Hunters from Jamnagar rocketed and strafed the sprawling storage farms at Keamari that housed about 100 tanks.[11] The licks of flame spread to adjacent tanks and in minutes, turned into a huge inferno that continued to burn for several days. Regrettably, PAF fighters as well as Pak Navy AAA were unable to react as there had been no warning of the attack, the Hunters having approached low from the seaward side to avoid the MOUs. While the psychological impact of the raging firestorm was devastating, the strategic reserves of POL remained largely unscathed. Notwithstanding the Indian bluster about lighting the 'biggest fires in Asia', only five storage tanks had burnt, causing a loss of about 15,000 tons of various oils.[12]

On 14 December, shortly past mid-day, a flight of four Hunters from Jaisalmer struck the country's major natural gas facility at Sui with rockets.[13] The attack portended the ominous direction the war was taking as the IAF operated with impunity, unchallenged from Keamari to Sui.

Hopeless Cause

For the air defence of VAs and VPs in the Southern Sector, the PAF flew a total of 253 sorties employing F-86E/F and F-104; these included 167 day sorties and a measly 23 night sorties from Masroor, while Talhar generated 63 day sorties. No intruding aircraft could be intercepted by PAF fighters, either over land or over sea, with the result that some strategic assets like oil storage farms, Karachi harbour, and the country's largest natural gas plant at Sui were targeted by the IAF with impunity. More than material damage, the psychological impact was devastating, and the national will to continue fighting was badly impaired. The railway network in the south was also targeted by the IAF, and the PAF never had timely warning to intercept any of these raids. The Army AAA, however, had a fair amount of success in being able to down five enemy aircraft during their vulnerable attack phase.[14]

A cloud of smoke rising from the area of Masroor AB after one of the Indian air strikes. (Albert Grandolini Collection)

Given the air defence assets whose quantity as well as quality left a lot to be desired, there were very few tactical tricks that could be pulled out of the proverbial hat. Air defence in the Southern Sector was, thus, a hopeless cause from the outset.

5
TACTICAL AIR SUPPORT

Helping Hand in Chamb

The General Staff at Rawalpindi felt that, besides the main strategic offensive in the Ganganagar-Suratgarh area, an additional secondary offensive was obligatory to lure the Indian strategic reserves, thereby improving the relative strength ratio favourably in that sector. It was surmised that control of nodes on communication lines in Kashmir could provide the quickest access to vital areas in the hinterland, while simultaneously choking the enemy by severing his main supply line. The Indian strategic formations were, thus, bound to be unhinged by the threat to its jugular, and the Pakistani main offensive could thence be unleashed.

The capture of Akhnur town, along with the vital bridge over Chenab, could sever the main road communication of Indian troops deployed in the western half of Jammu region. With the defending Indian troops thus choked off, operations could be developed towards Jammu from the western side. For Pakistan, however, it was important to properly secure the Chamb Sector before any plans for the capture of Akhnur could be put into action. The Grand Trunk Road and the main railway line ran close enough for the Indians to steal a jaunty ride towards either Lahore or Sialkot. This vulnerability dictated that the Pakistan Army improve its defensive posture before any further advance.

23 Division was, thus, tasked to first secure the line up to the Tawi River; to this was added the subsequent task of capturing an intermediate objective of Palanwala. Akhnur remained the ultimate goal, for which the task force was to 'remain prepared'. The division had five infantry brigades and one armoured brigade at its disposal. Artillery fire support included a large two-brigade sized group. All in all, 23 Division was a formidable force by any reckoning.

The Indian 10 Division, primarily organized for an offensive task, was purportedly re-tasked to defend against an impending Pakistani offensive. An infantry brigade was positioned west of the Tawi River while another one defended the northern reaches of Chamb. One infantry brigade stayed put at Akhnur, to ward off any attack on the bridge from the exposed southern direction of the Pukhlian Salient. An armoured and an infantry brigade at Akhnur made up the assault echelons of the division.

23 Division opened up with its offensive with two infantry brigades on the night of 3/4 December. The Indian forward brigade was pushed back, and over the next three days fierce fighting was witnessed, with Pakistani forays repeatedly countered by Indian forces. During the night of 4/5 December, a small bridgehead was formed by Pakistani infantry elements to enable the armoured brigade to break through. Heavy enemy air and artillery attacks, however, forced them back with

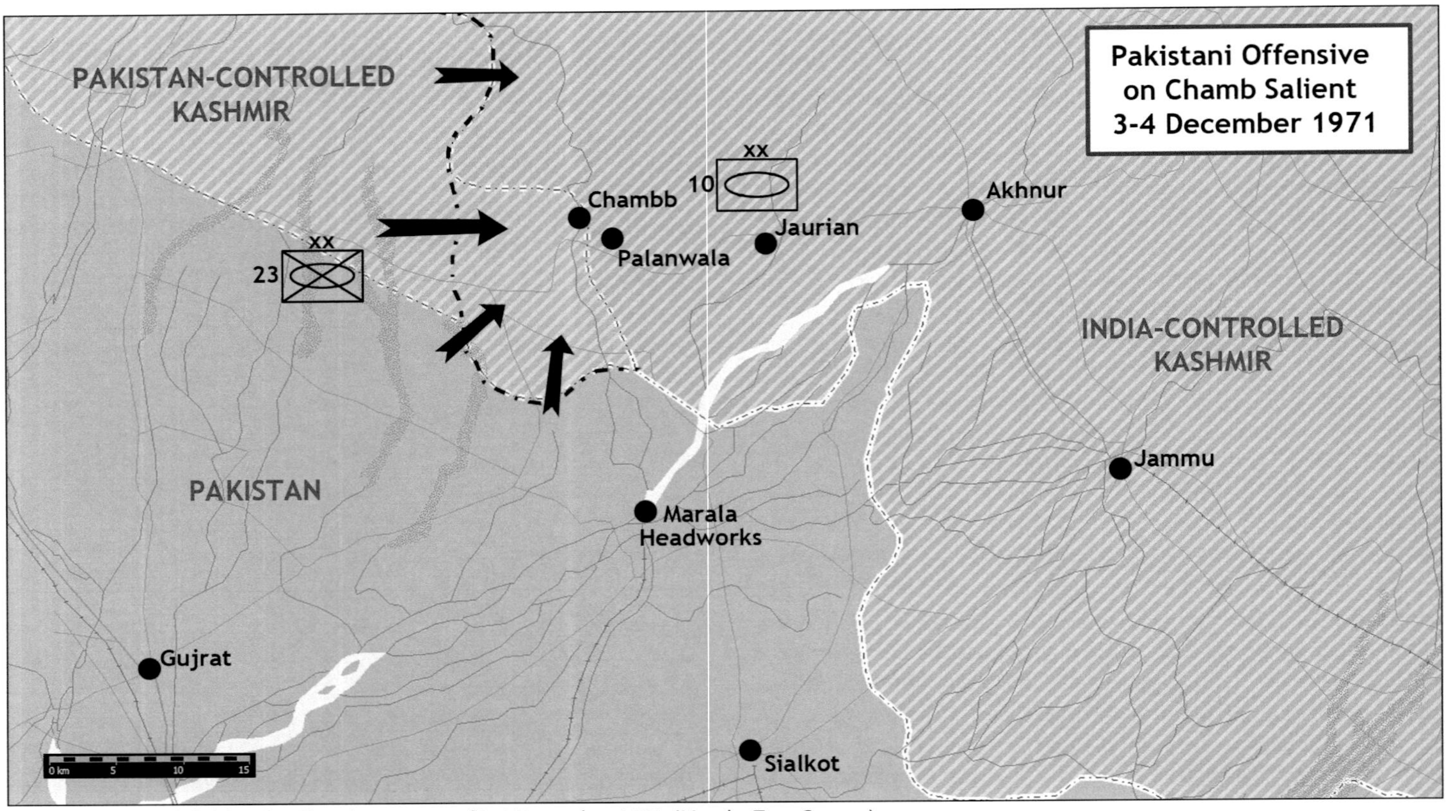

A map of the battlefield in the Chamb sector as of 3-4 December 1971. (Map by Tom Cooper)

An entrenched 106mm recoiled rifle captured during the initial advance of the Pakistan Army in the Chamb sector. (Albert Grandolini Collectionl)

heavy losses to armour. The maximum extent of advance was about 2,000 yards east of the Tawi River, before the withdrawal.

On 7 December, the indefatigable GOC of 23 Division, Major General Iftikhar Janjua, ordered the capture of Chamb and Manawar after regrouping the forces. Both objectives were easily achieved as Indian resistance west of the Tawi River had practically ceased. The gravity of the situation had forced the Indian 10 Division to prepare for a last stand at Akhnur.

With the primary mission accomplished, and seeing the enemy in complete disarray, Major General Janjua decided to expand the operation to the more ambitious phase. He ordered the capture of Palanwala, the springboard for a final hop to Akhnur.

Orders for the attack were issued on 7 December, but operations could not start until the night of 9-10 December for several reasons. Regrouping and positioning of certain units, and resting the fatigued troops took up vital time. A replaced brigade commander needed an extra 24 hours to size up the situation. Finally, the unfortunate loss of the GOC in a helicopter crash on the morning of 9 December robbed the division of a 'very bold and competent off' (according to an Indian assessment).[1] When the attack did commence, the impetus had already been lost. Fierce counter-attacks by the enemy, along with heavy air attacks, limited the extent of the Chamb offensive to the west bank of the Tawi River. The capture of 90 square miles of territory was Pakistan's most substantial gain. Its insignificance was, however, highlighted when India ceded most of it, as the occupied territories were being traded off in the post-war Simla Accord.

Close Air Support in Chamb

Three squadrons of F-86E/F at Sargodha, Murid and Peshawar made up the fighter element for air support in the Chamb Sector. T-6G trainers were also found handy for strafing convoys on moonlit nights, with the menacing whine of their engines providing a suitable overture to the staccato rattle of the .303" machine guns. F-6s, the better endowed fighters for tank killing, remained committed in the more critical Shakargarh Sector.

The first phase of 23 Division's operations that lasted from 4-7 December was vigorously supported by the PAF. However, weapon-target compatibility left a lot to be desired as neither the F-86's 0.5" guns, nor the general-purpose bombs were effective against armour. Luckily, the air support demands were not desperate, as the situation on the ground never went out of control.

A classic close air support mission was flown on the afternoon of 5 December with the help of an airborne Forward Air Controller. A Pak Army Aviation L-19 flown by Major Saeed Ismat had located guns of an Indian artillery regiment a day earlier, and 23 Division had requested an air strike to take them out. After establishing radio contact with Squadron Leader Sajjad Akbar, the leader of a five-ship F-86F formation, Saeed daringly acted as a pathfinder despite intense enemy ground fire, and guided the F-86s precisely for a very effective air attack in which eleven guns were claimed as destroyed. When the attack was over in a few minutes, Saeed led the leader of the F-86 formation to a nearby ammunition dump, which was also promptly destroyed. Saeed not only braved ground fire but was able to escape unscathed after being swooped upon by four MiG-21s that had arrived belatedly to tackle the F-86s.

While no photographs of PAF T-6Gs as deployed in combat during the 1971 War with India are available, this taken in 1959 is at least indicative of their general appearance. Their overall yellow colour was by then replaced by more suitable dark olive green. (via Tom Cooper)

The sprawling Akhnur ammunition dump was sporadically bombed, involving 21 sorties. Forward stocking of ammunition supplies in the field might have cushioned the blow for the short term, but had 23 Division's operations developed towards Akhnur, the Indian forces would have likely felt the ordnance deficiencies, if the smoke billowing from igloos was anything to go by.

T-6Gs flew 12-odd sorties during four nights. General area strafing was done on suspected enemy positions near Akhnur, though jammed guns and night visibility problems often dogged these intrepid attempts. In one mission on the night of 4/5 December, Flight Lieutenant Israr Ahmad got hit in the arm by ground fire, but he determinedly brought back the aircraft for a safe landing.

On 8 December, Flight Lieutenant Fazal Elahi of No 26 Squadron was fatally hit by ground fire, while performing a close air support mission in the Chamb area. Apparently, the AAA shell hit the bomb fuse, causing the F-86F to blow up in mid-air.

On 10 December, two F-86Fs of No 26 Squadron had a brief scrap with two Hunters of No 20 Squadron. Squadron Leader Aslam Choudhry and Flight Lieutenant Rahim Yousefzai had just arrived on an air support mission near Chamb, when they spotted two Hunters attacking ground targets. Rahim manoeuvred behind one and fired a lengthy burst, ripping the fuselage and drop tanks of the Hunter. In the meantime, the second Hunter flown by Squadron Leader R N Bharadwaj slipped in and responded with a massive fusillade of four 30mm cannon. The F-86 went down, with Aslam getting no chance to eject. The Hunter crippled by Rahim was able to limp back to Pathankot, with its pilot, Flight Lieutenant Karumbaya, surviving by a cat's whisker.

Also on 10 December, two F-86Es of No 18 Squadron manoeuvred to get behind two Su-7s while both formations were on air support missions in the Chamb area. Wing Commander Moin-ur-Rab and Flight Lieutenant Taloot Mirza claimed a Su-7 each in gun attacks, though it later transpired that both aircraft made it back to their base after having taken some bad hits.

The PAF flew a total of 146 sorties in the Chamb Sector, which was 20 percent of the PAF's total tactical air support effort. 89 sorties were considered successful, while 57 were rated as failures.[2] Just as in Shakargarh Sector, on many occasions the pilots found no enemy activity upon reaching the target area, resulting in wasted missions.

While interference by enemy fighters in the air was not of much consequence, the IAF had expended a heavy effort in support of their ground forces around Chamb. Ruefully, the PAF's complete lack of low level radar cover and fringe high level cover in the battle area, underscored the futility of flying blind CAPs to ward off the IAF's persistent attacks against 23 Division targets. Without effective air cover, ground offensive plans are as good as stalemated from the outset. This truism finally drove home as GHQ pragmatically decided to curtail the operation and be contented with an improved defensive posture at Chamb.

Beating Back in Shakargarh

The Shakargarh Salient juts into Indian territory in a particularly threatening way: the northern boundary of the salient runs not too far from the road between Pathankot and Jammu. The Kathua-Samba stretch is a mere 5-6 miles away, offering the possibility of developing operations astride the road towards the vital Madhopur Headworks. Such a manoeuvre could also serve as a ruse, while a major offensive was launched towards one of several important objectives like Gurdaspur, Batala or even Amritsar. The Pakistan Army appreciated that a riposte in this sector would likely draw elements of the Indian strategic reserves into the salient and embroil them, thus preventing or delaying their extrication to face the main Pakistani offensive in the Ganganagar-Suratgarh area. The configuration of the salient lends itself well to operations on 'interior lines,' whereby a Pakistani threat could be radiated from a single point in several directions with minimal logistic problems. The enemy, conversely, would be compelled to operate on 'exterior lines,' having to position a larger contingent of forces all along the periphery of the salient.

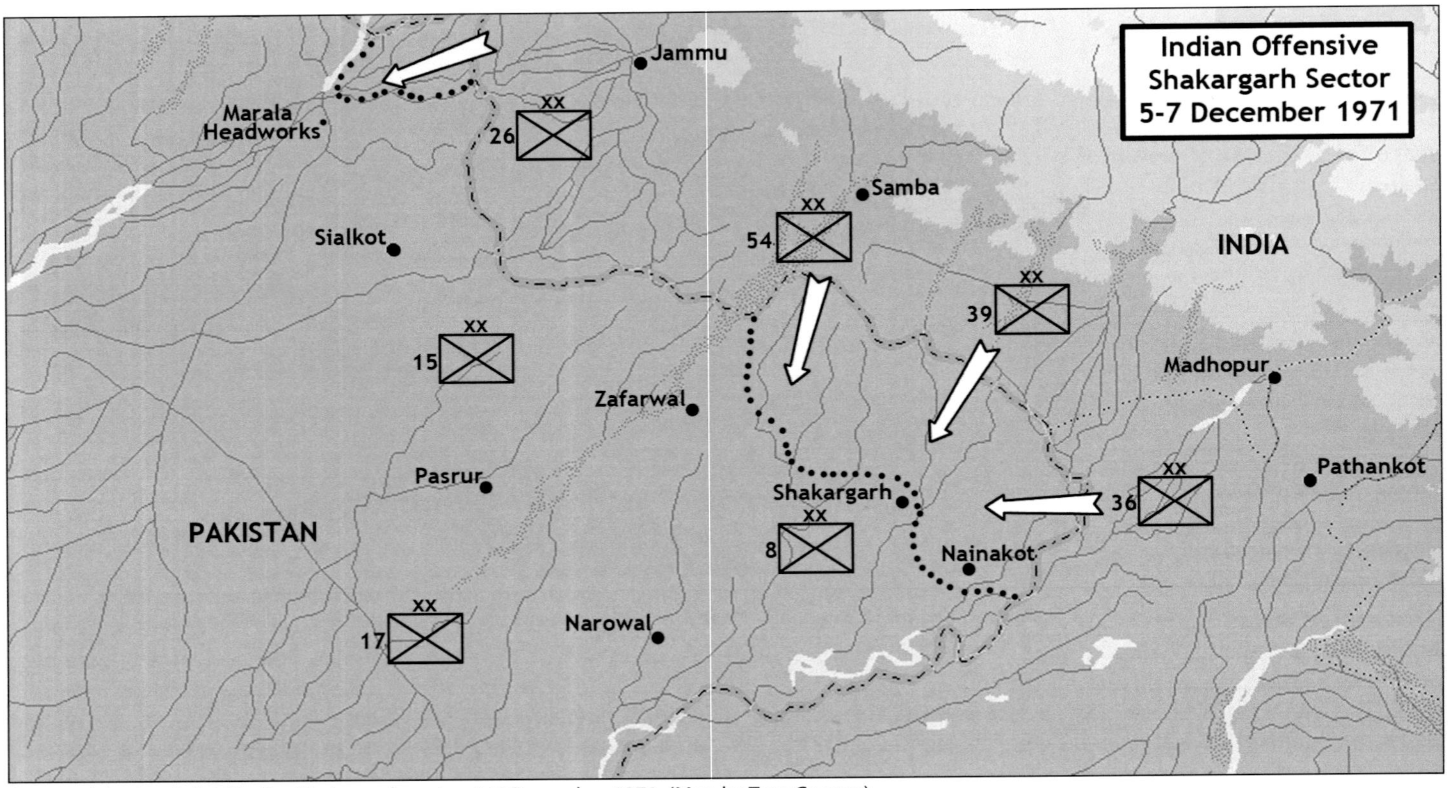

A map of the battlefield in the Shakargarh sector, 5-7 December 1971. (Map by Tom Cooper)

The Indian Army's overriding concern was to protect the vital Jammu-Pathankot artery while capturing important territory through its main offensive by I Corps. This formation had 39 Infantry Division and 54 Infantry Division, each supported by an armoured brigade, as the spearheads of its two-pronged offensive. 36 Infantry Division and two brigades of the ad hoc 'X-Sector' covered the flanks, while an additional brigade covered the central base, all in a holding role.

For the defence of Sialkot and the Shakargarh Salient, the Pakistan Army's (similarly numbered) I Corps had fielded 15 Infantry Division and 8 Infantry Division on the western and eastern sides of Degh Nadi respectively, both divisions supported by 8 Independent Armoured Brigade. The formation tasked to launch a counter-offensive at an opportune time was the so-called Army Reserve North. It consisted of 6 Armoured Division and 17 Infantry Division. Though nominally under I Corps, it was directly controlled by GHQ.

The Indian I Corps opened up with its offensive at dusk on 5 December. Facing the brunt of the Indian offensive was Pakistan Army's lone 8 Division, as 15 Division remained tied up against the 'X-Sector' force (guarding Indian I Corps' right flank) as well as 26 Division (XV Corps), on a wide frontage between Degh Nadi and Pukhlian Salient.

The Indian 39 Division, tasked to capture Shakargarh, crossed the international border from a north-easterly direction on the evening of 5 December, but the advance ran into trouble as it hit the first belt of a well-laid out minefield on 7 December. 'This, coupled with heavy artillery fire and air attacks frustrated the attempts … to make headway,' reasons the Indian *Official History of the 1971 India-Pakistan War*.[3] Another attempt to attack from the north on the following day was foiled when a second belt of the minefield was encountered. It was evident that the inability to breach the minefield, and stout resistance by Pakistani 8 Division had a demoralising effect. The 'standard of stage management for the battle so far displayed was uninspiring and weak,' was the assessment of 39 Division's performance by the Corps Commander Lieutenant General K K Singh.[4] He was compelled to abort his plan of investing Shakargarh, and decided to redeploy 39 Division's forces in another sector.

The Indian 54 Division launched its attack from a northerly direction on the night of 5 December, with the aim of capturing Zafarwal, and in the process, destroying Pakistani 8 Armoured Brigade. By 11 December, peripheral border villages and small towns had been captured, the flanks of the Corps' forces secured, and the minefield breached. A bridgehead was established for the final assault on Zafarwal by 15 December, but Pakistani forces counter-attacked fiercely, duly supported by the PAF. While 54 Division's effort was better planned and executed than that of 39 Division, it too failed to penetrate the main defences and was able to advance just eight miles in two weeks of fighting. The objective of capturing Zafarwal remained elusive as fighting ceased on 17 December. Pakistan's 8 Armoured Brigade paid a heavy price by losing as many as 50 tanks during the counterattack, but it was some consolation that the Zafarwal-Shakargarh chain of defence remained intact.

The Indian 36 Division had been performing a holding role on the eastern side of the salient. After the failure of 39 Division to take Shakargarh, 36 Division was hastily charged with an offensive task, with the aim of developing operations towards Shakargarh in yet one more attempt. A rear-guard brigade of 36 Division had secured a bridgehead across the border on 9 December. Together with an infantry brigade and an armoured brigade mustered from 39 Division, Indian forces advanced up to the Bein River, and an assault was planned on Shakargarh on the night of 14/15 December. Pakistani forces were rushed from other sectors to Nurkot-Shakargarh area, which was already well prepared with deep minefields. Intense artillery shelling and exploding mines caused heavy casualties to the Indian forces and exposed the troops to more precise fire from well-concealed platoons having adequate photo-reconnaissance support. The Indian armour got bogged down while attempting to cross the soggy bed of the Bein River, and the advance fizzled out as soon as it had commenced. 39 Division was thrown completely off-balance, its plight only worsened by the absence of the IAF which was said to be committed heavily in the Chamb Sector.

A Pakistan Army M48 main battle tank and infantry on advance in the Chamb sector. (Albert Grandolini Collection)

Lying within the area of responsibility of Pakistani 15 Division, on the western flank, was the narrow Pukhlian Salient. Its defences were sloppily left to the para-military 1 Wing of Rangers, along with a regular infantry company. The Indian 19 Brigade (ex-26 Division) attacked the salient on the night of 5 December, so as to pre-empt any threat to Akhnur materialising from the southern direction. The Rangers were easily pushed out, and a menacing threat was posed to the nearby Marala Headworks before the regular Pakistani troops salvaged the situation.

PAF Hastens to Help

With Murid, Sargodha and Risalewala optimally located in relation to Shakargarh Sector, air support could be made available promptly. Peshawar, though distant, could also chip in with the aircraft flying a modified flight profile. Altogether, two and a half squadrons of F-6s, and three squadrons of F-86E/Fs were available for air support operations. Seemingly an adequate force, the F-86s were, however, ill-armed to conduct anti-armour operations with their small calibre 0.5" Browning guns, and 2.75" FFAR or SNEB 68mm unguided rockets, the former acclaimed neither for accuracy, nor penetration. The F-86s were mostly configured with general purpose bombs to blast out armour, which was considered a suitable compromise by providing a safe stand-off distance, notwithstanding the ineffectiveness of general area bombing for destroying armour. It was surmised that relentless bombing would, at least, have some blast effect on personnel and equipment. The F-6s were relatively better endowed for close air support, having three powerful NR-30 30mm cannon which were absolutely lethal, as might be expected of the heaviest aircraft round (.93 lb) then in use on any aircraft. The F-6 also flew a few sorties with the S-5 57mm rockets.

As the Indian 39 Division ran into the first minefield belt, PAF F-6s and F-86s managed to get some good hits on the stalled armour. For the most part however, the PAF had to provide sporadic and knee-jerk air support which, in the given situation, was a godsend for the Army nonetheless. The vital and vulnerable bridgehead operations, and subsequent breakout of all three divisional offensives, escaped punishment from the air as these took place under cover of the night. A pontoon ferry bridge over the Ravi River was destroyed on 11 December, two days after crossing by the main elements of Indian 39 Division had already taken place. While the destruction of the bridge did not induce any delay in the commencement of this offensive, it did possibly hamper subsequent reinforcements, as the stalled offensive seems to indicate.

An exciting situation developed in one of the close air support missions on the morning of 7 December, when four F-6s of No 11 Squadron found themselves vying for airspace with four Su-7s, who also happened to be on a similar mission near Zafarwal. The moment the Su-7s sighted the F-6s pulling up for their attack, they lit afterburners and started to exit eastwards. At that time, the No 2 F-6 called that he had been hit by AAA so he was asked by the mission leader, Flight Lieutenant Atiq Sufi, to pair up with No 4 and recover back. Once sure that the situation was under control, Atiq smartly ordered a split, so that an F-6 each was chasing a pair of Su-7s. 'I remember accelerating to 1,100kph despite the rocket pods which were retained, as I could not afford to take my eyes off the prey to look inside for the selective jettison switches,' says Atiq. He barely managed to arrest his rate of closure, and opened fire on his target with the centre gun. 'I had expended the ammunition in the centre gun so I switched to the two side guns and continued firing. A well-aimed volley struck right behind the cockpit and the Su-7 rolled over its back,' remembers Atiq. It was later learnt that Squadron Leader Jiwa Singh, the senior flight commander of Adampur-based No 26 Squadron had gone down with the aircraft, south-west of Samba just over the border. The F-6 deputy leader, Flight Lieutenant Mushaf Mir also fired at one of the fast-receding Su-7s, but it accelerated away, apparently unscathed.

In another close air support mission on the afternoon of 11 December, a formation of three F-86Es from No 18 Squadron led by the enthusiastic Squadron Commander, Wing Commander Ali Imam Bokhari, had a scrap with a flight of Su-7s, also on a similar mission. Bokhari had just released a salvo of rockets on a cluster of vehicles in the battlefield near Nainakot when his No 2, Flight Lieutenant Momin Arif yelled 'Lead, three Su-7s at 2 o'clock.' Bokhari promptly ordered all to jettison their drop tanks and turned the formation hard right, to position behind the Su-7s. Bokhari then manoeuvred on to the tail of one Su-7 and was about to shoot when his No 3, Squadron Leader Cecil Chaudhry, came charging in from the other side, trying a pot shot at the same aircraft. Cecil requested, 'Leader, leave it for me, please.' Bokhari abandoned the attack and switched to the other Su-7 which was not too far off. Centring the enemy aircraft in his gun sight, Bokhari pressed the trigger and saw a stream of bullets rip into the Su-7. Moments later, there was an orange flash and then the aircraft exploded, with bits and pieces showering down. Commendably, this was the PAF's first subsonic versus supersonic aircraft kill. It was later learnt that Flight Lieutenant K K Mohan of Ambala-based No 26 Squadron went down with his aircraft. Cecil also fired at his quarry and claimed a Su-7 but firing from long-range resulted in a missed shot; no details of aircraft wreckage or pilot status have emerged since.

On 14 December, Squadron Leader Salim Gauhar of No 26 Squadron, while on a close air support mission in Shakargarh area, spotted a light observation aircraft and easily shot it down with his F-86's guns. There were some anxious moments for Salim after he returned from the mission, as a Pakistan Army L-19 was reported to have been flying in the area at the same time. There was immense relief when it was learnt that the L-19 had landed safely. It later transpired that the downed aircraft was an Indian Army Krishak. Its pilot, Capt P K Gaur of No 660 Squadron, went down with the flaming aircraft, though the co-pilot, Capt G S Punia, survived the crash.

Many exciting aerial scraps took place in Shakargarh Sector, though

The business end of an F-6, showing its three 30mm NR-30 cannon to advantage. These caused quite a flash, not to mention rattling the pilot, but also delivered a powerful punch – and proved a very useful weapon for ground attack. (Albert Grandolini Collection)

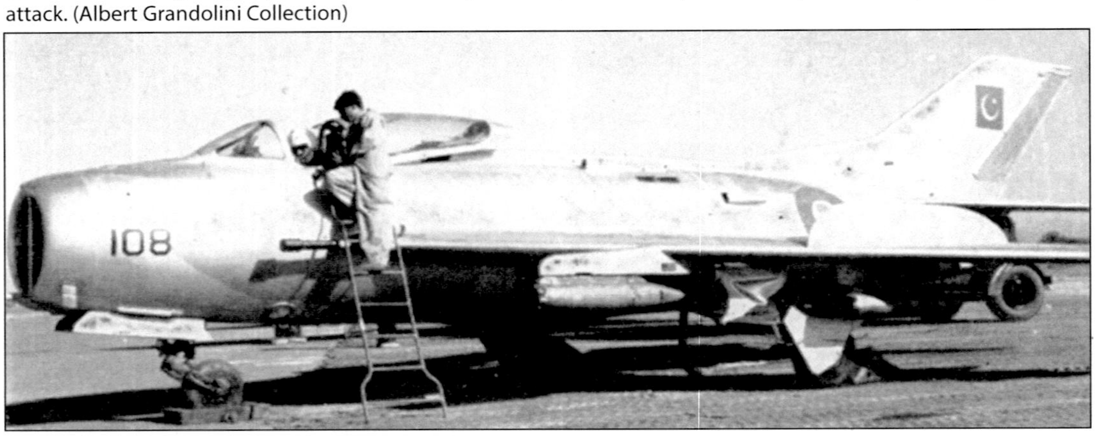

Another of PAF's F-6s: notable here is the ORO-57K rocket pod installed on the inboard underwing pylon: this contained eight 57mm S-5K unguided rockets. (Albert Grandolini Collection)

Many of the PAF's F-6s received makeshift camouflage patterns during the war, to better conceal them during low-altitude ground attacks. While most of the patterns in question consisted of light earth, brown and green, this aircraft received a grey livery on top surfaces and sides, and light blue on the undersides. (Albert Grandolini Collection)

some of them had uncertain results. Wing Commander Abdul Aziz, a senior pilot attached to No 26 Squadron during the war, was flying a ground attack mission at mid-day on 14 December. His formation of F-86Fs was bounced by four MiG-21s. A dogfight ensued in which several missiles were fired by the MiGs. The F-86s were not only able to evade them but managed to get into an advantageous position. Having no missiles, they were unable to catch up with the fast accelerating MiGs which exited, apparently low on fuel.

Flight Lieutenant Aamer Sharieff of No 11 Squadron was leading a flight of four F-6s on an armed photo-reconnaissance mission at mid-day on 14 December. Spotting a flight of four MiG-21s trying to manoeuvre behind his formation, he was able to out-turn one, and launched a Sidewinder missile at his quarry. The MiG-21 was seen to be flaming, but its ultimate fate remains unknown.

Flight Lieutenant Abbas Khattak of No 11 Squadron was leading a flight of four F-6s on an armed recce mission late in the afternoon of 14 December. He chanced upon a pair of Su-7s and was able to sneak behind one. Firing a Sidewinder missile in good range, Khattak was dismayed to see it nosedive into the ground. A second missile was fired, which appeared to explode in the proximity of the aircraft, but no more was known of it.

During the course of air support operations in Shakargarh Sector, the PAF lost three aircraft to ground fire. On 7 December, an F-6 flown by Flight Lieutenant Wajid Ali Khan of No 11 Squadron was shot down by AAA, as he was attacking ground targets near Marala. He ejected and was taken POW. The same day, Squadron Leader Cecil Chaudhry of No 18 Squadron was apparently hit by friendly AAA, near Zafarwal.[5] He was lucky to fall into Pakistan Army hands as he parachuted down after ejection only a few hundred yards away from Indian positions. Cecil was also fortunate to be in good shape and was able to fly again the very next day. On 17 December, the last day of the war, Flight Lieutenant Shahid Raza of No 25 Squadron volunteered for a mission from which he was fated not to return. During ground attack, his F-6 was hit by enemy AAA near Dharman, close to Shakargarh. He was heard to be ejecting, but sadly, nothing more was ever learnt about him.

The PAF flew a total of 298 sorties in Shakargarh Sector, which made up 40 percent of the PAF's total tactical air support effort.[6]

Interference by enemy fighters was not prohibitive, and the PAF was able to perform its task without let, by and large. The missions were mostly close air support and armed recce. 183 sorties were considered successful, while 115 sorties were rated as failures.[7] Poor visibility caused by winter haze was the bane of pilots, though an equally frustrating issue was the discovery of non-existent enemy activity on reaching the target area. Apparently, time delays – from air support request, until the fighters arrived over the target area – resulted in a completely changed situation than what was expected. The dense foliage and built-up areas also complicated visual pick-up.

Even if assessed on the basis of a high probability of 'one target hit per sortie' (assuming a single attacking pass), it can be seen that not more than 183 targets could have been possibly destroyed in the successful sorties flown in the sector. However, actual claims exceed this figure, and include 115 vehicles, 74 tanks, 13 tank transporters and six guns, besides a pontoon bridge. Since such claims cannot be verified accurately in a one-sided assessment based on fuzzy gun camera ciné film, it would only be fair to reduce these claims considerably. Attack parameter inaccuracies that got induced in the heat of the battle, unfavourable weapon-target compatibility, and weapon failures, are important factors that cannot be overlooked.

For an academic discussion, even if the claims are reduced by an arbitrary factor of half, the results still remain fairly impressive. It can be clearly seen that the Pakistan Army's 8 Division was effectively supported by the PAF, and was thus able to deny the Indian I Corps the twin strategic objectives of Zafarwal and Shakargarh, despite repeated Indian attempts to capture them. In the bargain, 8 Division suffered considerable losses in men and material, along with the loss of 265 square miles of territory in the Shakargarh Salient.[8] (Additionally, about 40 square miles were lost in the Pukhlian Salient.) Any plan to recoup the losses could not be put in place, as the Army Reserve North had already been denuded to the point of futility. Two brigades of its constituent 17 Infantry Division, along with the complete artillery assets, had been detached to other sectors that were confronted with equally critical situations.[9]

It is some consolation that the enemy was denied a foothold for developing operations towards the core areas of Punjab – a chilling prospect that could well have followed on the heels East Pakistan's loss.

Fighting a Desert Storm

Spiny-tailed lizards scamper across the dunes that make up the vast Thar Desert straddling the Sind-Rajasthan Border. Buzzards soar on the desert currents during day, and caracals prowl the scattered scrub at night. Staking out territory is no easy matter, and every creature treads prudently in this desolate and forbidding expanse.

The 1971 War saw rival armies face off in the inhospitable Thar Desert, each aiming to unbalance the other's strategic formations, and capturing vital territory in the bargain. The desert offered few objectives of strategic value, as these lay deeper, away from the border. The Indian Army's formidable Southern Command, consisting of two regular infantry divisions (11 Division and 12 Division), and two brigade-sized formations ('Bikaner' and 'Kutch' Sector HQs) of the Border Security Force and Territorial Army troops, was arrayed against the Pakistan Army's single 18 Division required to cover a frontage of over 700 miles. Both of India's infantry divisions were poised to create footholds inside southern Pakistan for threatening deeper objectives; this, in turn, was expected to unhinge the Pakistani strategic reserves, whose elements would have been detached helter-skelter to cope with the dangerous situation thus obtaining.

The predicament of 18 Division was well-understood by the GHQ at Rawalpindi, and it was decided to pre-empt any Southern Command incursion by undertaking a most unexpected foray into Indian territory. A two-pronged offensive of brigade-strength each was hastily put together for the capture of Ramgarh, and for neutralising Jaisalmer airfield – the latter, a rather quixotic task in view of absence of the PAF from the area. It is also open to conjecture if the Pakistan Army's GHQ had wishfully imagined the dislocation of Indian strategic reserves as a consequence of the daring 18 Division sortie. In the event, the offensive bogged down at Longewala soon after initiation on midnight of 4 December. However, due to the boldness

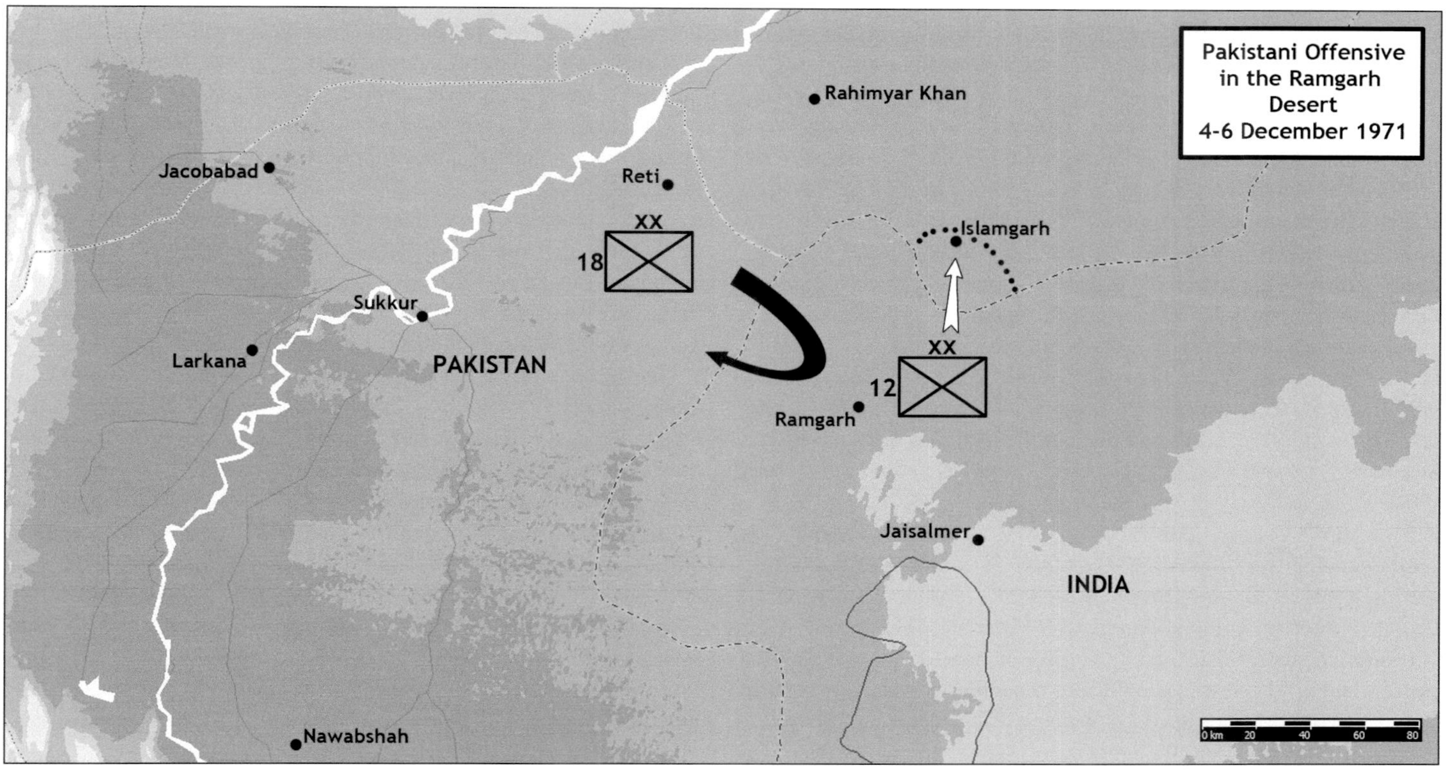

A map of the battlefield in the Longewala sector on 4-6 December 1971. (Map by Tom Cooper)

A Type-59 tank of 18 Division, knocked out during the failed advance on Jaisalmer in the Ramgarh desert (Longewala sector). (Albert Grandolini Collection)

and surprise of the move, Indian 12 Division was completely knocked off-balance; it remained mired in efforts to counter the Pakistani offensive, as well as screening the area for any more surprises. Charged with the ambitious objective of severing the rail-road link to northern Pakistan, it could not progress beyond the initial capture of a desert outpost of Islamgarh and failed to develop operations towards Rahim Yar Khan. There is also evidence of the panic entraining of some elements of the crack Indian 1 Armoured Division for providing relief, a task that was quickly taken over by a detachment of six IAF Hunters belonging to the Hunter OCU stationed at Jaisalmer.

With no air opposition to menace them, the Hunters carried out textbook strafing and rocketing attacks during the 38 sorties flown over two days, in which they wreaked havoc on Pakistani tank columns caught in the open desert.[10] By 7 December, the Pakistani brigades were in full retreat, having suffered heavy losses including at least 20 tanks and scores of other vehicles destroyed or abandoned. [11] At the end of the venture, Major General B M Mustafa, the ill-starred Commander of 18 Division, stood relieved of his command for an undertaking that went awry under his watch.

The rout of 18 Division armour at the hands of the IAF has been partly blamed on Air HQ for not providing air cover during the operation. This is despite the fact that Air HQ had asked GHQ for at least four days' notice (and preferably, ten days) for activating the airfield with all the operational, logistic and air defence wherewithal. In the absence of such notice, PAF fighters could not be positioned at the nearest airfield of Jacobabad. Even if a fighter complement was deployed, there was no low-level radar to provide early warning against intruders coming for the base, much less for the 400nm swathe of airspace from Pir Patho to Shorkot that had no radar cover whatsoever.

The PAF C-in-C, Air Marshal A Rahim Khan, who was accompanying the Army Chief of Staff (COS) General Abdul Hamid during a visit to Rahim Yar Khan in October, must not have failed to notice the utter vulnerability of 18 Division elements to air attack. It is another matter that the 18 Division offensive had been planned hastily, had not been war-gamed, and the logistics requirements had been treated most superficially. It was easy to see why it floundered as it did. Even though some diehard strategists make much of the initial advantage of surprise, it must be realised that, had the overstretched Pakistani force somehow reached its objective at Ramgarh, it would have been eventually destroyed by a realigned 12 Division charging in from the left flank.

Despite the battering that it took at Longewala, it can be said that 18 Division's venture, foolhardy though it was, did not go in vain, and it was somehow able to prevent a befuddled 12 Division Commander, Major General R K Khambata, from achieving his main task of truncating West Pakistan. The Indian *Official History of the 1971 India-Pakistan War* succinctly sums up 12 Division's disappointment thus: 'Had it detected the Pak thrust on 4 December, the Division could have met and dissipated it, and gone ahead with its offensive as originally planned.'[12]

Action at Naya Chor

Further south, Indian 11 Division was tasked to capture Naya Chor by launching an offensive along the Monabao-Khokhrapar-Naya Chor axis with the help of two brigades, and subsequently, to develop operations into the green belt of Sind. Additionally, the division's third brigade was to outflank and capture Chachro along the Gadra-Khinsar-Chachro axis. Apparently, no link-up of the two widely divergent incursions was planned, and neither complemented the other. The Indians had envisaged that a threat to towns like Mirpurkhas and Umarkot would force Pakistan's II Corps to detach its elements for the assistance of 18 Division's single brigade in this sector, thus depleting the former's offensive potential.

As the two Indian brigades advanced towards Naya Chor on the night of 4 December, they met little resistance at first. The disrupted rail link between Monabao and Khokhrapar was repaired, and it was hoped that a regular logistics supply chain would hasten progress of the onslaught. The rail connection, which had been disused for years, had many more snags than expected. The vulnerable rail link proved to be the very bane of the Indian brigades as the PAF swung into action, and started a concerted day and night interdiction campaign that precipitated the 'overstretch' which the *Official History of the 1971 India-Pakistan War* much bemoans.[13]

The Base Commander at Masroor, Air Commodore Nazir Latif, along with the OC of No 32 Wing, Group Captain Wiqar Azim, responded swiftly and decided to throw in everything the base could muster. Composite missions, including different types of aircraft, were ingeniously flown. The OC Wing and two of his Squadron Commanders, Wing Commander Shaikh Saleem of No 19 Squadron and Wing Commander Asghar Randhawa of No 2 Squadron, were at the forefront of this air action and led many missions themselves. Several interdiction and armed recce missions targeted trains laden with fuel and ammunition along the Khokhrapar-Naya Chor railway line. Tanks and vehicles exposed in the open also turned out to be lucrative targets, and in the surprising absence of air opposition, multiple attacks were carried out without much trouble.

One daring mission involving the only daylight B-57 sortie of

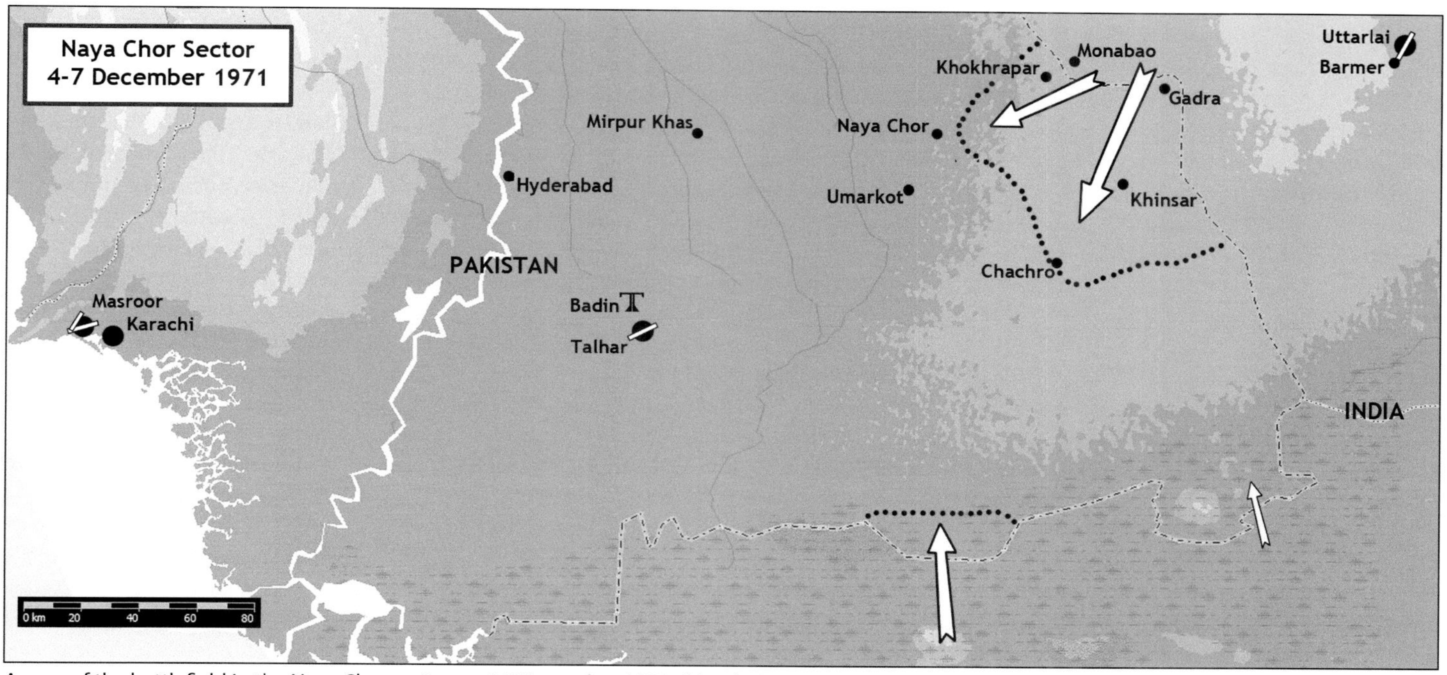

A map of the battlefield in the Naya Chor sector on 4-7 December 1971. (Map by Tom Cooper)

the war, manifestly inspired the pilots of the Wing to fight fearlessly. On 7 December, Flight Lieutenant Shabbir A Khan, along with his navigator Squadron Leader Shoaib Alam, carried out an afternoon bombing raid on a concentration of tanks and vehicles, and followed it up with several strafing passes on a stationary train. Such was the fervour that Shabbir spent nearly twenty minutes taking steady pot shots, as if on a training sortie at his home firing range.

The same night, Wing Commander Asghar Randhawa bombed an important POL bulk supply node that served the theatre of operations, while flying in a T-33. 'The oil tanks at Barmer railway station were hit and set on fire,' reports the Indian *Official History of the 1971 India-Pakistan War*.[14]

Another remarkable mission involved a motley of aircraft flown by No 32 Wing, and it was boldly led by its enthusiastic OC, Group Captain Wiqar Azim. In the afternoon of 14 December, a nine-ship composite formation of four F-86Fs and four T-33s, escorted by a lone F-86E, and covered on top by two F-104s, struck three trains laden with POL and explosives near Naya Chor. In the same mission, a convoy was struck and many vehicles destroyed.

In all, 189 sorties (including 26 night sorties by B-57s, T-33s, and C-130s) were flown in support of 18 Division in Chor, Ramgarh and Kutch Sectors; this formed almost 26 percent of the total air support effort provided by the PAF during the war.[15] In addition, 43 CAP sorties were flown by F-86E and F-104 to cover the vital troop and armour reinforcements arriving by train from the central zone to Naya Chor. The inability of the IAF to interfere with the reinforcements only underscores the effectiveness of the PAF's air umbrella. The *Official History of the 1971 India-Pakistan War* succinctly sums up the causes of the stalemate in Naya Chor: 'As the PAF was very active and as it was becoming increasingly apparent that the Division had overstretched itself, it was decided to give up the piecemeal nibbling of enemy defences and put in a more concentrated effort after proper build-up.'[16]

Unlike the PAF's air support in the northern battle zones, where as many as one-third of the air support sorties were unsuccessful (mainly because the enemy tanks and vehicles could not be sighted in the natural camouflage of Punjab), the success rate in Thar was a remarkable 92 percent as the desert offered the enemy no sanctuary.

A total of 20 tanks, 63 vehicles, five trains, three bulk fuel stores and an ammunition dump were claimed by the pilots, according to the PAF's official history.[17] During the course of the tactical air support campaign by the PAF, no aircraft were lost to ground fire.

It is evident that the PAF was able to operate with such impunity in the Thar Sector because IAF planners had not paid heed to countering it in earnest, both on the ground and in the air. An incessantly disruptive campaign against Masroor Base, along with aggressive fighter sweeps in the Naya Chor area, could have surely helped the Indians. After all, IAF had four fighter bases which directly served the Southern Sector, and there was no dearth of air effort. Had the IAF's counter-air campaign been more whole-hearted, Major General R D Anand, Commander 11 Division, may well have been planning his next moves from the district headquarters at Mirpurkhas!

Own Offensive Foreclosed

The third Indian brigade which had Chachro as its objective, was able to overcome minor resistance at various points on the way and managed to capture it by the afternoon of 8 December. Later, on 13 December, a battalion-sized foray towards Umarkot was launched from Chachro but was soundly beaten back by a Pakistani counterattack. The Indian raid did, however, raise concerns at GHQ in Rawalpindi as the 'green belt' had been trespassed, as it were. So as not to distract 55 Brigade which was putting up a brave stand at Naya Chor, and to provide it with much needed relief, it was decided to bolster it with a brigade pulled out from II Corps' 33 Infantry Division. 55 Brigade and the newly arrived 60 Brigade, with zealous air support from the PAF's No 32 Wing, were thus able to repel renewed Indian efforts to push forward towards Naya Chor.

Earlier, another of 33 Division's brigades had been detached to I Corps in Shakargarh, where the ground situation was equally grim. This all but meant that Lieutenant General Tikka Khan's offensive stood aborted. II Corps, which had been somehow hoping for an improvement in the relative strength ratio of forces, actually found itself denuded to the point of impracticality as far as launching its offensive was concerned.

Though vast stretches of desert amounting to over 1,740 square miles were captured by 11 Division in the Naya Chor and Chachro

A Canadair CL.13 Sabre, known in the PAF as the F-86E: 90 of these ex-Luftwaffe fighters were acquired to circumvent US sanctions. This example was one of few to receive only an overall coat of grey, instead of the usual camouflage pattern in green, prior to its delivery 'to Iran' (for details, see the colour section). (Albert Grandolini Collection)

sub-sectors, it is of academic interest to know that the Indian division commander was still denied his operational objective. As stated earlier, the significance of Pakistani forces being able to hold on to Naya Chor lay in the enemy being denied a foothold for developing operations deeper into the core areas of Sind. This apparently came at the cost of Pakistan's main offensive, but in retrospect, it can be clearly seen that II Corps' elements had a 'fire-fighting' role chalked out from the outset, and the much talked about offensive was rather delusory in its strategic conception.

Sundry Assistance

Besides the raging battles in Shakargarh and Chamb, two other sectors in Punjab saw fierce exchanges resulting in minor, but potentially useful gains by the Pakistan Army's IV Corps. Both in Sulaimanki and Hussainiwala Sectors, land operations were overlaid by negligible, and largely inconsequential, air support.

Sulaimanki Sector

The precarious proximity of Sulaimanki Headworks to the international border dictated that the Pakistan Army take offensive action at the outset, so as to pre-empt any Indian designs against the vital Southern Punjab waterworks. For Pakistan, any territorial gain would not only threaten nearby Fazilka, it could also provide a firm supporting base for the impending main offensive as it swung due north-eastwards into the Indian heartland.

The Pakistani 105 Independent Infantry Brigade (IV Corps) was pitted against Indian 67 Infantry Brigade ('Foxtrot' Sector).[18] On the twilight of 3 December, the Pakistani brigade, under cover of intense artillery fire, charged through the Indian troops with such speed and ferocity that it was able to establish a foothold on the tank obstacle line of the Sabuna Distributary six miles inside, within an hour. The Indian troops struck by total 'pandemonium and bewilderment,' had destroyed all but one of the 22 bridges on the distributor while withdrawing; this desperate action also foreclosed any chances of success of a subsequent counterattack.[19] The Indians counterattacked five times over the subsequent nights but each operation resulted in complete failure, mainly due to intense and accurate artillery shelling by 105 Brigade.[20] Such was the intensity of the artillery fusillade, that the enemy granted undue strength to the attacking troops by imagining two attacking brigades. It was, thus, unable to plan properly and counter-attack confidently, much to the chagrin of the Major General Ram Singh, Commander Foxtrot Sector who thought that 67 Brigade was 'discomposed and flustered, its men demoralised and put out.'[21]

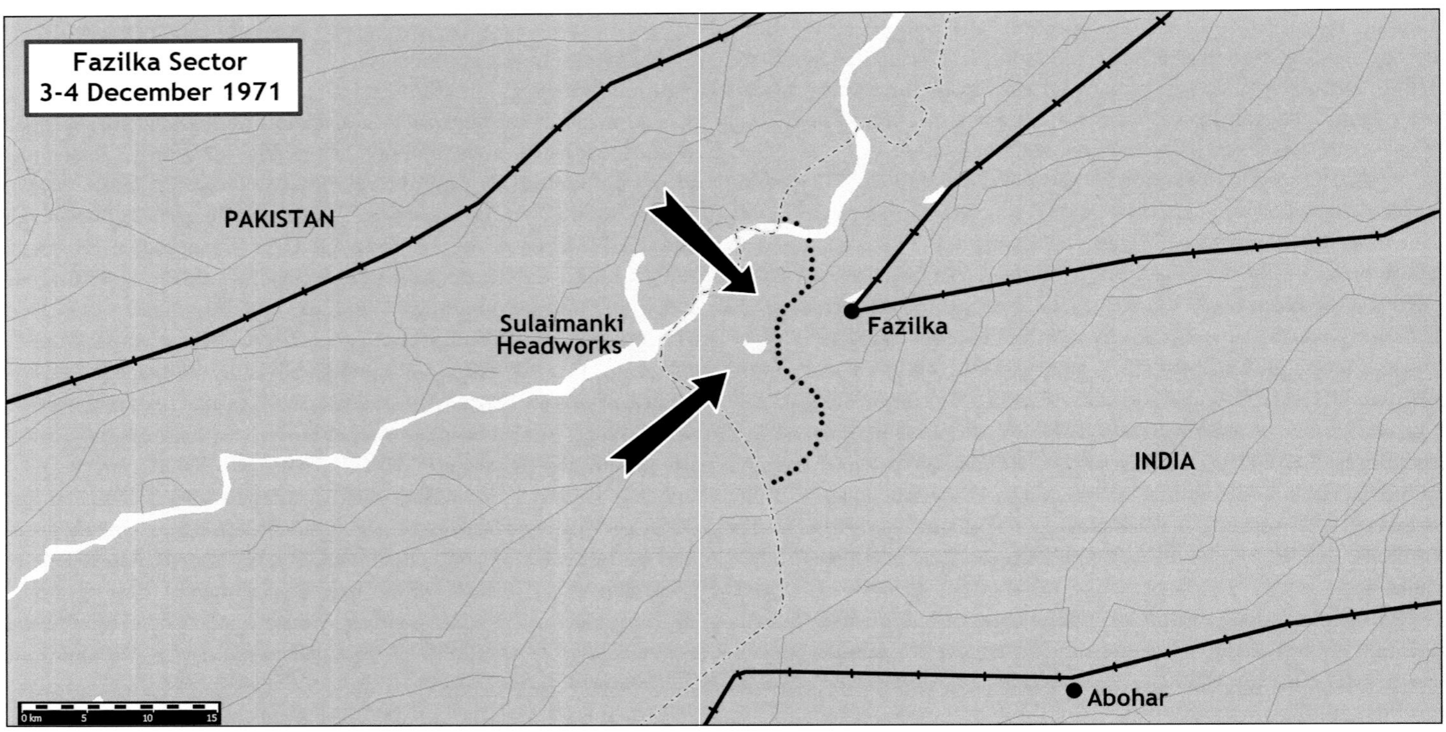

A map of the battlefield in the Fazilka sector on 3-4 December 1971. (Map by Tom Cooper)

A Type-59 tank assigned to 105 Independent Infantry Brigade, knocked out during its fast advance through the positions of 67 Indian Brigade in the Sulaimanki sector. (Albert Grandolini Collection)

The brigade saw two of its successively changed commanders ram their heads, as it were, against the dogged resistance by Brig Amir Hamza's brilliantly-led outfit.[22]

Since all Indian counterattacks were foiled within hours of darkness, air support during daytime largely served to mop up any stragglers, besides boosting friendly troops' morale. No 17 Squadron, based at Rafiqui, flew 55 F-86E sorties, of which 33 were considered successful. In 22 sorties, either no targets could be found or, bombs were released on dead reckoning with questionable results. Half a dozen tanks and some vehicles were claimed as destroyed.

Hussainiwala Sector

Several enclaves nestled in the meandering loops of the rivers Ravi and Sutlej came to be exchanged during minor operations by either side. Difficult to defend across rivers, one such Indian enclave was Hussainiwala, which housed important canal headworks by the same name. The psychologically significant Indian town of Firozpur lay a tantalising six miles from Hussainiwala.

At twilight of 3 December, Pakistani 106 Infantry Brigade (11 Division) attacked with two infantry battalions and a troop of armour. The opening barrage of artillery fire completely surprised the Indian 15 Punjab (35 Brigade), a reinforced two-battalion strength unit tasked to defend the enclave. Consternation amongst the defenders knew no bounds when the Hussainiwala Bridge, which had been wired up by them for demolition, just in case, purportedly blew up under Pakistani artillery fire. The Officer Commanding of 15 Punjab, safely ensconced in his headquarters south of the River Sutlej, was too overcome by the devastating situation and pleaded with his superiors for a withdrawal. 'Infected by his pessimism' (as the Indian official historian puts it), the Brigade Commander was able to convince Commander 7 Division to pull back to the south bank of the river after having conceded about 20 square miles to Pakistani forces. Within 24 hours of start of the operation, Hussainiwala lay at the mercy of Brigadier Mumtaz Khan's unstoppable brigade.

With the grave threat to the headworks having developed in no time, the IAF responded swiftly, and in full force, to keep 106 Brigade from making any further headway. Without low level radar cover, the PAF's presence in the air meant little, and IAF fighters had virtual freedom of action which they used to some advantage. It is easy to see

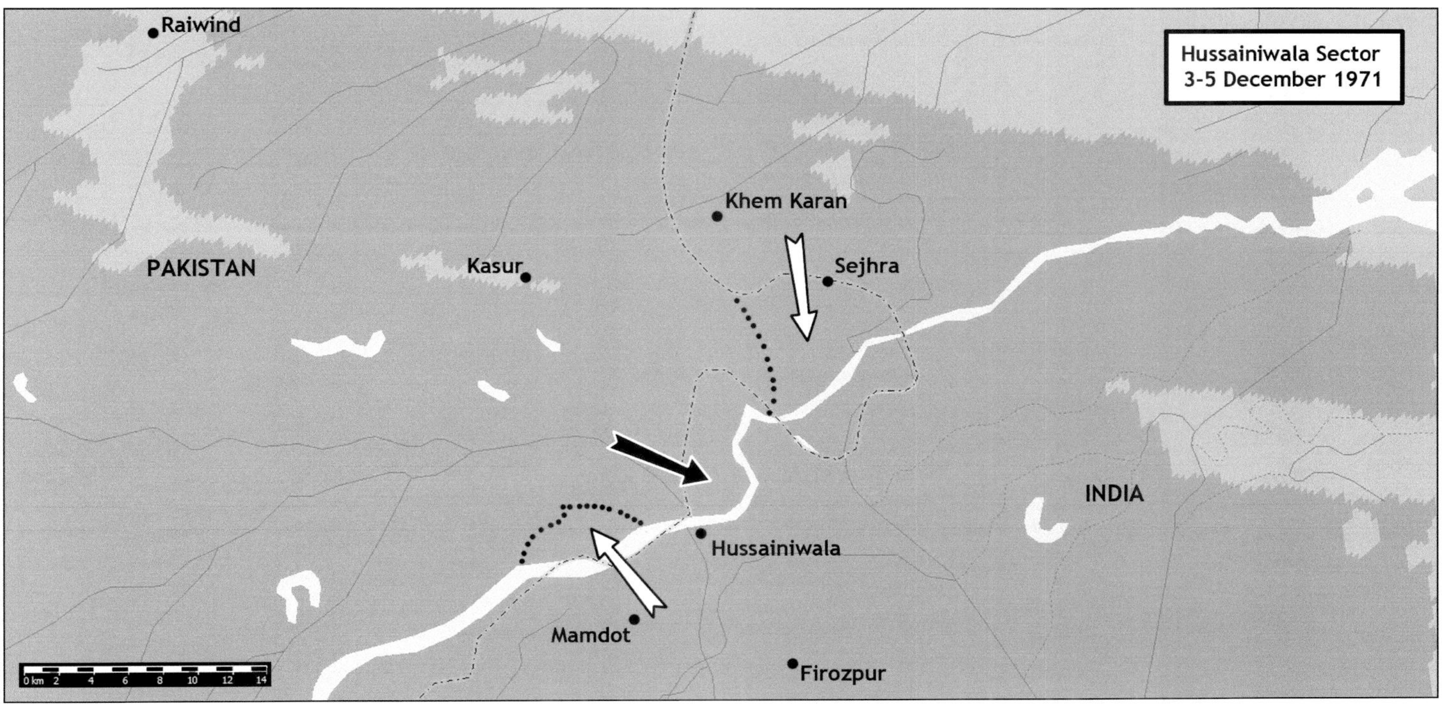

A map of the battlefield in the Hussainiwala sector on 3-5 December 1971. (Map by Tom Cooper)

why any advance towards Firozpur would have been disastrous. As in Chamb Sector, GHQ wisely decided not to expand the operation, since the basic objective of improving the defensive posture had been achieved.

With the Indian ground troops having hunkered down, PAF fighters on air support missions were unable to spot any worthwhile targets. A nominal 29 sorties were flown on the following days, and other than a mission claiming to have targeted an ammunition dump, all others were unsuccessful.

While 106 Brigade was successful in capturing the Hussainiwala enclave, the Indians were able to clear the protrusion known as the Sehjra Bulge, as well as an enclave near Mamdot, without much opposition. Battles involving these latter two enclaves did not entail any air support.

Scouting the Troops

The PAF had three Mirage IIIRPs which were equipped with five OMERA Type 31 optical cameras each, all mounted in the nose. With Doppler navigation radar available, getting to a destination was fairly easy. Magnesium flares provided enough illumination at night to confer a round-the-clock tactical reconnaissance capability. The number of aircraft was, however, on the low side and did not sufficiently cater for unserviceability.

A month prior to the outbreak of all-out war, the PAF had started to fly cross-border photo-reconnaissance sorties, some of which were in the vital Chamb Sector, where Pak Army's 23 Division had planned a secondary 'diversionary' offensive. With the disposition of forces well-known, the attack resulted in significant advances that threatened India's overland links to Kashmir. It also deprived the Indian forces of establishing a launch pad for offensive operations towards the vital lines of communication passing through nearby Gujrat.

Early in the war, another important breakthrough came in the Sulaimanki-Fazilka Sector, where 105 Independent Infantry Brigade (IV Corps) was able to surprise the Indian 'Foxtrot' Force and made a firm foothold in the area of Pak II Corps' planned main offensive. While the Indian forces desperately carried out repeated counterattacks, PAF Mirages conducted regular photo-reconnaissance missions in the Firozpur area to update the ground commanders about Indian reinforcement efforts aimed at vacating the incursion. In the event, a badly demoralised and confused Foxtrot Force could not make any headway, and the Pakistani brigade was able to safeguard the vital Sulaimanki Headworks which was only a mile from the border.

In preparation for the main offensive, PAF Mirages fervently conducted photo-reconnaissance missions along the railway networks Firozpur-Kot Kapura, Firozpur-Fazilka and Fazilka-Muktasar, as well as in the general areas of Firozpur and Sri Ganganagar, for the latest disposition of forces. An important mission involved reconnaissance of crossing points over Gang Canal, for a careful scrutiny of obstacles across the waterway that could possibly impede the movement of II Corps. The main offensive would, however, not materialise, and most of the photo-reconnaissance effort was rendered worthless. Two pilots who played a sterling role in the photo-reconnaissance operations were the squadron's 'slide-rule wizards', Squadron Leader Farooq Umar and Flight Lieutenant Najib Akhtar. Of the 36 photo-reconnaissance sorties flown by No 5 Squadron during the war, 22 were considered successful. Although most of the singleton reconnaissance Mirages were escorted by another Mirage, yet some of the missions had to be aborted due to intense enemy air activity. In Shakargarh Sector, a few

One of three Mirage IIIRPs operated by No 5 Squadron, PAF, seen while still in France. During the 1971 India-Pakistan War, these jets conducted a total of 36 photo-reconnaissance missions over the frontlines, of which 22 were considered successful. (Albert Grandolini Collection)

Another view of a Mirage IIIRP, together with a row or Mirage IIIEPs: this example is configured with 1,300-litre drop tanks. Take-offs of jets heavily loaded with fuel and weapons, and at high temperatures, were often tricky. (Albert Grandolini Collection)

night reconnaissance missions were attempted with partial success. In one such mission on the night of 11 December, an IAF MiG-21 scrambled to intercept a Mirage flown by Squadron Leader Farooq Umar, ended up shooting down one of its own MiG-21s which was patrolling in the vicinity.

The IAF's 'fighter-bomber trio': a HF-24 Marut (left upper corner), a Mystère IVA (leading aircraft), and a Hunter (here two two-seat conversion trainer variant), as seen after the war. These types bore the brunt of ground-attack sorties in December 1971. (Albert Grandolini Collection)

A flight of four Mirage IIIEPs over the Salt Range, not far from their home-base at Sargodha. (Albert Grandolini Collection)

Red Patrols

An important though abortive effort, involved the move of 1 Armoured Division from its concentration area in Arifwala-Okara to its forward assembly area east of Bahawalnagar. This vulnerable move by rail and road was provided with top cover by standing patrols between 15-17 December. The aptly named 'red' CAPs lasted a duration of 30 daylight hours, and involved F-86E, F-6 and Mirage aircraft from Rafiqui, Sargodha and Risalewala. Given the paucity of resources, this was a commendable effort indeed. Its efficacy stood out in relief as no enemy aircraft were able to interfere during any of the 81 sorties flown. In all likelihood, the move completely eluded the enemy due to bad intelligence. Intriguingly, the unusual and intense air activity also failed to ring alarm bells, and the IAF missed an opportunity to undertake a profitable hunt that could have seen the susceptibly entrained armour thoroughly routed. Perhaps, the IAF commanders were completely overtaken by the imminence of the much-hyped Pakistani offensive that never came about.

Inadequate Interdiction

Apparently influenced by the Army's notion that interdiction missions within the raging battlefield were more lucrative from the point of view of immediacy of results, the PAF paid much less heed to severing the supply lines beyond the frontline. A known problem of interdiction within the battlefield that had to be contended with, pertained to the location of well-concealed stocks of ammunition and fuel during a single attacking pass. On the other hand, an indirect approach of attacking nodal points like railway stations and marshalling yards, over which replenishments of the consumed vital stocks were bound to transit to various sectors, would have been a more profitable option. While deferring to the Army, who did not seem to have the patience to wait for the effects on the battlefield delayed by up to 72 hours or even more, the PAF still undertook a belated and half-hearted interdiction campaign that should have started in earnest from Day-1.

Of a total of 24 sorties (including 5 night sorties by B-57 and C-130) flown against deeper railway stations or rail segments, most were reported to have produced satisfactory results. The targeted railway stations that were of consequence to the critical Shakargarh Sector included Gurdaspur and Mukerian, while those serving the equally stressed Chor Sector included Vasarwah and Monabao.

One of the very successful missions of the war was an attack by Mirages on Mukerian Railway Station. On 15 December, Wing Commander Hakimullah was tasked to lead a four-ship mission to attack Bhangala Railway Station on the Jalandhar-Pathankot railway line. After pulling up for the attack, he was dismayed to discover that there was no rolling stock in sight, but he decided to try his luck further south along the railway line. Having flown a mere 30 seconds, he overflew Mukerian Railway Station which was bustling with trains. Peeling off into the attack pattern, the four Mirages set themselves up for single-pass dive attacks with two 750lb bombs each. According to Hakimullah's estimate, there were at least 100 freight bogies latched to different trains berthed adjacent to each other. The Mirages released their bombs one by one though No 4, who had hung ordnance, pulled off dry. The impact of bombs on the fuel and ammunition laden trains was so furious that the blasts shook the aircraft; No 2's drop tanks sheared off with the shock wave, but he was able to fly back without any further damage. It was ironic that of all the interdiction missions, this was the only one flown by the ideally-suited Mirages.

6 HELPLESS AT SEA

Maritime Air Support

At the outbreak of the war, the PAF's maritime support capability of any consequence was limited to night bombing of a couple of the Indian Navy's coastal installations on the Saurashtra coast and daytime strafing and rocketing of not-too-distant surface vessels. Measures to locate these vessels were largely of a passive nature and rested on the Pak Navy's shore and sea-based signals intelligence gathering network. Unhappily, at the outbreak of hostilities, much of the communications and radar transmissions had gone discrete, and signals intelligence had all but dried up. Active measures included surface surveillance by a SUPARCO-loaned radar located at Manora, which had been picking contacts as far as 100nm on occasions, when the somewhat irregular phenomenon of 'anomalous propagation' was experienced. [1, 2] Ships at sea were good only for more localised flotilla surveillance, and at great risk of giving away their position while their radars transmitted.

Airborne maritime reconnaissance was the optimum and most reliable method, but with the Pak Navy lacking any organic air capability, employing the services of the PAF's small transport fleet of six C-130s remained the next best alternative. However, with the planned commitment of the C-130s for unconventional bombing missions, these could not be spared, reportedly. Instead, the C-in-C directed the Managing Director PIA, Air Vice Marshal Zafar Chaudhry to make some assets available to the Pak Navy. One Fokker F-27, along with its volunteer civilian crew, was put at the disposal of the Navy before the war started. The weather radar of the F-27 aircraft could provide a rudimentary search capability over a calm sea, and could, therefore, be utilised at night as well. The Indian Navy, of course, understood that in practical terms the Pak Navy's search capability was of little consequence, and it was surmised that the window of the night offered the maximum chances of sneaking in unobserved.

According to the Indian Navy's appreciation, if it could take the battle to Pakistani waters at the outset, it would force the Pak Navy to abort any offensive plans, and bottle up her surface fleet inside the harbour for the remaining period of war. The planners were also confident that such a move could wipe off the Indian Navy's craven image going back to the 1965 War, when the puny Pak Navy had carried out a daring, morale-shattering raid on the naval establishment at Dwarka without being challenged.

Borrowing a leaf from the Dwarka annals – but planning more cerebrally – the Indian Navy decided to hit Pak Navy warships patrolling the outer and inner cordons of Karachi harbour. With the newly-acquired Soviet Osa-I missile boats, there was no need to get close and discharge broadsides in the old manner. The task force remained within 60nm of the Saurashtra-Kutch coast, and got even closer at later stages, while trying to avoid Pakistani submarines that may have been prowling in deeper waters. Arrival at nightfall was a clever safeguard against visual spotting from the air, as the flotilla broke off westwards to take up battle station south of Karachi. A night visual attack on the ships by PAF aircraft was, thus, also out of the question.

By 2 December, the main body of the Western Fleet comprising 13 ships had already set sail for an area 200nm south of Karachi and beyond, to interdict merchant shipping, but with a more immediate purpose of diverting attention from Operation 'Trident' that was to unfold shortly.

The Cordon is Pierced

On the night of 4 December, at 20:10hrs, the duty officer at the Manora radar picked up a surface contact at a distance of 75nm on a bearing of 165° from Karachi. The contact was immediately reported to Maritime Headquarters (MHQ). Half an hour later, another contact was picked up at a distance of 100nm south of Karachi and was duly reported. After an inexplicably long delay, a signal was issued by MHQ at 22:00hrs, warning ships at sea of two surface groups heading towards Karachi; PNS *Khaibar*, a destroyer which was patrolling the outer cordon, was ordered to investigate.[3] Apparently not responding due to radio silence measures on board, it headed south, as per orders.[4]

At 22:45hrs, watches on board *Khaibar* reported what appeared like a bright light heading towards them at high speed; everyone took it to be an attacking aircraft with afterburners. The Commanding Officer, Commander M N Malik, who had rushed to the bridge, ordered the ship's anti-aircraft guns to open fire. Just then, a deafening explosion was heard as the glowing object slammed into the aft galley, below deck, and blew up the boiler room. Flames leapt upwards as sailors rushed helter-skelter, some trying to jettison the torpedoes, others trying to put out the fires. A hasty message was transmitted to MHQ, informing that, 'enemy aircraft attacked…, boiler hit, ship stopped.' A few minutes later, another eerie glow was observed heading towards the stricken ship, and in no time, it tore into the second boiler room with an intense explosion. Uncontrollable fires enveloped the ship, and ammunition started to explode. As it started to list, some men jumped overboard from the sinking ship. PNS *Khaibar* finally went down, taking with her 222 ill-fated hands.

PNS *Muhafiz*, a minesweeper, sailed out to relieve the survey vessel PNS *Zulfiqar* which was patrolling Karachi harbour's inner cordon. Arriving on station at 22:45hrs, she was just in time to witness the fireworks in the outer patrol area. Altering her course and heading south to investigate the fiery glow on the horizon, Lieutenant Commander M S Usmani, the Commanding Officer of *Muhafiz* feared the worst. Suddenly, a speeding light was seen to be headed towards his own ship. Moments later, a swishing object smashed into the minesweeper, and exploded with such force that it disintegrated the wooden vessel into pieces. Some of those who had been thrown overboard on impact managed to swim away, but 33 others went down in this second deadly attack, barely twenty minutes after the first one.

The Indian Navy task force had included two frigates for submarine screening, and three missile boats for the actual attack. INS *Nirghat* was the first to engage, and it fired two Styx missiles that hit PNS *Khaibar*. The next to fire two missiles was INS *Nipat*, but its victim remained a mystery for some time until the sunken wreck of SS *Venus*

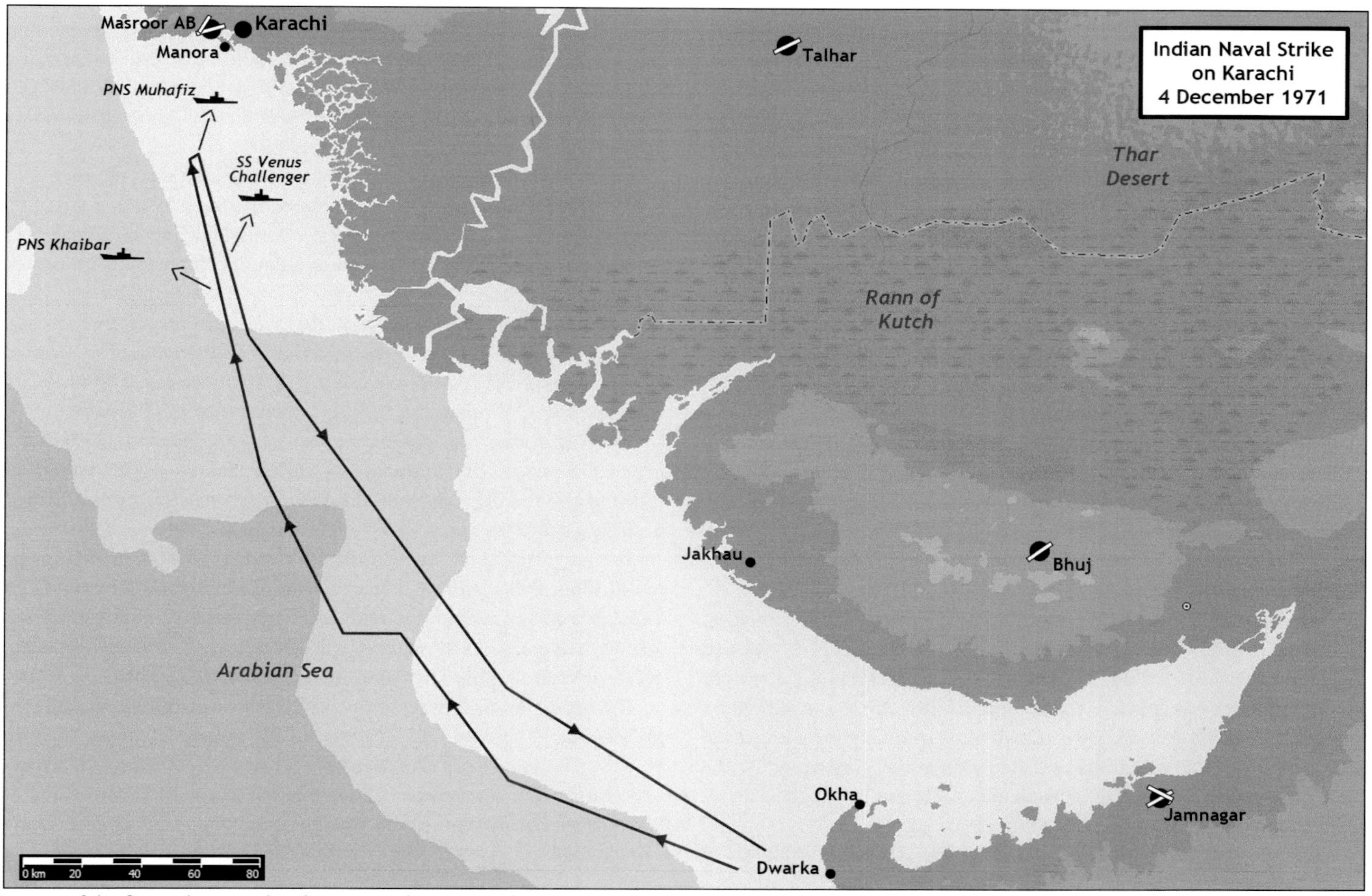

A map of the first Indian naval strike on Karachi, 4 December 1971. (Map by Tom Cooper)

Challenger, a Liberian merchant ship, was found by navy divers 26nm south of Karachi, some days after the war ended. The next to attack was INS *Veer*, whose single missile hit PNS *Muhafiz*. INS *Nipat* also fired a third missile at the harbour a little later, which hit some oil storage tanks at Keamari terminal.

Having resoundingly achieved its objective, the task force sped back under cover of darkness to rendezvous with a waiting tanker for refuelling. By dawn of next day, the task force had cleared the estimated strike range of PAF fighters and was homeward bound. An IAF fighter patrol had been arranged to cover the task force just in case, but no PAF fighters were encountered.

Shocked and demoralised by the surprise attack, a hapless Pak Navy struggled to cope with the crisis that had literally exploded at her doorstep. The PAF, none too happy about its own plight in the south, could only sympathise with its sister service in this sombre situation.

In the aftermath of the attack, an urgent Air Priority Board meeting was asked for on 5 December. As a result, the Pak Navy was able to muster a motley of aircraft including some more from PIA and different government departments, for the purpose of enhancing maritime reconnaissance measures.[5] Most of them were light aircraft, and might have been suitable for daytime 'coast guard' duties, at best. Nonetheless, with the warships bottled up in the harbour or hidden away around Cape Monze and Gaddani, additional aircraft for patrolling were considered a welcome help for the overworked PIA F-27. It was to be seen if the desperate measure meant anything.

Hitting Back

In the wake of the missile attack, the Pak Navy felt – almost as an afterthought – that the home base of the missile boats at Okha needed to be taken out. In all likelihood, the tit-for-tat raid serving as retribution of sorts would have been uppermost in the minds of the Naval Staff. In any case, the necessity of tackling the threat of missile boats also sank in at PAF's COC, and it was agreed to attack Okha harbour. Of course, it was not expected that the missile boats would still be berthed at the quayside in Okha. As a matter of fact, these had already been dispersed to smaller locations along the Saurashtra coast, even before the war had started. Nonetheless, it was the considered opinion of the Pak Navy that a hit on the infrastructure could hamper missile boat operations to some extent.

On the evening of 5 December, Flight Lieutenant Shabbir A Khan was standing out on the tarmac watching preparations for the night missions, when he was informed about being detailed for a strike on Okha harbour. He, along with his navigator, Squadron Leader Ansar Ahmad, rushed off to the operations room to start planning the mission. Two hours after moonrise seemed like a good selection of the TOT, as the glimmering sea would clearly outline the edges of the darkened harbour.

Taking off at 22:10hrs, the B-57 got a fiery send-off as the AAA opened up in the nearby Karachi harbour, signalling an air raid. Continuing the take-off, Shabbir and Ansar settled down to watch – with unnerving anticipation – the moonbeams dazzling the creeks and estuaries of Kutch coast to their port side. Finally, turning to the attack heading, they picked up a sizeable flotilla on their radar, about 20nm to their starboard. There was a temptation to go for the ships, but discipline prevailed and they continued to the designated target. Reaching the pull-up point, Shabbir pushed the throttles to 100 percent power, while Ansar started to guide him into the attack. Just when Shabbir pressed the bomb release button and there was no release, Ansar realised that he had forgotten to arm the release switch. In a fraction of a second he flipped the switch on and Shabbir pipped the button again, pulling out of the dive narrowly. After some ten-odd seconds, there was a tremendous flash of light and the aircraft shook up with the blast. A direct hit had been achieved as nine 500lb bombs slammed into fuel tanks and other stores at the harbour. In the meantime, AAA had started to fire and the sky seemed ablaze. Shabbir and Ansar saw the shells continuously exploding along the aircraft's flight path but luckily, the bomber escaped unscathed.

The attack had been a tremendous success, and news that the home base of the missile boats was in flames turned out to be thoroughly cathartic for all and sundry in the Pak Navy and PAF. A pair of F-104s, which visited Okha for another attack four days later, reported that the harbour was still smouldering, and the smoke could be seen from as far as 60nm. The Indian *Official History of the 1971 India-Pakistan War* notes that, 'two air attacks were also carried out on Okha and some fuel tanks were set ablaze, thereby denying the missile boats any furter use of this port as a forward base.'[6]

Harbour in Flames

Seeing the success of Operation 'Trident' which had resulted in huddling up of the Pak Navy ships in harbour, the Indian Navy decided that the main force of the Western Fleet would carry out a similar attack from an unexpected south-westerly direction, the very next night. However, the breakdown of two vessels forced the withdrawal of a group of five, which sailed back home, and consequently, the attack had to be postponed.[7] Subsequent snags, and then bad weather, delayed the operation further.

On the night of 8/9 December, at around 22:45hrs, lookouts at Manora suddenly picked up the infamous glow hurtling towards them, then crossing overhead and slamming into the nearby oil tank farms at Keamari.[8] A tremendous fire engulfed the terminal and the whole harbour lit up, visible for miles. Distressingly, fires lit by an earlier air attack on the morning of 4 December had been laboriously put out just a day earlier.

A few minutes after the first attack, another missile hit the anchored British-owned merchant ship *Harmatton*, causing it to sink in no time. This was immediately followed by a third missile which hit the SS *Gulf Star*, also anchored, flying the Panamanian flag. It survived the attack with serious damage.[9]

A fourth missile hit PNS *Dacca*, the Navy's supply ship which was idling in the harbour, having been out at sea for 25 days at a stretch. A portion of the ship caught fire, but due to the courage and presence of mind of its Commanding Officer, Commander S Q Raza, the steam smothering system was operated and a major explosion averted; the fires were put out by midnight. By next evening, power had been restored and the ship was moved further inshore, where she remained until the end of the war.

The attacking force had consisted of three frigates escorting the missile boat INS *Vinash*. All four missiles were fired by this boat from a distance of 12nm from the harbour. After the attack, the group was able to make a getaway without a hitch and rendezvoused with the Western Fleet flagship INS *Mysore* for a return to Bombay.

The operation had again been thoroughly successful and rendered the Pak Navy's surface fleet incapable of any operation during the war. However, it must be said that if international conventions on declaring and enforcing a blockade had been heeded to by the Indian Navy, at least the loss of lives on-board foreign merchant shipping could have been avoided.

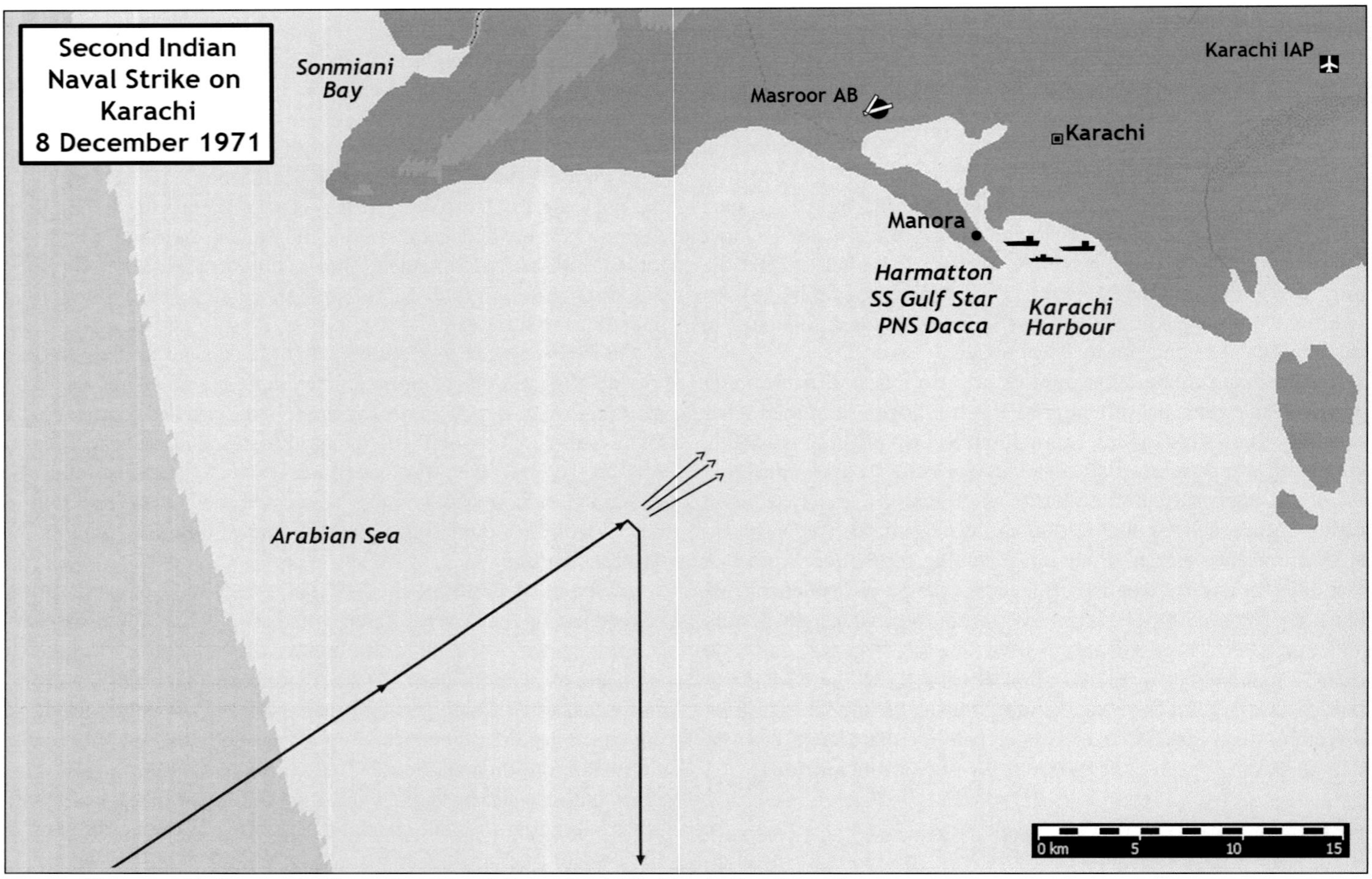

A map of the second Indian naval strike on Karachi on 8 December 1971. (Map by Tom Cooper)

While a flight-sized group of Alizés of the Indian Naval Aviation were embarked on the aircraft carrier INS *Vikrant*, the majority of others flew anti-submarine warfare patrols – so also over the Gulf of Kutch. This is how one of them was intercepted and shot down by a PAF F-104 on 10 December 1971. (Albert Grandolini Collection)

Whither PAF?

With 'do-it-yourself' maritime reconnaissance in the hands of PIA and Pak Navy, the PAF was expected to only carry out anti-surface vessel attacks during daytime. It is alleged that the PAF was called out many times but the usual refrain was that 'effort was not available'. What is known is that the PAF flew 22 day missions (F-86E and F-104), and ten night missions (B-57 and T-33) searching for enemy missile boats and other ships, none of which were successful. Regrettably, the reports of sighting of enemy ships were either bogus, or the ships were incorrectly located. On one occasion, for instance, PNS *Zulfiqar* was strafed west of Cape Monze by a pair of F-86s, after the target was repeatedly confirmed by a frantic MHQ as being hostile.

It is evident that the fundamental problem of maritime support lay in the inadequacy of airborne maritime reconnaissance, as the platforms were under-equipped and crew untrained. With Pak Navy officers on-board the F-27 aircraft having no prior experience in this role, and their PIA pilots literally finding themselves at sea, the outcome could not have been any better. Sadly, but not surprisingly, the PIA Fokker F-27 (AP-ALX) crashed on the night of 12/13 December off the Makran Coast while on a reconnaissance mission, killing its crew of four.[10] In all probability, the fatigued pilots were disoriented in a pitch-dark night, as the aircraft descended uncontrollably into the coastal Ras Malan Hills. The wreckage was found after the war.

On at least three occasions at night, Indian Navy task groups were reportedly located by the reconnaissance aircraft, but these reports could not be followed up with actual strikes as PAF aircraft were not equipped with any aids for sighting and attacking ships at night.[11] In all three cases, the ships had broken off from the area by daybreak after taking evasive measures, and were not traceable. It is open to question if the attacking aircraft would have been able to successfully penetrate the formidable AAA screen of the task groups for a close-in dive attack in daytime. Not the least, lacking any practical training in the anti-shipping role whatsoever, PAF pilots were not expected to blast away bridges and boiler rooms during their first lessons at sea.

It may also be opportune to clarify that of the 127 visual reconnaissance sorties that were 'made available,' as *The Story of the Pakistan Air Force* states, PIA flew 59 sorties while other civilian aircraft flew 68 sorties, all with their own crew.[12] Even though the effort did not yield any concrete results, the dedication of the volunteer pilots is, indeed, commendable.

On one occasion on 10 December, while on an unusual maritime reconnaissance mission in a F-104 searching for Osa boats, Wing Commander Arif Iqbal chanced upon an Indian Navy Alizé maritime patrol aircraft off Jakhau on the Saurashtran Coast. The hapless aircraft jinked and thrashed about very low over the water, as Arif settled behind it with some difficulty. Soon after Arif opened fire with his gun, the Alizé was seen to tumble into the sea, as the gun camera clearly recorded the event.[13] The patrolling Alizé was part of a massive hunt for the Pak Navy submarine PNS *Hangor* in the eastern Arabian Sea, after she had sunk an Indian Navy frigate INS *Khukri* the previous morning, and escaped successfully.

The sum total of all the help that the PAF could provide to the Pak Navy was only one successful strike against the enemy missile boat facility at Okha harbour. Planners at both services' headquarters must have rued their vacillation in striking a couple of harbours on Saurashtra coast as an opening gambit of the war. An audacious and imaginative planner might have included an attack on Bombay harbour too, staged-through like the Agra strike.[14] Arguably, the Styx missile attacks of 4/5 December may have been preventable after all, if the later raid on Okha was anything to go by.

7
FEARLESS LAST STAND

Air Operations in East Pakistan

The disparity between the air forces arrayed against each other in the Eastern Wing was nothing but grotesque: one PAF combat squadron operating out of a single base, versus twelve of the IAF operating from eight bases all around East Pakistan.[1] Even the Bay of Bengal was well covered by a squadron of fighters on the aircraft carrier INS *Vikrant*. One cannot but agree that the idea of 'defence of East lies in the West' reflected a realistic appraisal of the grim situation by Pakistani military strategists. With the PAF's air element not expected to last beyond two-odd days at best, and the outnumbered Pak Army hopelessly encircled by the Indian Army and *Mukti Bahini*, strategic compulsions demanded that a front be opened in the West at the earliest. Only the capture of Indian territory would redeem some lost honour. Occupation of Indian territory was no less important from the point of view of bargaining the release of POWs that were bound to be captured in East Pakistan, en masse. Sadly however, this line of thinking meant that the Pakistani forces in the East were sacrificial lambs and would have to submit to the inevitable sooner or later. The only challenge

The Indian Navy's task force centred on the aircraft carrier INS *Vikrant* – seen in this post-war photograph – and carrying an air wing consisting of Sea Hawk fighter-bombers, Alizé submarine-hunters, and a few helicopters. It dominated the Bay of Bengal and the entire coast of East Pakistan during the 1971 India-Pakistan War. (Albert Grnadolini Collection)

A row of Sea Hawk fighter-bombers as seen while parked on the rear deck of INS *Vikrant*, prior to the next mission. In the foreground is the opening of the lift shaft of the ship. (Albert Grandolini Collection)

for the unfortunate soldiers, sailors and airmen was to delay the impending disaster as much as they could, in the dim hope of some miracle occurring on the geo-political front at the eleventh hour. If ever there was a pathetic and despondent situation at the outset of a modern-day conflict, the one faced by Pakistani armed forces in East Pakistan was beyond compare.

In the utterly distressing circumstances, the PAF did well to designate one of its most accomplished officers to oversee operations in East Pakistan. Air Commodore Inam-ul-Haque Khan was appointed as the Air Officer Commanding (AOC) East Pakistan, with the dual hat of Base Commander Dacca, a few days after the military operation that commenced on the night of 25/26 March. He took over from Air Commodore M Zafar Masud, yet another outstanding officer, who was unfortunately relieved of his command due to an elemental disagreement with the military junta about the course of action to be followed. Masud had been doggedly advocating a negotiated political settlement in the prevailing civil disobedience movement and widespread insurgency in East Pakistan.

A Sea Hawk about to launch from the sole steam catapult of INS *Vikrant*. (Albert Grandolini Collection)

The PAF's Plight

In the wake of the military's counter-insurgency operation, Air Commodore Inam-ul-Haque had some very pressing operational issues to attend to. The direct Islamabad-Dacca route, which involved flying over India, had been closed down following the hijacking and subsequent blowing up of an Air India F-27 in February 1971. Pakistan was implicated for supporting the Kashmiri-origin hijackers, and the incident was used as a pretext by India to suspend over-flights. Timely availability of logistic support for No 14 Squadron was, thus, rendered

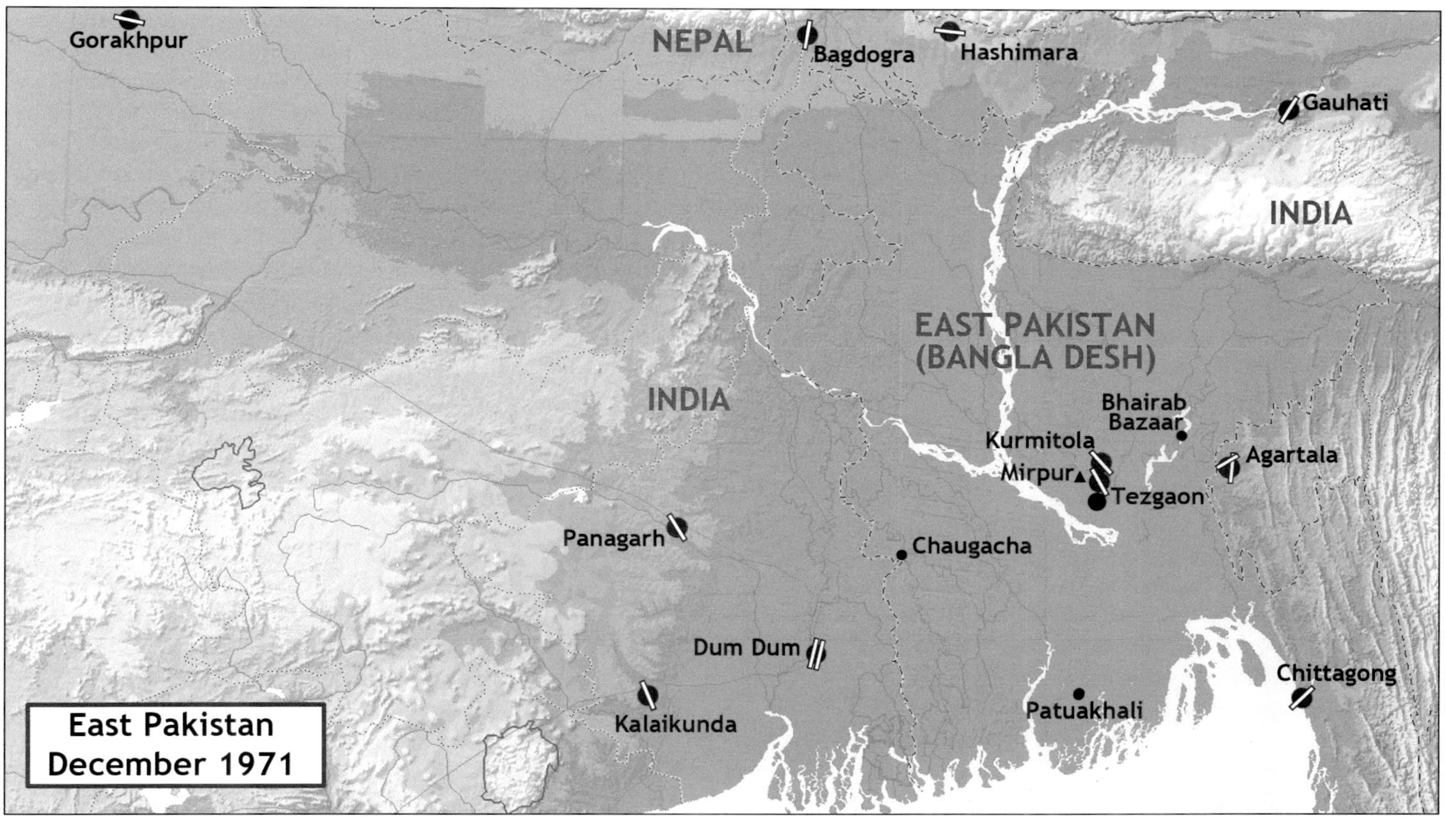

Map of major air bases in East Pakistan (Bangla Desh) and north-eastern India as of December 1971. (Map by Tom Cooper)

extremely difficult to manage across 3,000 miles, via the circuitous Ceylon (Sri Lanka) route. Spares and supplies had to be carefully conserved, even more so in view of the looming threat of all-out war.

Transfer of fuel from Narayanganj fuel depot to Dacca airfield in bowsers also became impractical due to the poor law and order situation. One C-130 was, therefore, permanently positioned at Dacca to bring in fuel supplies directly to the home base, via Colombo, until as late as the end of November. Reinforcements of men and material were, however, out of the question once the war began.

A significant setback to the PAF's operational capability occurred when all its MOUs had to discontinue operations, following the sporadic killing of airmen while deployed on duty. Noting that the MOUs were deployed in the field in hostile surroundings, and were sitting ducks for the insurgents, the previous AOC, Air Commodore Masud, had ordered withdrawal of the vulnerable MOUs back to Dacca. During recovery of one of the flights consisting of twenty airmen led by the OC of No 246 MOU Squadron, Flight Lieutenant Safi Mustafa, it was ambushed by the *Mukti Bahini*. All personnel were arrested and consigned to an underground dungeon in Mymensingh Jail. The whole lot were then brutally massacred by the *Mukti Bahini* in retaliation following the Army's military operation that started on 26 March. The Bengali Superintendent of the jail claimed to have been helpless in preventing the massacre as his staff were badly outnumbered. When confronted later by an irate Air Commodore Inam-ul-Haque, he is said to have sheepishly muttered a rather strange *mea culpa*: 'Hindu blood still runs in our veins!'[2]

Following the non-availability of the MOUs, the PAF's low level early warning came to rest on a single AR-1 radar located at Mirpur, about 10 miles north-west of Dacca. With the low-level radar constrained by an inherent line-of-sight limit of about 25 miles, the reaction time available after initial detection was barely three minutes, which was insufficient for a ground scramble. Constant patrolling by fighters was, thus, the only option for intercepting intruders before weapons release. Had the MOUs been available and deployed 50 miles out of Dacca, the reaction time could have been doubled, allowing a more economical utilisation of the limited air effort when the time came.

A high level P-35 radar that was earlier located near Dacca was withdrawn to Malir in October, to improve the coverage in southern West Pakistan. The assumption that most of the attacks against Dacca would be at low level was not altogether unfounded, as things turned out, so any criticism of denuding Dacca of radar coverage was unwarranted.

Yet another setback suffered by the PAF soon after the 26 March operation was the loss of Bengali manpower, which was about 20 percent of its total strength. These Bengali officers, airmen and civilians had to be laid off, as their loyalties were considered suspect. In East Pakistan, the situation was even graver, as 52 percent of the 1,222 PAF personnel were Bengali and their services were dispensed with, leaving only 577 loyalists. Not only had the PAF to make do with shortage of manpower, it had to face the wrath of the laid-off airmen who promptly joined the *Mukti Bahini*, and took to harassment, ambush and sabotage. Most damaging for the PAF was the compromise of operational information that resulted when these Bengali airmen collaborated with the Indian authorities and passed on vital secrets.

No 14 Squadron had 16 F-86E, of which only four were modified with launchers for the carriage of AIM-9B Sidewinder missiles. The unit's aircraft strength was barely adequate for carrying out the widespread task of counterinsurgency, and its response time was not expected to be swift, particularly near the border areas.

A T-33 was utilised for pilot check-outs and for maintaining instrument flying currency, while a RT-33 was used for photo reconnaissance to determine the insurgents' location in the naturally camouflaged areas. The Rescue Squadron was made up of two Alouette III helicopters.

Counter Insurgency Operations

Soon after the commencement of the military operation codenamed 'Searchlight', the PAF was required to flush out those well-defended clusters of insurgents which could not be tackled by the Army alone. The months of March and April were particularly busy, during which period, 170 air support sorties were flown.

A significant air support operation took place on 15 April, to help the Army recapture Bhairab Bridge over Meghna River, which had fallen into the hands of *Mukti Bahini* with the active support of Indian troops. The major railway bridge was the only link between Dacca and the Sylhet-Comilla-Chittagong Sector east of Meghna, and its capture by the insurgents meant that elements of 14 Division stood isolated. Equally worrying was the prospect of major grain stores on the outskirts of the nearby town of Bhairab Bazaar falling into the hands of the insurgents. It was planned that initially a bi-directional assault by 50 Special Services Group (SSG) commandos, transported by two Mi-8 and two Alouette III helicopters, would capture the bridge. Subsequently, reinforcements would be airlifted by the helicopters shuttling between the makeshift forward base and the target area, for consolidating the operation. The PAF was tasked to soften up the target before the operation, and later, provide air cover for four to five hours. Accordingly, four F-86s led by Flight Lieutenant Abbas Khattak arrived in the area at 06:20hrs and began strafing and rocketing the insurgents' known strongholds in the Bhairab Bazaar area for about ten minutes. Under cover of the aerial onslaught and the mayhem caused by jet noise, two crack commando teams led by Lt Col Shakur Jan and Maj Tariq Mahmood (the legendary Brig 'TM' of later years), were able to disembark close to the bridge. They assaulted it with such speed and fury that the enemy did not have any time to organise a meaningful retaliation. The Bhairab Bridge was captured

A little-known fact about the Pakistani armed forces in East Pakistan of 1971, is that they operated a handful of Mi-8T helicopters obtained from the USSR. (Albert Grandolini Collection)

intact, and the insurgents were completely neutralised. For the better part of the day, Army Aviation helicopters continued bringing in reinforcements and evacuating casualties, flying 51 sorties in the process. The F-86s were at hand to suppress any pockets of resistance. By dusk, the operation had culminated in a resounding success. The operation was also an example of flawless coordination between the PAF, Army Aviation, and the SSG commandos.

All the Sabres assigned to the Dacca-based No 14 Squadron as of December 1971, were the powerful, Canadair-built CL.13B or Sabre F.Mk 6s, obtained via Iran in the late 1960s. They were easily recognizable by their camouflage pattern consisting of grey and green (for details, see the colour section) – like this example, photographed at Sharjah, in the future United Arab Emirates, in 1969. (Albert Grandolini Collection)

The PAF provided vital support in yet another operation on 26 April in Patuakhali, where the insurgent elements, defeated two days earlier in nearby Barisal, were known to have regrouped. The PAF was called upon to pound the rebels' sanctuaries, before a company of SSG commandos and other troops arrived to take control. At 08:00 hrs, four F-86s led again by the battle-hardened Flight Lieutenant Abbas Khattak – who had thrice survived small arms fire while attacking insurgents – pulled up for a rocket attack in the area. The enemy fire was completely suppressed, but not before Khattak's F-86 took a nasty hit from ground fire, yet again. The bullets missed the elevator actuator by half an inch, or else he would have had to eject into very unfriendly territory, to put it mildly. The four Mi-8 helicopters carrying the commandos were able to land and disembark without a hitch. In the meantime, three companies of 6 Punjab Regiment which were being transported by river, and duly covered by Pak Navy gunboats PNS *Comilla* and PNS *Rajshahi*, also disembarked in the vicinity of the rebels. Such had been the suddenness and accuracy of firepower delivered by the F-86s that the insurgents were thoroughly routed. Any rebels that remained were mopped up by the ground troops. The unique tri-service operation was a complete success.

No significant air support operation took place in the subsequent months, other than routine counter-insurgency missions. The advent of monsoons in June, with the dreary low clouds in intimidating attendance, curtailed flying activity for the next couple of months. As the soil started to dry out from late September onwards, insurgent activity also started to pick up menacingly, as before. Intelligence reports also indicated the movement of Indian Army formations to forward locations, in what could clearly be seen as a 'tightening of the noose' around East Pakistan. By November, air support operations had once again spiked up considerably, with as many as 100 sorties flown during the month. These included escort missions for PIA Fokker F-27s transporting troops to the Jessore Sector, where the first Indian intrusion had taken place.

An Unlucky Strike

On 19 November, the PAF swung into action against troops and gun positions that were part of Indian 9 Division, which had brazenly violated the international border, and penetrated several miles deep in Jessore Sector. Several sorties were flown against them until the afternoon of the next day. Well camouflaged tanks were spotted by an RT-33 on a reconnaissance sortie near Chaugacha, and action against them was again initiated by F-86s starting from the morning of 22 November.

In the third mission of the day, around 15:30hrs (all times EPST), three F-86s led by the Squadron Commander, Wing Commander Afzal Chaudhry, with Flying Officer Khalil Ahmad as No 2 and Flight Lieutenant Parvaiz Mehdi Qureshi as No 3, attacked a couple of tanks that had been reported in the area. Subsequent to the attack, ground control asked the leader to look for more tanks that were suspected to be concealed around. Loitering over the battlefield amounted to inviting trouble, especially when flying without radar cover. Trouble came swiftly when four ground-scrambled Gnats, of Dum Dum based No 22 Squadron, were able to sneak in and bounce the F-86 formation. At that time, the leader, Wing Commander Chaudhry, was attacking an AAA battery that was noticed to be firing at them. Pulling out of the dive, Chaudhry broke into the Gnat pair flown by Flight Lieutenant R A Massey and Flying Officer S F Suarez, and managed to ward off the attack. Chaudhry then reversed to take a pot shot at one of the Gnats. During a brief scrap, both Massey and Chaudhry claimed firing at the other, but their aircraft remained unscathed. Massey later stated that gun stoppage prevented further firing, and he had to give up the chase. Scattered, and without visual cross cover, Khalil and Mehdi fell prey to another pair of Gnats flown by Flight Lieutenant M A Ganapathy and Flying Officer D Lazarus, who picked off the two wingmen with professional ease.[3] Both F-86 pilots ejected

A view into the cockpit of a Gnat F.Mk 1 of the IAF: with the entire aircraft being very small, the cockpit was a tight squeeze for most pilots, too. Nevertheless, the type proved highly popular amongst those who flew it. (Albert Grandolini Collection)

and were captured by the insurgents, who handed them over to the Indian Army, eventually ending up as POWs. For No 14 Squadron, it was like losing the opening batsmen in the first over. Notwithstanding Chaudhry's misperception of having been outnumbered by as many as ten Gnats, the reality is that his formation was simply surprised by the nimble interceptors. It might have been instructive if Chaudhry had somehow known that the two previous missions of the day had survived interception, only because the Sabres had not lingered around, and each time the Gnats had arrived in the area just a little too late. The kills by No 22 Squadron also helped wash away the Squadron Commander's lingering ignominy of force-landing his Gnat at the Pakistani strip of Pasrur, when rushed by an F-104 during the 1965 War.[4]

Determined Fight Back

Vacillating for a full twelve days after the Indian intrusion into East Pakistan, General Yahya and his junta reluctantly responded on the evening of 3 December by opening a front in West Pakistan. In the East, the outcome was dismally clear, but No 14 Squadron was determined to put up a fight to the last. Next morning, everyone was in high spirits, eagerly awaiting the drama that was to unfold as the curtain of fog gradually started to lift from the runway.

The first CAP mission of the day led by Wing Commander Afzal Chaudhry took-off at first light. Perhaps the weather at the IAF bases was not yet clear, so Chaudhry returned without encountering any intruders. The next mission led by the much-respected Flight Commander, Squadron Leader Dilawar Hussain, also returned without having seen any action.

Soon the third CAP mission took-off at 07:30hrs and a flight of three Hunters of No 37 Squadron based at Hashimara was reported to be heading towards Tezgaon airfield from the north. Squadron Leader Javed Afzaal, along with his wingman, Flight Lieutenant Saeed Afzal, picked up visual contact with a pair of Hunters approaching their 2 o'clock position. Turning in a wide arc, Afzaal easily settled behind the lead Hunter which had not yet reacted. Just as Afzaal jettisoned his drop tanks, both the Hunters broke towards the right, and after completing a 180-degree turn, rolled out on a northerly heading for home. At that moment, Afzaal came upon another unwary Hunter and promptly manoeuvred behind its tail. Like many other observers excitedly watching the dogfight from the ground, Flight Lieutenant Ata-ur-Rahman was also riveted to the fighters turning and twisting in the sky. He recalls, 'I saw the lead F-86 behind two Hunters over the airfield, in line with the runway. Next, I could see leader's bullets hitting a Hunter, and it started to trail heavy smoke, though it didn't go down as far as I could see.'[5] Afzaal too, recalls, 'I saw the bullets hitting the aircraft, and the last I remember is that it was still flying, trailing smoke.'[6]

Saeed, who was separated from his leader and may have been looking out for him, was oblivious to what was going on in his rear quarters. A third member of the Hunter formation, Flying Officer Harish Masand, who had been straggling behind due to an earlier malfunction, emerged from nowhere and latched on to Saeed's F-86. Firing a short, well-aimed burst from very close range, Masand was able to hit his target before it could react. Saeed ejected from the stricken aircraft, but sadly, was lynched by *Mukti Bahini* insurgents soon after coming down by parachute.

Afzaal had, by this time, switched to a MiG-21 that he had spotted in the vicinity. It was part of a pair escorting yet another raid, this time by MiG-21s from Gauhati-based No 28 Squadron. A brief turning fight with one of the escorts ensued, while the strike aircraft went through with a successful attack on hangars and other airfield infrastructure. The MiG-21 escort then hastily disengaged to re-join the strike aircraft on their way back.

With three different IAF formations totalling 13 aircraft having converged over Tezgaon in a matter of a few minutes, it is virtually impossible to retrace their tracks in the air.[7] What is known is that the first two formations of five Hunters, along with two MiG-21 escorts, were unable to carry out the attack in the face of determined opposition from the F-86s. It also transpires that the Hunter Afzaal had been firing at was actually from the second formation belonging to No 17 Squadron, which had reached its target somewhat early. Its pilot, Flying Officer Bains, was lucky to escape with 42 bullet hits that were counted on his aircraft after landing. All the IAF aircraft were reported to have landed back. The PAF had put up a gallant fight in the first encounter of the war. An undaunted Afzaal had audaciously shown that an even a vastly large aggressor could be taken on fearlessly.

As Afzaal was being swamped by the MiGs, he had asked for immediate relief. The Staff Operations Officer, Wing Commander S

MiG-21FLs from multiple units assigned to the Eastern Air Command of the IAF, eventually overpowered the Sabres from No 14 Squadron, PAF in the skies over East Pakistan. Subsequently, the type was deployed for ground attack. (Albert Grandolini Collection)

M Ahmed, who was visiting No 14 Squadron to cheer up the pilots, thought that he could lend a helping hand in the grave situation. On the spur of the moment, he decided to fly, and took along young Flying Officer Salman Rasheedi as his wingman. The Squadron Commander and Flight Commander were not yet back after flying; otherwise, they might have had a different opinion about sending Ahmed up in the air, as he was not a regular flier in the squadron, and had mostly been performing staff duties with the base. Nonetheless, Ahmed's eagerness saw the pair in the thick of the action in no time. Getting airborne at about 07:45hrs, Ahmed was vectored towards a strike approaching Kurmitola airfield that lies about five miles north of Tezgaon. A Hunter flown by the Squadron Commander of No 17 Squadron, Wing Commander N Chatrath, broke off and engaged Ahmed's F-86. After a brief dogfight, Ahmed disengaged, but was chased right up to Tezgaon, where the pursuing Hunter finished him off. Ahmed ejected, but like Saeed Afzal in the previous mission, was hauled up by *Mukti Bahini* on landing. His fate was never known, but it was presumed that he too met an unfortunate end at the hands of a furious mob.[8] Rasheedi, in the meantime, managed to extricate himself, and landed back safely. No 14 Squadron had suffered yet another casualty, but driven by an indefatigable determination, its pilots seemed unstoppable.

The next mission of consequence was flown by Flight Lieutenant Iqbal Zaidi and Flight Lieutenant Ata-ur-Rahman who took off at about 08:20hrs.[9] Incidentally, Ata was a Bengali pilot who had opted to stay on with the PAF, and had been cleared to fly only one week earlier, after many months of pleading with the authorities to quash his grounding. Zaidi and Ata had barely picked the landing gears up, when four Hunters were spotted pulling up for an attack on the airfield. On the leader's instruction to split and take on a pair each, Ata was quick to position behind one of the Hunters. Closing into a textbook range of 2,000 feet and ready to open fire, he was abruptly warned by Killer Control about two Hunters perched on his tail. Breaking viciously to ward off their attack, Ata was horrified to see tracers from the guns of both Hunters whizzing past his aircraft. He continued a hard turn until the Hunters overshot, tempting him to reverse his turn and pursue them. The Hunters, however, outran Ata's F-86 and managed to escape at treetop height. Low on fuel and barely able to keep their wits in the prevailing confusion, Zaidi and Ata hastily recovered before yet another reported raid arrived. Reflecting on the dicey mission flown four decades ago, retired Air Vice Marshal Ata-ur-Rahman credits the Killer Control, manned by the late Squadron Leader Aurangzeb Ahmad, for having saved his life. He thinks that Aurangzeb played a pivotal role in many a dogfight over Dacca.

By the time Zaidi's F-86 pair had landed, the next one was getting airborne; the time was 08:45hrs. Led by a junior Flying Officer Shams-ul-Haq, with an even more junior Flying Officer Shamshad Ahmad as his wingman, they had been eagerly waiting for their turn to scramble since early morning. Immediately after taking-off, they were vectored by the radar onto an intruding pair which turned out to be Su-7s, as Shams spotted them promptly. Jettisoning their drop tanks, the F-86s prepared for the engagement, but were surprised to see the still-laden Su-7s split and throw in a sharp turn. As Shams was manoeuvring to shake off the Su-7 which was fast turning towards his rear, he saw the other one shoot off what appeared to be two missiles in quick succession, at Shamshad's F-86. While Shams watched the missiles swish past his No 2, he was dumbfounded to see another one being fired at his own aircraft. Shams broke into a defensive turn and was much relieved to see this missile miss its target as well. Stupefied at the strange turn the dogfight was taking, Shams immediately pulled up behind the Su-7 that was now zooming past him. Instantly selecting his guns, Shams started firing at the Su-7 which was about 1,800 feet away. Continuing the shooting until he was close enough to pick up ricochets, Shams saw the bullets land around the canopy. At this time, the heavily smoking Su-7 selected its afterburner and tried to accelerate away. Shams claimed that soon afterwards, he saw the aircraft spiral and eventually go down. He then immediately switched to the other Su-7 which was still in his No 2's rear quarters, but it too lit afterburner and sped away. While confirmation of the Su-7 downing by Shams remains moot, the F-86s had been successful in intercepting them before weapons release. Shams and Shamshad need not have been bothered about the flurry of missiles launched at them, as these were 57mm unguided ground attack rockets cleverly fired off by theSu-7s when their mission stood aborted after being intercepted.[10]

Barely finished with shaking off the menacing Su-7s, Shams heard the radar controller call out that there were four Hunters turning for them. Outnumbered this time, Shams decided to split so that each F-86 was to engage a pair of Hunters, while foregoing mutual cross cover. To Shams' good luck, the pair he was engaged with also split up, and one of the Hunters inexplicably pulled away out of sight. Shams then manoeuvred behind the other Hunter and managed to close in to 600 feet before opening up with his six guns. Accurate fire got the Hunter smoking, and a few seconds later, he saw the pilot eject out of the stricken aircraft.

Looking around for his wingman, Shams was more than relieved to spot Shamshad firing at a Hunter. At this time, the radar called out the position of another bogey and Shams was able to spot it in a few seconds. Apparently warned about his presence by the other Hunters, Shams saw his quarry diving down in a westerly direction towards West Bengal. With his bullets spent, Shams decided to use the Sidewinder missile, which he had earlier decided not to use due to its uncertain performance in a tight-turning dogfight. Crossing about ten miles into Indian territory, Shams was able to close in to a mile behind the Hunter. Getting down below his target, Shams heard the unexpected growl of the seeker head at tree-top height and let off the missile. According to Shams, 'the aircraft immediately turned into a ball of fire like a napalm explosion. I saw the pilot being thrown out at an angle of 45 degrees to the right.' Shams then orbited over the area and directed the radar controller to mark his position so as to be able to apprehend the downed Hunter pilot, if possible.

At the limits of their endurance, Shams decided to recover back, and asked his No 2 to land first. Subsequently, as Shams was setting up for his landing, he saw a Hunter to his left side. Trouble seemed to know no end as Shams was out of ammunition; in a show of bravado, he broke off and chased the Hunter for several minutes while Dacca scrambled another pair. When yet another raid was reported by the radar, Shams thought it wise to grab the first opportunity to land back.

Just two hundred feet from the landing threshold, Shams couldn't believe his ears when the radar controller's radio crackled a warning about two intruders 8,000 feet behind him. If he continued with the landing, Shams thought to himself, he was sure of presenting his aircraft as an easy target to be shot at in merry good time. Instead, he peeled off from the landing approach, cleaned up his aircraft's 'dirty' configuration, and broke into a MiG-21 that he saw less than a mile behind. Turning hard into the MiG with whatever little speed he had been able to build up, Shams managed to force an overshoot, but his quarry accelerated away. Going by Killer Control's instructions to the leader of the new F-86 pair that had just taken off, Shams was able to pick up the engagement nearby. However, with his fuel tanks almost dry, Shams finally came in for a long overdue landing.

In a matter of a few gut-wrenching minutes, the rookie F-86 pilots had managed to ward off attacks by three successive formations. It was a wonder, not only that they survived an incessant onslaught by eight aircraft, but that they were able to keep their wits, and managed to shoot at several of them. Squadron Leader K D Mehra of Dum Dum based No 14 Squadron was one of Shams' victims, who ejected near Dacca, and was able to evade capture with the help of the omnipresent *Mukti Bahini*. Details of Shams' second Hunter victim are hard to come by but going by his story of having seen his victim eject inside Indian territory, followed by an orbit over the location for a radar fix, his claim may not be totally unfounded. Shamshad's victim was last seen by ground observers to be trailing smoke is considered as 'damage'.[11]

A reconnaissance photograph showing the runway of Kurmitola airfield cratered at at least nine points. (Albert Grandolini Collection)

At 09:30hrs, the next pair, led by Flight Lieutenant Schames-ul-Haq, with Flying Officer Mahmood Gul as his wingman, took off for their turn to participate in the aerial drama that had been going on ceaselessly for the last two hours. Scanning the skies, they picked up a pair of Hunters in battle formation and pulling up for the attack over Tezgaon airfield. One of the Hunters broke off and started to tangle with Schames' F-86. Schames found himself overshooting the rapidly decelerating Hunter and put his speed brakes out. With his rate of closure still high, Schames did something unthinkable: he lowered his landing gear to pick up much needed drag. The trick worked and Schames gradually started to get behind the Hunter – wisely remembering to pick up his landing gear while he was at it!

The other Hunter continued with its strafing attack, with Gul in trail. Gul continued to chase his prey but lost visual contact as he pulled up to avoid getting in line of the Hunter fighting with Schames. Instead of a futile chase, Gul broke off and looked for his leader who was engaged in a dogfight right overhead Dacca. Gul settled behind his leader to keep his tail clear, and intently watched the scissoring fighters. As expected of the slatted F-86 scissoring at slow speed, Schames was gaining advantage with every snip. Finally tail-on, he opened fire on the Hunter which started to trail heavy smoke. Gul's situational awareness commentary was interrupted by Schames wondering out aloud, as to why the Hunter pilot wasn't ejecting from his stricken aircraft. Apparently incapacitated, the Hunter pilot went down with the aircraft in full view of the onlookers.[12]

After an exciting first round in which the PAF was able to parry most of the blows, a lull prevailed until the afternoon, during which period two CAPs were flown without any encounter.[13] Around 16:00hrs, Squadron Leader Dilawar Hussain took off with Flying Officer Sajjad Noor on his wing. Soon, the radar was reporting bogies at their 11 o'clock position, but neither Dilawar, nor his No 2 could spot them. Suspecting that the radar had been unable to resolve the blips in close proximity as friend or foe, he did a belly check by banking to either side. To his horror, he spotted a Hunter well set to shoot at him from about 1,500 feet. Breaking into the Hunter, Dilawar was not only able to shake it off, but found it opportune to reverse, and get behind it after it had overshot.

In similar fashion, the IAF's MiG-21s heavily bombed and cratered the runway of Tezgaon AB, outside Dacca. This reconnaissance photograph shows at least a dozen craters. (Albert Grandolini Collection)

Aiming carefully, Dilawar fired a short burst which set the left wing ablaze. Soon after, the pilot ejected from his burning aircraft.

Sajjad, in the meantime spotted another pair of Hunters pulling up into the sun. Intent on keeping them in sight, Sajjad forgot about his own tail, a most frequent mistake in air combat. Dilawar too, was fixated to this new sighting, and singled out one of the Hunters for a chase as it seemed to be running away. With both F-86s split, and Sajjad completely engrossed in his front quarters, it was not long before his aircraft was rattled by cannon fire. The immensely destructive fusillade of the Hunter's four 30mm cannon had spared none of its victims in the other dogfights, so Sajjad was lucky to manage an ejection. It was all the more so for Sajjad, as Wing Commander R Sunderesan, the Squadron Commander of No 14 Squadron, had scored his kill with his pipper remaining on the centre of the canopy as recorded on his film, according to IAF sources.

IAF ground crew seen while preparing a British-made 1,000lbs (454kg) general purpose bomb for deployment from a Canberra bomber, the left engine exhaust and centre fuselage of which are visible in the background. (Albert Grandolini Collection)

Dilawar's victim, Flight Lieutenant Kenneth Tremenheere, was picked up by the same PAF helicopter that had rescued Sajjad from the vicinity a few minutes earlier. Tremenheere was fortunate to have a chivalrous rescue crew at hand just in time, for he had ejected near a pocket of a pro-Pakistan mob which was baying for his blood. While discussing the dogfight with Dilawar soon after his apprehension, a disconsolate Tremenheere revealed that he was the one who somehow happened to be ahead of his leader and was visual with both F-86s at the beginning of the dogfight. His leader, who was perched somewhere behind, disallowed him to fire until he had himself spotted the hitherto unseen F-86s, a delay which turned out to be consequential for Tremenheere.

Writing on the Wall

From the IAF's standpoint, the proceedings of 4 December have been succinctly summed up by the then OC of Gauhati based No 28 Squadron (MiG-21), Wing Commander B K Bishnoi, when he states that, 'perhaps we were achieving little except for harassing the Pakistanis.'[14] He goes on to say that it was difficult to pick out aircraft in camouflaged shelters and then destroy them. He had suggested to the Eastern Air Command, 'to make the runways unusable, thus grounding the enemy aircraft.' The decision to that effect seemed like an afterthought, when it came on the evening of 5 December. Apparently, it was not the foremost priority in the minds of IAF planners, as one can glean from Bishnoi's lament.

A view inside the bomb-bay of an IAF Canberra, with weapons specialists hoisting general purpose bombs into their position, prior to the next combat sortie. (Albert Grandolini Collection)

IAF Canberras carried out night raids but failed to deposit a single bomb on Tezgaon runway or the infrastructure in the technical area. Instead, one of the stray bombs fell on the Officers' Mess causing several casualties including a pro-Pakistan Bengali officer, Squadron Leader Ghulam Rabbani. Another officer injured in the raid and given up for dead was pulled out of the hospital morgue by the AOC himself.

While the IAF mulled new tactics, attacks against Tezgaon fell down considerably on 5 December, which is also evident from an absence of aerial engagements on that day. Both air forces mostly concentrated on providing air support to ground troops, though the IAF flew a couple of missions against Tezgaon, including one involving a napalm attack against AAA gun positions.

On the morning of 6 December, an air sweep mission of four F-86s, led by Squadron Leader Dilawar, was sent up to ward off air attacks

While most of the PAF officers were evacuated form Dacca by a sole DHC-2 Beaver, others managed to reach safety in Burma with the help of these two Mi-8T helicopters. (Albert Grandolini Collection)

against the desperately cornered Pakistani ground troops in Comilla Sector, south-east of Dacca. The F-86s encountered four Hunters, of which one was claimed as downed by the wingman Flying Officer Shams, though confirmation has been hard to come by. The inevitable attack on Tezgaon runway came shortly after the F-86s had landed at 10:00hrs. A formation of four MiG-21s led by Bishnoi, was able to place eight 500kg bombs along its entire length, in an accurately delivered dive attack. The runway was hastily patched up by the PAF's diligent repair teams, but their efforts came to nought when a midday raid by Bishnoi's team neutralised the runway yet again.

Just to be sure that a desperate 14 Squadron might not move its assets by road to nearby Kurmitola, it too was administered the same treatment as Tezgaon.

The night of 6 December saw virtually all personnel of Dacca Base put in their efforts at repairing Tezgaon runway. They were successful in preparing a stretch of about half the length and width of the standard runway, which was considered sufficient for F-86s to take-off in an air defence configuration. 'The squadron crew was very excited and kept waiting for the first light to get airborne and challenge the enemy one more time,' recalls retired Air Marshal Dilawar.

At first light of 7 December, as 14 Squadron pilots were going to the Air Defence Alert hut, they saw a MiG-21 pulling up for an attack. Well-placed bombs resulted in bisection of the repaired stretch into two unusable halves. Dilawar says that when he went to the runway to inspect the state of damage, tears rolled down his cheeks. 'The fate of East Pakistan has been decided,' he muttered to himself, sentimentally.

Escape by Aircrew

With air operations all but over for No 14 Squadron, the Air Staff decided to put the aircrew to good use on the Western Front, where the war was in full fury. Early at 03:00hrs on 9 December, eight pilots and several other personnel who were considered indispensable to the war effort, were seen off by the AOC East Pakistan as they boarded PIA's lone remaining Twin Otter (AP-AWG).[15] Bravely piloted by the airline's senior Captain Zia Mohammed and Captain Shahnawaz Dara, the aircraft made a dangerous take-off from a 3,600 foot long looping taxiway that was actually bent by 10° in three segments. The aircraft's destination was Akyab (now known as Sittwe), a manned airfield in Burma, about 300 miles SSE of Dacca. It was surmised that the Burmese government would not be unduly obdurate in allowing safe passage to the Pakistanis, who were at least putting up a pretence of being civilians faced with some exigency of dire nature. The pilots gate-crashed their way in and managed to land safely after an eventful mission.

At daybreak, Squadron Leader Dilawar who had stayed back, broke the news to the three remaining pilots of No 14 Squadron about the early morning exodus on-board the Twin Otter. Dilawar explained that in the event of Tezgaon runway being repaired by the Army Engineers and the MES, there was a need for some pilots to stay back for one last round. Perhaps the brash victory roll by a MiG-21, a day after the runway was neutralised, was weighing too heavily on the minds of the authorities, and it was thought that a retort might be curative. Before Ata, Schames and Shams could ask, 'why us?' Dilawar came up with a bizarre reason, which could have been intensely funny if it wasn't wartime: all of them had dark complexions, and they would be able to blend in with the locals while escaping, after the aerial deed was done! Mercifully, the imprudence of the plan showed through in no time, and it was decided that the remaining four pilots would also leave the following day.

The AOC was again at the taxi-track at 03:00hrs next morning to see off the four pilots who were to fly off to Akyab, this time in a DHC-2 Beaver aircraft belonging to the Department of Plant Protection. The department's senior pilot Zafar was in the captain's seat, Squadron Leader Dilawar was sitting as the co-pilot, and the three other pilots were squatting on the floor in the rear, as the seats had been removed to lighten up the aircraft. The curved taxiway, which was faintly lit up by airmen with hand-held torches, complicated matters for Zafar who was not even qualified to fly at night from a straight runway. The yellow Beaver managed to take off shakily in the darkness, though after lift-off, it narrowly missed ramming into the ATC building. Getting into combat mode, Dilawar took over the controls of the aircraft and ducked down low for the rest of the flight. After flying over Chittagong Hill Tracts, the Beaver entered Burmese airspace, at which stage the pistols, ID cards and other papers were tossed overboard as the PAF officers got ready to put up a charade of being civilians. After a flight of two-and-a-half hours, Dilawar called up Akyab for a landing clearance, which was denied. Nonetheless, the Beaver forced its way onto the airfield. As the Beaver taxied to the parking area, the welcome sight of the PIA Twin Otter that had arrived the previous day, greeted them. Troops from the Burmese Army surrounded the aircraft, and its occupants were herded away to a large thatched cottage for some mild interrogation. After a week of internment in the same cottage, all Pakistani personnel were smuggled out by the Pakistani Embassy in Rangoon, in obvious collusion with the Burmese authorities. From Rangoon, they flew out to Bangkok, then to Teheran, and finally Karachi. Unfortunately, by the time the PAF aircrew reached their squadrons, the war had been over for many days.

Denial Plan

When it was all over on 16 December, the AOC directed his staff to implement what is known as the Denial Plan, i.e. the destruction of assets so as to deny them from falling into enemy hands. Of the sixteen F-86s at the start of war, eleven remained, besides one T-33 and one RT-33, so these were earmarked for demolition by explosives at the last moment. In the event, Indian troops had moved into Dacca city, and the air base was surrounded by hordes of trigger-happy *Mukti Bahini*. Any explosions in that tense situation were likely to result in retaliation of grave consequences. It was, therefore, decided to damage them with hammers, crowbars, etc. That a few of the F-86s (possibly five) were recovered by the newly-formed Bangladesh Air Force, and actually flown in the new colours for some time, has generated some criticism about the rationale behind the delay in their destruction. It appears that there was hesitation in destroying them earlier due to sensitivities about the morale of airmen, who had been working most diligently on these very aircraft to keep them airworthy.

Indian troops with one of 11 F-86Es captured intact at Tezgaon AB. (via Albert Grandolini)

Stocks of assault rifles and mortars captured by the Indians from the Pakistani Army in East Pakistan. (Albert Grandolini Collection)

No 4071 Squadron's AR-1 radar located on the outskirts of Dacca was the PAF's only high value asset that was destroyed as per plan.

Of the two Alouette III helicopters of the PAF's Rescue Squadron at Dacca, one had been damaged by small arms fire before the outbreak of hostilities, so it was left behind in an unserviceable state. The remaining helicopter managed to take-off for Akyab well before dawn on 16 December, with Squadron Leader Sultan Khan and Flight Lieutenant Rasheed Janjua at the controls. It was part of the Pak Army Aviation's staggered aerial convoy that included its three Mi-8 helicopters, one Alouette III helicopter, and three Beavers of the Department of Plant Protection seconded to the Army. (Two more of the Army's Alouette III helicopters flew out of Dacca later in the afternoon). All of these assets were later retrieved from Burma.[16] Besides the aircrew, there were 123 passengers, mostly women and children, all of whom made it back from Rangoon to Karachi via Colombo, in a PIA aircraft.

An Ignoble End

With the PAF having lasted a mere 72 hours after commencement of IAF operations in East Pakistan, the Army was left to fend for itself without air cover. Wearied for the past eight months in the counter-insurgency role, and much bloodied since the Indian intrusion on 20/21 November, Lieutenant General A A K Niazi's Eastern Command troops had been falling back, quite literally, from a forward posture to a last stand for Dacca. In line with the government's objective of preventing loss of any territory on which Bangladesh could be proclaimed – unrealistic as it was – the thinned out Eastern Garrison had been defending the 1,800 miles of an intensely convoluted land border with India. Niazi's plan had the tacit approval of the General Staff at GHQ, which had looked at the complex situation from beyond a merely operational standpoint.

Badly outnumbered in men and material, fighting in the midst of a hostile population that was constantly betraying their locations to the Indians, and with a completely broken-down logistics and communications infrastructure, the Eastern Command managed to hold out for a remarkable 26 days. Any chance of a last stand for Dacca was, however, rendered worthless when staggering territorial losses at the edge of core areas of West Pakistan had started to threaten the very existence of the country. Under the calamitous circumstances, it fell to the lot of the unfortunate Lieutenant General Niazi to have to accept a cease-fire under dishonourable terms, and to unconditionally surrender all Pakistan Armed Forces in East Pakistan (consisting of 45,000 uniformed personnel, including 11,000 paramilitary forces and police) to the 'GOC-in-C of Indian and Bangla Desh Forces in Eastern Theatre' on 16 December 1971.[17]

Outcome of Air Operations

The PAF in East Pakistan did not have the wherewithal to be of any consequence in a full-scale war, and it came as no surprise that it was grounded within three days, despite the heroic performance in aerial battles while it lasted. It had already outlived its utility when the war morphed from counterinsurgency against *Mukti Bahini*, to a full-scale Indian invasion with regular troops, mightily supported from the air.

The effort put in by No 14 Squadron, with sterling support from No 4071 Radar Squadron, can however, be looked at from an academic viewpoint as a classic performance in a fight against the odds. Despite the looming futility of the exercise, there was no lack of grit and determination, with everyone contributing to the best of his professional ability. At least three enemy aircraft (and possibly four) were downed by No 14 Squadron pilots. Complementing the kills by fighters, batteries of the Pak Army's 6 Light Anti-Aircraft Regiment deployed in various sectors, shot down ten enemy aircraft between 4-16 December. Against a loss of five aircraft, the PAF and the AAA element together destroyed almost three times as many Indian aircraft; this was an impressive exchange from an air defender's standpoint, though it could do nothing to prevent the secession of East Pakistan.

8
THE WAR ASSESSED

Given the superior performance of the PAF in the 1965 War, it was only natural for the Pakistanis to expect a similar repeat in any future conflict. However, to a keen student of military history, it would have been clear that the PAF's sterling performance emanating from decisive leadership and better aircrew training were only partial reasons for the success in 1965. Equally persuasive reasons lay in the failure of the IAF to take the initiative at an operational level, as well as several blunders at the tactical level. For instance, not neutralising Sargodha on the morning of 6 September, when the Indian Army had launched an offensive on the Lahore front, was a major mistake as three-fourths of the PAF could have been grounded. Similarly, not dispersing their aircraft that lay openly parked on the airfields cost the IAF gravely, with 39 aircraft claimed destroyed and another 17 damaged in air raids by the PAF, as opposed to the loss of only one confirmed PAF aircraft destroyed on the ground.

Since the IAF's shortcomings had more to do with leadership decisions than any training or material shortcomings, these were addressed straightforwardly within the intervening years. The IAF of 1971 was, thus, a far cry from that of 1965. This is not to say that the PAF had slackened any bit; on the contrary, qualitative and quantitative improvements in aircraft, early warning radars and new airfields with hardened shelters continued apace. It is, however, noteworthy that by 1971, the difference in capabilities of the two air forces had narrowed considerably.

In 1971, the PAF also found it challenging to live up to its much-hyped image of a mythical force in the eyes of the populace, which was obviously well fed on patriotic stories and songs harking back to the heady days of 1965. Thus, any expectation of the PAF to repeat past wonders in 1971 needed to be tempered with a realistic appraisal of the changes that had come about over the years.

The 1971 India-Pakistan War represented the swan-song of the PAF's F-104-fleet: although at least six examples survived the conflict, and despite reinforcements from Jordan, combat losses and lack of spares resulted in their subsequent withdrawal from service. This was the wing of Squadron Leader Amjad Hussain's F-104A shot down by ground fire near Amritsar on 5 December 1971. (Albert Grandolini Collection)

A Critique of the PAF's Operational Plans

The PAF's Concept of Operations for the 1971 War had clearly underlined all-out air support to the Army's main offensive in West Pakistan. As a prelude to this support, it was appreciated that some degree of control of the air was necessary, and the PAF was content with being able to prevent any prohibitive IAF interference with the Pak Army's operations. During the critical phase of the main offensive, the enemy airfields serving the concerned land sector were to be kept suppressed. Additionally, air defence in the Northern Sector, including the main sectors of land battles, was to be ensured by mutually supportive bases with sufficient redundancy for providing complete daylight and selective night time patrols, as well as round the clock scrambles.

It is important to note that the air defence of each and every VA and VP had not been called for, as the PAF was cognizant of the limitations of aircraft numbers as well as the radar coverage. Large swathes of the country thus stood compromised and were vulnerable to enemy air attacks. The Karachi Port complex, including vital POL stores, stood exposed to seaward attacks against which there was no early warning. Some of the refineries, the Sui gas plant and the rail/road network, particularly at the narrow-waisted centre of the country, also lay at the mercy of the IAF because of lack of air cover in the central region. These strategic target sets were immensely critical, and a dedicated campaign against them could threaten the very integrity of the country. The PAF hardly had any antidote to these vulnerabilities, except a credulous hope that the Army's objectives would have been achieved before matters came to a sordid end. Even if the PAF were to attempt air defence operations whose success was questionable, it would have amounted to frittering away the scant resources that had to remain inseparably dedicated to the II Corps offensive.

The high intensity of operations of the PAF F-6 units required high intensity of their maintenance too. This photograph shows ground crews maintaining the Wopen-6 engines of this aircraft, the aft fuselage of which has been removed. (Albert Grandolini Collection)

The Concept of Operations talked about 'providing air support for holding actions with the aim of tying down as many of the enemy's resources as possible, and to achieve a favourable tactical posture in the process.' The overriding priority of the PAF was 'to give maximum support to the proposed offensive into India.' It is not difficult to glean from these statements that other than the planned main offensive, the rest were considered routine holding operations. Content with the Army's assumptions regarding likely enemy courses of action, the PAF's concept was silent about one or more of these holding operations turning into major reverses, requiring the PAF's maximum support, of a magnitude similar to that envisaged for the II Corps' offensive. In the event, unexpected reverses at Shakargarh and Naya Chor were of exactly such a nature, and required the fullest attention of the PAF, as the core areas of Punjab and Sind lay threatened. If the main offensive had gone through, the PAF would have been hard-pressed in supporting it, along with the two operations that were now critical to the integrity of Pakistan. A well-thought out contingency brief in the Concept of Operations would have been helpful in such a critical situation.

For want of a dedicated anti-shipping platform and weapon, the PAF's maritime air support capability was limited. A tri-services meeting held in February 1971 at Air HQ apparently settled the issue of air support to the Pakistan Navy, with the PAF agreeing to 'engage some targets of importance, subject to availability of air effort, and during day time only.' In reaction to the Indian Navy's devastating attack against PN ships at sea on the night of 4/5 December, the PAF did strike Okha harbour, a coastal Indian facility for small vessels, and put it out of operation in a single strike; it was, however, too little and too late. The PAF also planned a daring, albeit abortive, response against Bombay harbour by B-57s, modified with four F-86 200 gal drop tanks carried under the wings. Ruefully, such imaginative tasks should have been considered by the Pakistan Navy and PAF jointly, so that initiative could be seized, and the battle taken to the enemy at the outset. Apparently, naval operations and associated air support were not on the highest priority, when the Pakistani response to Indian aggression mainly centred on the capture of territory.

According to the PAF's official history, there was talk of the PAF having to fight a war for as long as six months. This, however, does not figure out in the calculation of the war effort, which catered for just about half a month. The incongruity seems to indicate that the Air Staff was being fearful to a fault, as the PAF had the means to fight only a short war. Owing to US sanctions and tight budgets, war reserves of all three services were not exactly at the target of 30 days stipulated in the War Directive. These reserves varied over a wide range of 15 to 45 days, at the planned consumption rates for various weapon systems in each service. Conservation of resources under these constraints is one thing, but talk of a six-month long war raises the valid question if a 'go slow' was envisaged at some point in time.

Air Effort Generation

The PAF had planned an optimal aircraft Utilisation Rate (UR) of 2.2 sorties per aircraft per day, for an envisaged war of 14 days. This rate was based on an average of three daily sorties per aircraft for the first three days of the war, and two daily sorties per aircraft for the remaining eleven days. Also, all aircraft types were expected to generate a similar effort. The planned UR was, however, an average figure, taking into account the different effort generation capabilities of various aircraft types.

It may also be noted that the planned UR glossed over an important requirement of an increase in effort generation, to cater for enhanced air support requirements during the critical phase of the Pak Army's main offensive. For purposes of comprehensive logistics planning, it was vital to have incorporated a second surge of three daily sorties per aircraft, lasting at least three days, if not more.

The PAF flew a total of 2,955 sorties from the time India commenced hostilities in East Pakistan on 22 November, until the ceasefire on 17 December. Of these, 2,911 sorties were flown in West Pakistan between 3 and 17 December, while approximately 44 sorties were flown in East Pakistan between 22 November and 5 December. It goes to the credit of the PAF to have managed this air effort generation despite extremely adverse circumstances, foremost of which was the critical shortage of spares. The loss of 20 percent of the Bengali technicians who had been grounded, or had defected to India before the war, was also overcome without any substantial strain. Most reassuring was the fact that air and ground crews maintained their potential, ready to launch in support of a meaningful response to the Indian aggression.

Compared to the three-week long 1965 War in which the PAF flew 2,279 sorties, it flew 23 percent more during the two weeks of 1971 War.

The total sorties flown during the war were 60 percent of the planned effort of 4,960 combat sorties. The shortfall is understandable considering the fact that the Army's main offensive, which was to take up the bulk of air effort for its support, had failed to materialise. The PAF was obviously conserving its effort while concentrating on air defences and support to the Army in critical sectors. It would be opportune to clarify here that the PAF did not hold back any part of its fighting force in reserve, as has been imputed occasionally. As an instance, the otherwise reputable writer, Major General Fazal Muqeem Khan, grossly errs when he asserts that, 'four squadrons out of 10½ in West Pakistan were not utilised at all.'

The workhorses of the PAF turned out to be the F-6 and F-86E which were acquired soon after the 1965 War. Each type flew 29 percent of the total war effort.

The best Utilisation Rate – though still a lowly 1.6 daily sorties per aircraft – was achieved by Mirage III and F-6, both having been the more recent inductions in the PAF (three and five years old respectively). These figures also contradict criticism in some quarters that the Mirages were not utilised fully, for fear of loss of these prestigious assets.

Aircraft Attrition

The IAF lost a total of 60 aircraft to combat-related causes while flying 6,542 combat sorties, resulting in an attrition rate (loss per 100 sorties) of 0.91 percent. The PAF lost 27 aircraft while flying 2,955 combat sorties, also resulting in an attrition rate of 0.91 percent. Although by no means a comprehensive assessment criterion, attrition rate is a reasonably fair indicator of an air force's (and AAA's) performance during war. On this basis, both air forces were at par, though this result must be tempered with the truism that the IAF flew many more ground attack sorties in a vulnerable air and ground environment. For both air forces, the number of aircraft lost was 9.3 percent of their respective inventories.

For the IAF, its performance in 1971 was a considerable improvement over the 1965 War, when it got soundly beaten, having an attrition rate of 1.67 percent versus the PAF's 0.7 percent.

The IAF was at the receiving end of the Pak Army's AAA, with 60 percent of all IAF aircraft downed by the Army's guns, while the PAF notched up 30 percent, mostly during the interception of egressing raiders. The preponderant role played by the Pakistan Army's AAA in the country's air defence, was one of the reasons that eventually led to the birth of a separate Army Air Defence arm in 1989.[1]

Twenty-six percent of the PAF's aircraft losses were entirely avoidable as slipshod dispersal led to the loss of five aircraft on the ground in Murid in a single IAF raid; two more were lost on the ground in other raids.

Air Defence

The PAF invested heavily in air defence, apportioning 62 percent of the total air effort to this vital mission. Of this effort, seven percent of the missions were flown exclusively over the battlefield to cover the troops, albeit without any radar visibility, thus diluting the effect of the effort considerably. The sectorial performance was lop-sided, as the Northern Sector had better concentration of resources – both aircraft and radars – compared to the Southern Sector. The reason was obvious, for the major land battles, as well as the planned major offensive, were localised in Kashmir and Punjab.

Despite the considerable air defence effort expended in West Pakistan, raiders were intercepted by fighters only after weapon release in the Northern Sector, while none was intercepted in the Southern Sector either before, or after weapon release. In the battle area, a couple of enemy aircraft were intercepted following chance pick-up by the pilots on air support missions. The AAA gunners mostly picked off the raiders as they pulled up and exposed themselves during the vulnerable attack phase.

Deployment of low level radars in the Northern Sector was too far in the rear, and only provided an early warning of about three minutes. This warning time turned out to be insufficient even for aircraft already patrolling in the vicinity. Murid and Chander air bases, for instance, could not be defended effectively because of the limited early warning. Apparently, the locations of three (out of four) AR-1 radars atop hills at Cherat, Kallar Kahar and Kirana, which could provide up to 50 percent additional pick-up range, were considered a big bonus. This deployment scheme still left the extremely important lines of communications, the forward-located concentration areas of the strategic reserves, and all of the battle areas without any early warning. The PAF stood frustrated and helpless when the IAF started to target the railway network, including trains. Forward deployment of radars, which was not constrained by terrain or any other limitation, could have provided timely warning against raiders coming for most of these targets, as well as PAF installations. Under positive cover of forward positioned radars, the CAPs could also have been anchored further ahead to improve the intercept possibilities, but with some risk of being surprised by enemy fighter sweeps. With the Air Staff's response options overly swaddled in layers of caution and safety, such risk-taking was an improbable prospect. As long as IAF aircraft were being shot down, even though after weapon release, the PAF seemed quite content with the rear deployment of radars.

The coverage pattern and search limitations of most radar had been compromised by the defecting Bengalis, so the IAF had fairly good information to help chart safe routes for ingress. This was also a significant setback to the PAF's already limited air defence coverage.

The deployment of aircraft for air defence in the Northern Sector was generally optimal, except an odd case. In Mianwali, a half-squadron detachment of F-6s deployed solely for air defence could not perform their equally well-suited mission of tactical air support, as Mianwali was too far removed from any of the battlefields. A swap with the relatively longer-ranged F-86s based at Sargodha, would have helped in better utilisation of both types in the air support role, as well as air defence.

In the Southern Sector, a small detachment of four F-86E at Talhar was at the complete mercy of any intruder, for the base was only 32nm from the border, and had no low-level early warning. This reality was understood too late, when a scrambling pair was surprised by IAF Hunters, and one of the F-86s was promptly shot down over the airfield. The base had little utility other than emergency recoveries, or for some stage-through strike operations.

In East Pakistan, where air defence may have been a futile effort in the overall scheme of things, the PAF's intrepid band of pilots and air defence controllers kept the IAF fighters at bay for over two days. Once the PAF was grounded with the destruction of the runway at Dacca, Pak Army AAA continued to batter the IAF. The net bag of at least 13 aircraft downed by both arms, under the most adverse circumstances, speaks volumes about the 'never say die' spirit with which the air warriors and the gunners were imbued. Sadly, valour alone could add little meaning to the eventual outcome of the war.

Offensive Counter Air

The meagre 10 percent of the total air effort that went into airfield strikes and a few anti-radar missions need to be seen in proper perspective. As stated earlier, the PAF's airfield strikes were part of a disruptive counter air campaign, aimed at overburdening the IAF's effort generation capabilities. It also served the purpose of demonstrating an offensive resolve, while employing the full spectrum of air power. Damage inflicted to the runways was, however, not very substantial, and the airfields were seldom closed for more than one day or night. The main reason was that shallow dive angles during attack – dictated by the compulsion of minimising exposure to AAA fire – caused only slight penetration of the bombs into the runway surface, which was easily repairable. Especially designed runway attack weapons like the hard-nosed Durandal, which can be delivered in level flight and is rocket-boosted to assist in deeper penetration, did not exist at that time.

With their greater payload and accurate navigation, the B-57 bombers were able to cause significant damage during night strikes. The attacks on Uttarlai and Bhuj were particularly devastating, as both the runways remained under repair for at least one week. The attacks on distant Agra – distressful as these might have been for the reposing souls in the nearby Taj – were certainly alarming for the IAF, as PAF had struck unhindered at India's very heartland.[2] The more intense phase of the Offensive Counter Air campaign was planned to be overlaid with the Army's main offensive, which never came about; as a result, the effort put in by the PAF appears to be small.

Tactical Air Support

A sizeable 25 percent of the total air effort went into Tactical Air Support missions which included Close Air Support, Battlefield Air Interdiction and Armed Reconnaissance. Since these missions were sometimes logged interchangeably, an accurate textbook breakdown of the sub-divisions has not been possible; the bulk of them were, however, of the classic Close Air Support variety which targeted armour, artillery guns and vehicles. Sixteen percent of these missions were flown in the 'escort' role, in which ammunition was expended by the escorts if the opportunity arose after sanitising the airspace over the battlefield.

Overall, about two-thirds of the air support effort was considered successful. The main reasons for unsuccessful missions included inability to locate well-camouflaged targets (especially in the wooded areas of Punjab), unfavourable target-weapon compatibility, weapon failures and poor visibility due to winter haze. Most frustrating for the pilots was to discover 'no enemy activity' on arrival at the battle location. This problem was attributed to the inordinate delay from the time the air support request was put in by the Army, until the fighters reached overhead the target area. Equally exasperating was the poor radio communication with the Forward Air Controllers who were to guide the fighters to their targets in the terminal phase of the mission; many a mission was wasted due to faulty radio contact.

In an effort to stay clear of AAA fire, F-86s were configured with general-purpose bombs in most of the missions, which was a rather unconventional way of destroying tanks and armoured vehicles. The choice of weapon was considered a suitable compromise by providing a safe stand-off distance, notwithstanding the ineffectiveness of general area bombing for destroying armour with gravity and wind-prone bombs. On the other hand, using the 2.75" rockets had two pitfalls: firstly, the attack profile entailed approaching the target closer than in a bombing attack, rendering the aircraft more vulnerable to AAA fire; secondly, these rockets were inherently not very accurate, in which case if it missed even by 10-odd feet, the damage to armour by its puny warhead would be negligible. In case of a bomb, even if the hit was not direct, its extensive blast effect could still immobilise a tank by disabling its engine, communications systems, or even the crew if caught with an open hatch. In any case, both the 2.75" FFAR, as well

Table 9: Summary of War Effort

Aircraft	Air Defence (General)	Air Defence (FEBA)	Offensive Counter-Air	Tac Air Support	Air Interdiction	Photo-Recce	Maritime Air Support	Total
	Day/Night	Day	Day/Night	Day/Night	Day/Night	Day/Night	Day/Night	
B-57B/C			0/104	1/15	0/4		6	130
F-6	632/0	42	8/0	139/0				821
F-86E	381/9	58	20/0	294/0	15/0		14	791
F-86E (E Pak)	20/0	4		20/0				44
F-86F	317/0		70/0	228/0			2	617
F-104A/B	23/18	22	22/0	5/0			6	96
Mirage IIIE/R/D	208/96	8	38/0		4/0	36/0		390
T-6G				0/12				12
T-33A			0/21	12/6			4	43
C-130B/E			0/5	0/5	0/1			11
	1,581/123	134	158/130	699/38	19/5	36	32	2,955

Notes:
This table shows all combat sorties flown in West Pakistan between 3-17 Dec, and in East Pakistan between 22 Nov – 6 Dec.
Besides 36 Photo Recce sorties flown between 3-17 Dec, nine operational sorties (not included here) were flown during October and November.
The 44 F-86E sorties flown in East Pakistan are based on estimates of 14 Squadron aircrew, as all written records were left behind in Dacca.

The six available C-130B/E transports of the PAF flew a total of 11 combat sorties during the 1971 War with India: five of these were extremely dangerous air strikes on IAF air bases. (Albert Grandolini Collection)

as the more accurate SNEB 68mm rockets were used by the F-86s in a limited number of missions.[3]

It is quite understandable that a fine balance had to be maintained between the need to conserve aircraft and weapons for the Pak Army's promised main offensive, and the disagreeable possibility of consuming them beforehand. As long as it is appreciated that the PAF responded to most of the requests for tactical air support, the odd choice of weapons should be seen in the context of the need to stay viable for the impending major air support campaign.

The PAF did not treat on-going operations in various sectors as 'lesser actions of holding formations', as *The Story of Pakistan Air Force – A Saga of Courage and Honour*, awkwardly tries to argue in favour of taking the safer approach; nor did the debate about the cost of an airplane versus a tank inhibit any air support, as the official history seems to imply. The fact of the matter was simply a desire to remain a 'force in being' for the impending Army offensive, which it considered as its primary task. Even so, it was without any prejudice to the routine air support being called for in various sectors. As an instance, when the situation in Shakargarh Sector needed a helping hand, the PAF threw in the F-6s which were the most suitable platforms available. Arrayed with three powerful 30mm cannon, and on a few occasions with S-5 57mm rockets as well, these aircraft carried out close-in attacks at low heights, without any consideration of AAA hazards.[4]

When it came to the use of bombs against troop concentrations and ammunition dumps, the F-86s did quite well, and the effort resulted in the desired destruction, as expected.

A motley of bomber, trainer and transport aircraft also chipped in audaciously at twilight and during the night, but generally with unspectacular results. The best that was expected out of them were chance hits, of which there were a few.

Interdiction

These are missions flown to interdict supply of replenishments on rail and road transportation routes beyond the battlefield. Attacks against choke points on the rail and road networks like railway stations are the preferred targets, as their destruction can induce harmful delays in the scheme of things on the battlefield. These targets are much bigger and more visible compared to the well concealed and camouflaged stockpiles of supplies in the battlefield. Aircraft flying relatively deeper interdiction missions also have the advantage of remaining clear of the surface-to-air defences that infest the active battle area.

Ostensibly, these deeper missions were kept pending for the main offensive phase, and less than one percent of the total air effort – a mere 24 sorties – went into interdiction beyond the immediate battlefield. Perhaps the desire to stay out of harm's way and conserve the assets for the upcoming Army offensive, led to this course of action. This cautious line of thought was of little help, as it only gave the enemy a freer hand in bolstering the much-needed supplies of ammunition and fuel in various battle sectors. A comprehensive 'near-and-far' interdiction campaign, targeting communications nodes serving the enemy's main and secondary efforts in Shakargarh and the Desert sectors, should have started at the outset of air operations. Any delay

Table 10: Aircraft Utilisation Rate, PAF[6]

Aircraft[7]	Inventory	Operational	Sorties	Utilisation Rate
B-57B/C	18	18	130	0.7
F-6	90	48	821	1.6
F-86E[8]	74	62	835	1.3
F-86F	65	44	617	1.3
F-104A/B[9]	8	8	96	1.1
Mirage IIIEP/RP/DP	23	23	390	1.6
T-33A	12	12	43	0.4
Total	290	215	2,932	Average: 1.3

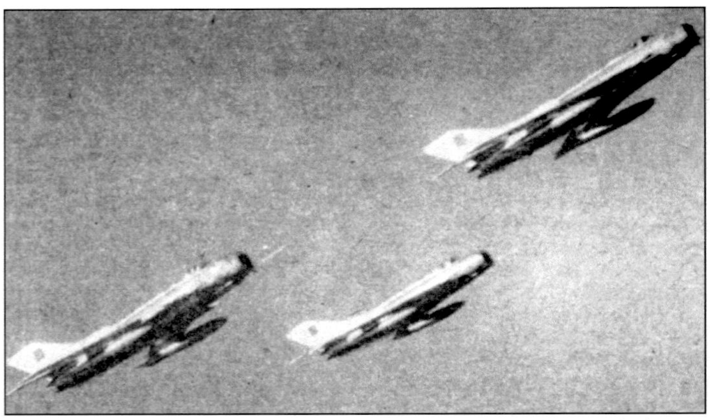

With 1.6 sorties per day per airframe, the PAF's F-6 fleet, along with the Mirage III, had the highest utilisation rate of the entire combat fleet of the force during the 1971 War with India. (Albert Grandolini Collection)

in such a campaign would not have had the desired effects, as the pre-stocked supplies would continue to sustain the enemy's ground operations for some time.

The highly successful attack on Mukerian Railway Station two days before the war ended showed the nature and extent of damage that could have been inflicted over the previous two weeks.

A Mirage IIIEP of No 5 Squadron, PAF. This squadron flew 390 combat sorties during the 1971 War with India, achieving one of the highest utilisation rates in the fleet. This example was photographed after the war, while having a JL.100 combined pod for unguided rockets and a fuel tank installed on the inboard underwing pylon. (Albert Grandolini Collection)

Table 11: Analysis of Combat-Related Aircraft Losses, IAF & PAF, 1971[11]

IAF	1971 War (21 Nov – 17 Dec)	PAF
18	Air Combat	10
36	Enemy AAA	7
-	Own AAA	1
3	Destroyed on the ground	7
3	Accidents (combat related)	2
60	OVERALL ATTRITION	27
6,542	TOTAL COMBAT SORTIES FLOWN	2,955
0.91%	ATTRITION RATE	0.91%
	AIRCREW CASUALTIES	
36	KIA	16
13	POW	4
7	Ejected and recovered over own territory	4
6	Ejected and escaped from enemy territory	-

Performance of Operations Personnel

The front-line players in the PAF's operations were the pilots and the air defence controllers, who were diligently supported by highly skilled engineers and technicians, logisticians, and air traffic controllers in keeping the aircraft, weapons and radars functional. During the war, as in peacetime, PAF personnel galvanised as a team, which was testimony to a cohesive and well-organised service.

The high standards of training and discipline stood out, and the results were in keeping with the sterling performance of 1965 War. The enthusiastic fighter pilots were seen to be particularly adept in interception and air combat, despite limitations of the airborne and ground radars. The air defence controllers displayed innovative skills in enhancing the situational awareness of the pilots and were instrumental in the achievement of almost all aerial kills. Functioning as proficient pilot-controller teams, they were able to affect a Kill Exchange Ratio of 1.8:1 in favour of the PAF in interception and air combat missions.[5] This was not too far behind the Kill Exchange Ratio of 2.1:1 in the 1965 War.

'Leading from the front' has never been an overused cliché in the PAF and is taken very seriously. In the 1971 War, just as in 1965, some of the most difficult and dangerous missions were led by the Squadron Commanders themselves. Four of them had an aerial kill each, which served as perfect examples of heroics for their young sub-ordinates to emulate.

The bomber aircrew deserve special mention as their lumbering platforms were slow and defenceless. Flying deep into enemy territory in the dark of the night against well-defended airfields, they carried out their missions bravely, and with complete resoluteness. Their effort helped PAF maintain round-the-clock pressure on the IAF's effort generation capability.

In a Nutshell

When the war ended in West Pakistan on 17 December, the PAF was still 'in the ring and on its feet'.[10] It had parried the enemy's blows and had been ever so careful in its offensive responses. It continued to be fixated with remaining viable for providing complete air support to the Army's all-important battle, which flowed out of the overarching dictum, 'defence of the East lies in the West'. The PAF's overall performance can be gleaned from the fact that it managed to keep its aircraft attrition rate at par with the IAF. The PAF unmistakably denied a much stronger IAF the distinct possibility of delivering a knock-out punch to it. In the circumstances obtaining, this was a commendable achievement. Yet, there were prospects which, if exploited with a measure of audacity, could have inflicted far more damage to the IAF and Indian Army formations, and also reduced losses to the PAF and the Pakistan Army.

The air defence system lacked forward orientation in the Northern Sector, whereby radars could not provide sufficient early warning to CAPs for timely interceptions. This oversight rendered friendly air bases, ground forces, as well as lines of communications susceptible to unimpeded air attacks. Considering the large IAF effort that went into tactical air support, the PAF could have accrued big dividends by being more up front and intercepting the intruders well in time; it's also quite evident that a lucrative opportunity to raise the IAF's attrition rate to unacceptable levels was missed.

The tactical air support provided by the PAF was adequate and largely met the Army's demands but should have also included interdiction beyond the battlefield in earnest, so as to cause a debilitating effect on supplies for the engaged enemy formations.

Maritime air support was not well thought out, and neither service came up with 'out-of-the-box' solutions for coping with the difficulties at hand. While the onus of brainstorming lay in large part on the Navy, the PAF could have filled in with an array of options.

The War at Large

It would be instructive to learn in this closing account that at GHQ, most of the Principal Staff Officers were in complete discord with the General Staff. Quarter Master General: Major General A O Mitha; Adjutant General: Major General Khuda Dad; and Master General of Ordnance: Major General Eftikhar Janjua were either not on speaking terms with the Chief of General Staff (CGS), or spoke only if they absolutely had to. Similarly, within the General Staff, the COS and CGS did not see eye to eye on any matter. 'The tensions between Hamid and Gul, and Gul and all the other PSOs undoubtedly affected the efficiency of the GHQ,' bemoans Mitha.[12] As can be gleaned, one of the glaring reasons for failure to lay down coherent aims and objectives, and plan and prosecute the war professionally, lay in an utterly disorganised and incoherent higher military leadership then at the helm in GHQ.

Defence of East Pakistan

The Commander of Eastern Command, Lieutenant General Niazi had intended to fight delaying actions so as to trade space for time, and then fall back to 'fortresses' in important border towns. His baffling orders, however, to continue fighting in the forward posture 'till seventy-five percent casualties had been sustained,'[13] meant that a completely emaciated and spent force was to fall back and defend the fortresses. With virtually no forces for the defence of Dacca Sector, it was as good as leaving it to Divine intercession that had purportedly routed the enemies of many a Sultan and Shah in the past. This was despite a reassertion by GHQ, (after an in-situ review by the COS, General Hamid, in early September) that 'Dacca should be treated as the lynch-pin for the defence of East Pakistan.'

A more pragmatic plan would have focused on embroiling the invading Indian forces in delaying actions from a forward defensive posture, and gradually falling back to the 'fortresses' or well-defended strongpoints in important towns. The defence of Dacca Sector could be left to a dedicated force that was not to be dependent on the fallback of forward elements. Those elements could, thus, continue to attrite and harass the Indian forces in a retrograde battle, as the latter headed towards Dacca. The forward elements could not be expected to execute a timely withdrawal all the way to the Dacca Sector, as their lines of communication would have been severed by the *Mukti Bahini* saboteurs, as well as by IAF's air attacks.

The success of such a plan mainly rested on the ability of Lieutenant General Niazi to correctly gauge the timing for transition from the counter-insurgency mode to a conventional defensive posture. The forces could, thus, be promptly redeployed and organised for their new tasks in the forward zones and Dacca Sector. There were sufficient indicators in the beginning of November to have spurred the operational reorientation of forces, which could have been completed soon after the Indian incursion started.

With the forces in the forward zones not encumbered with having to defend every inch of the territory, their strength could have been rationalised commensurate with their more focused task, while that of Dacca Sector could have been bolstered proportionately.

Reality dawned rather late on Lieutenant General Niazi when on 9 December, he sent a despatch to GHQ bemoaning his plight:

Owing to enemy action and hostility of rebels, cannot extricate force to defend Dacca. Enemy force causing large-scale destruction. Air strikes to be arranged against enemy based around East Pakistan and airborne reinforcements to be dropped to defend Dacca.[14]

That the PAF had been grounded three days earlier had pitiably escaped Niazi's notice, and clearly indicated his complete loss of situational awareness.

The GHQ must be faulted for failing to outline a broad concept of defence of East Pakistan. In the absence of such a guideline, it was left to a field commander who was not quite renowned in the Army for matters concerning operational strategy. 'Professionally, his ceiling was no more than that of a company commander,' laments the former C-in-C of Pakistan Army, Lieutenant General Gul Hassan in his memoirs.[15] An equally critical, former armoured division Commander Major General Wajahat Husain confirms thus: 'Tiger Niazi, an arrogant commander, was known for his limited professional knowledge of low-level tactics and no comprehension of high-level strategy and command.'[16]

Unfortunately, Niazi's stratagem, which was more bluster and less guile, was considered good enough by the GHQ, where listlessness and confusion prevailed. A fateful oversight by the General Staff – whose collective acumen and experience should have been invaluable – led to the squandering away of whatever little chance there was to salvage the situation.

When faced with the deteriorating situation in East Pakistan within the first few days of the war, Niazi was falsely assured by GHQ with a cryptic message rich in racial overtones: 'Yellow and White help expected from north and south shortly.'[17] Self-deception of this kind reached a climax when GHQ flashed a message to an impatient and desperate Niazi on 12 December, stating that Chinese activities had actually begun! That Yahya had deluded himself with a ludicrous hope of the international community bailing him out, speaks volumes about the bankruptcy of ideas to save East Pakistan.

Offensive in West Pakistan

In the GHQ at Rawalpindi, there were two points of view about conducting the main offensive. The CGS, Lieutenant General Gul Hassan, felt that an offensive spearheaded by II Corps should be launched immediately after an Indian incursion into East Pakistan, concurrent with preliminary offensive operations by the holding formations that are normally required for improving their defensive posture. To Gul, such a scheme would not only keep the enemy guessing about the location of the main offensive, thus retaining the vital element of surprise, it would also help avoid the wrath of the IAF by submerging any large-scale movements of the main offensive 'when the entire Western front [would] burst forth like an uncontrollable flood.' Gul was quite sure that the plan was loaded with prospects of achieving the objectives of the main offensive at the earliest, especially if it could develop a pincer in concert with the Army Reserve North. In his view, any delay in launching the main offensive would defeat its very purpose, by allowing Indian forces to complete their mission in the Eastern Theatre, and then, be mustered by the Indian Western Command to be unleashed on to West Pakistan.

In reaction to multiple Indian claims for Mirages shot down, after the war the PAF demonstratively lined up all 23 of its delta-winged jets on the tarmac of Sargodha AB and showed them to the foreign journalists. (Albert Grandolini Collection)

Surprisingly, Gul did not dwell on the stratagem required for dislocating the enemy's strategic reserves without which the Pakistani main offensive had little chance of getting past the Indian holding formations at the border.

The Army COS, General Abdul Hamid, was of the opinion that the launch of the main offensive should be delayed until the preliminary operations had stabilised, and the wind had been read, as it were. Hamid was apprehensive that if the strategic reserves were committed for the offensive operation at the outset, there would be none available to deal with any operational setbacks; it was, therefore, prudent to delay the main offensive until the situation had crystallised. Gul countered his boss by insisting that besides II Corps, there was the separate ARN which could handle any contingency, and it was to be committed for a strategic task only after the main offensive had made some headway.

Like Gul, Hamid also failed to address the issue of how the main offensive could be launched if ARN was engaged in firefighting elsewhere and was unable to create the necessary conditions for II Corps' main offensive.

Apparently, both the Principal Staff Officers pinned their hopes on the success of the preliminary offensive efforts in fulfilling the rather daunting task. With none of these efforts designed to threaten any major objective – this being outside the scope of such operations – it was hard to see how the Indian strategic reserves could be unhinged by something that could not have been more than a minor distraction.

Unfortunately, the twain could not meet, and no consensus emerged amongst the top brass until the eve of full-scale war. General Hamid's cautious approach, indicative of a taciturn nature, contrasted with the urgency borne of impetuousness in Gul's thought process. It was ironical that the C-in-C, General Yahya, remained nonchalant about the operational impasse at a most critical juncture; the result was that the Army went to war without a cogent plan of action and kept stumbling from one crisis situation to another.

Before the main offensive could be launched, II Corps and ARN had already been denuded of their fighting strength, with their infantry and artillery elements having been rushed to other sectors that were facing critical situations. General Hamid's apprehensions were not totally unfounded, it seemed, after all. A catastrophic situation was averted by not committing the reserves at the outset, as their timely withdrawal, transfer and re-insertion in another sector would have been impossible, subsequently.

With no reserves available for undertaking a meaningful manoeuvre to lure away the Indian strategic formations from the Ganganagar-Abohar area, an exasperated GHQ resorted to a desperate ruse one week into the war. ARN's 88 Brigade (ex-17 Division), was despatched with bridging equipment to Maqboolpur on the banks of River Ravi, seemingly the advance party of a surprise offensive that was about to undertake a river crossing. The Indians either did not notice the new arrival, or simply remained unmoved. This left the GHQ much befuddled for not achieving any results, despite detaching yet one more formation from its reserves, rendering them operationally useless for their primary task.

Going by the number of units permanently detached from the strategic reserves, it can be seen that, at a minimum, the Pak Army's deficiency was equivalent to one infantry division (i.e., three infantry brigades and an artillery brigade). Any plans to overcome such an operational shortcoming at the expense of either of the two strategic reserves, clearly meant that the main offensive was a non-starter. Additional reserve troops for the vulnerable formations like 8 Division (Shakargarh Sector) and 18 Division (Thar Sector), on whose turf strong enemy offensives were inevitable, should, therefore, have been adequately catered for at the outset. Unfortunately, as no collective field exercises had been held at Division or Corps level since 1969 due to involvement of the senior Army echelons in Martial Law affairs, such operational shortcomings of field formations remained largely unnoticed, and hence, unremedied.

Assuming that II Corps and ARN had somehow been able to maintain their integrity, would these formations have been able to accomplish their assigned tasks before Lieutenant General Niazi's Eastern Command eventually gave up? After all, it was important that GHQ not be disheartened by bad news from the Eastern Command Headquarters while in the middle of a crucial campaign in the West.

By most estimates, it would have taken at least two weeks for ARN's counter-offensive in Shakaragarh to roll back the Indian offensive, and another one week before it re-oriented itself and started pushing towards a vital Indian objective. If all went according to plan, the objective had to be threatened impudently enough for some of the Indian reserves in Ganganagar-Abohar to scamper northwards to provide relief. That such a displacement of Indian strategic formations could actually take place while their originally assigned sector was left vulnerable, beggars belief, but may be assumed for purposes of an academic discussion. It can, thus, be seen that something like three weeks were required before the Pak Army's main offensive could materialise. Once launched, however, the morale in Niazi's Eastern Command would have been buoyed immensely, and with a dedicated fortress defence plan in place, it might not have been altogether impossible to hold out until the offensive in the West had made some worthwhile gains.

The issue of the how the IAF would have dealt with a hunkered down force defending Dacca Sector remains moot. Nonetheless, with no extensive ground manoeuvres involved which could have greatly exposed the troops to air attacks, it can be surmised that they would have been dug-in, well-concealed and thus, far less vulnerable. The Pakistan Army AAA batteries were also largely intact, and there is every reason to believe that they could have contributed immensely to the effort to hold out longer.

Higher Direction of War

The President of Pakistan, General Yahya Khan, wore three additional hats including that of the Chief Martial Law Administrator, the Defence Minister, and C-in-C of the Army. Thus, to all intents and purposes, decision-making, with unchecked powers in all four domains, rested with him. With no consultative body to render sober advice, the country was at the mercy of his judgements and actions.

Based on his past association with Yahya, Gul recalls him to be 'professionally competent, decisive, confident, and possessing a high IQ, a remarkable memory and sharp perception.' Despite these impressive attributes, the burden of soldiering and governing at the same time, especially the latter sphere in which wily politicians had him twisted around their fingers, eventually proved too much for him.

In a move which was understandably a personal expedient, Yahya had retained General Abdul Hamid, his senior batch-mate, as the Army COS. Not willing to relinquish his real power base as the C-in-C, Yahya expected Hamid to play second fiddle which, as a superseded officer with a lackadaisical outlook, the latter did not find too intolerable to accept. The resulting situation was intensely detrimental to the Army for whose interests, Hamid had little inclination, and Yahya had little time.

With the war looming, Yahya did, however, find time to spell out his thoughts on the course of action he wished to adopt, in the fast aggravating military situation. Summing up a discussion after presentation of the National Strategy Paper by the National Defence College students in early November, Yahya declared, much to the surprise of officers of various syndicates, 'I am not so stupid as to go to war with India. I will do my best for a political situation to avoid war.'[18] The statement would have been considered a stroke of genius if it had come six months earlier, but it was dreadful to learn that he had failed to read the ill winds blowing from India, which were now gathering into a vicious storm. Quite evidently, Yahya was out of his elements at this critical stage, had not kept him abreast of the goings on, and was clueless about what to do. Instead of turning dovish, as if he was playing to a gallery of Western press reporters, he should have unequivocally outlined the broad contours of his strategy for war fighting at the highest seat of military learning. His statement was as confusing as it was defeatist; in fact, if one reads between his seemingly sagacious lines, Yahya had already lost the will to fight.

Table 12: Indian Air Force Losses of the 1971 India-Pakistan War

Date	Aircraft	Tail No	Pilot	Unit	Cause	Notes
4 Dec	Hunter		S/L K D Mehra	No 14 Sqn	Air combat	Shot down by F/O Shams-ul-haq while flying F-86E; Tezgaon area, pilot EOT and recovered
4 Dec	Hunter	BA252	S/L A V Samanta	No 37 Sqn	Air combat	Shot down by F/L Schames-ul-haq while flying F-86E; Tezgaon area, pilot KIA
4 Dec	Su-7	B849	F/L Harvinder Singh	No 222 Sqn	Air combat	Shot down by F/L Javed Latif while flying F-6; Rurala area, pilot KIA
4 Dec	Hunter	A490	F/L Sudhir Tyagi	No 27 Sqn	Air combat	Shot down by Mujahid Salik while flying F-86F; Duman/Chakwal area, pilot KIA
4 Dec	Hunter	A462	F/L K P Muralidharan	No 20 Sqn	Air combat	Shot down by F/L Salim Baig while flying F-86F, Peshawar area, pilot KIA
4 Dec	Su-7		F/L D R Natu	No 108 Sqn	Air combat	Shot down by S/L Rasheed Bhatti while flying F-104A; Amritsar area, pilot EOT and recovered
4 Dec	Hunter		F/L K Tremenheere	No 14 Sqn	Air combat	Shot down by S/L Dilawar Hussain while flying F-86E; Tezgaon area, pilot POW
4 Dec	Hunter	A479	F/O V S Chati	No 27 Sqn	Air combat	Shot down by F/L Qazi Javed while flying F-6; Sakesar area, pilot POW
4 Dec	HF-24	D1193	F/L P V Apte	No 220 Sqn	Ground fire	Shot down by AAA, Naya Chor area, pilot KIA
4 Dec	Su-7		F/L M S Grewal	No 32 Sqn	Ground fire	Shot down by AAA, Rafiqui Base, pilot POW
4 Dec	Su-7		F/L P N Saksena	No 222 Sqn	Ground fire	Shot down by AAA, Sulaimanki area, pilot ejected and escaped
4 Dec	Su-7	B839	F/L V V Tambey	No 32 Sqn	Ground fire	Shot down by air AAA, Rafiqui Base, pilot KIA
4 Dec	Hunter	BA295	F/L A R Da Costa	No 7 Sqn	Ground fire	Shot down by AAA, Lalmunirhat area, pilot KIA
4 Dec	Hunter	BA287	S/L S K Gupta	No 7 Sqn	Ground fire	Shot down by AAA, Lalmunirhat area, pilot EOT and recovered
4 Dec	Hunter	BA266	F/L S G Khonde	No 37 Sqn	Ground fire	Shot down by AAA, Tezgaon area, pilot KIA
4 Dec	Su-7		F/L S V Bhutani	No 221 Sqn	Ground fire	Shot down by AAA, Tezgaon area, pilot POW
4 Dec	Hunter	A940	?	No 20 Sqn	Ground fire	Shot at by AAA, pilot survived, aircraft wrecked on landing

Table 12: Indian Air Force Losses of the 1971 India-Pakistan War

Date	Aircraft	Tail No	Pilot	Unit	Cause	Notes
4 Dec	Su-7	B907	F/L Gurdeep Singh	No 101 Sqn	Ground fire	Shot down by AAA, Chamb area, pilot EOT and recovered
4 Dec	Canberra	IF916	F/L M Sasoon + F/L R M Advani (N)	JBCU	Air combat	Shot down by F/L Naeem Atta while flying Mirage IIIE at night; Jabbi/Chakwal area, crew KIA
5 Dec	Mystère IV	IA954	F/L A V Pethia	No 31 Sqn	Ground fire	Shot down by AAA, Chishtian area, pilot POW
5 Dec	Su-7		S/L D S Jafa	No 26 Sqn	Ground fire	Shot down by AAA, Lahore area, pilot POW
5 Dec	HF-24		F/L J L Bhargava	No 220 Sqn	Ground fire	Shot down by AAA, Naya Chor area, pilot POW
5 Dec	Hunter	A482	F/L G S Rai	No 27 Sqn	Air combat	Shot down by W/C Sa'ad Hatmi while flying F-6; Sodhi/Khushab area, pilot KIA
5 Dec	Hunter	A488	F/L K L Malkani	No 27 Sqn	Air combat	Shot down by F/L Shahid Raza while flying F-6; Katha Saghral area, pilot KIA
5 Dec	Hunter	A1014	S/L J M Mistry	No 20 Sqn	Air combat	Shot down by F/L Safdar Mahmood while flying Mirage IIIE; Katha Saghral area, pilot KIA
5 Dec	Chetak		-	No 114 HU	Air raid	Destroyed on the ground by F-86F (No 26 Sqn)
5 Dec	MiG-21FL	C764	F/L Harish Sinhji	No 29 Sqn	Ground fire	Shot down by AAA, Sulaimanki area, pilot POW
5 Dec	Canberra	IF923	F/L S C Sandal + F/L K S Nanda (N)	No 35 Sqn	Ground fire	Shot down by AAA, Arabian Sea, crew KIA
5 Dec	Canberra	IF960	F/L S K Goswami + F/L S C Mahajan (N)	No 5 Sqn	Ground fire	Shot down by AAA, Bhalwal area, crew KIA
6 Dec	Su-7	B868	F/L. V K Wahi	No 101 Sqn	Air combat	Shot down by F/L Salimuddin while flying Mirage IIIE; Samba area, pilot KIA
6 Dec	Su-7		F/L Bhattacharya	No 101 Sqn	Ground fire	Shot down by AAA, Chamb area, pilot ejected and escaped
6 Dec	Su-7		F/O K C Kuruvilla	No 222 Sqn	Ground fire	Shot down by AAA, Jassar area, pilot POW
6 Dec	MiG-21FL		S/L D P Rao	No 4 Sqn	Ground fire	Shot down by AAA, Gauhati area, pilot EOT and recovered
6 Dec	Vampire	BY925	-	No 121 Sqn	Air raid	Destroyed on the ground by B-57
7 Dec	Su-7		F/L Jiwa Singh	No 26 Sqn	Air combat	Shot down by F/L Atiq Sufi while flying F-6; Samba area, pilot KIA
7 Dec	Gnat	IE1075	F/O M M Singh	No. 9 Sqn	Combat accident	Hit ground while reacting to fake interception conducted by PAF radar controller, S/L Farooq Haider
7 Dec	Hunter		F/L S Dasgupta	No 14 Sqn	Ground fire	Shot down by AAA, Dum Dum area, pilot EOT and recovered
8 Dec	Su-7	B910	F/L R G Kadam	TACDE	Air combat	Shot down by W/C S M H Hashmi while flying F-6; Jaranwala area, pilot KIA
8 Dec	MiG-21FL		S/L Denzil Keelor	No 45 Sqn	Ground fire	Shot down by AAA, Chamb area, pilot ejected and escaped
8 Dec	Hunter	BA329	W/C B A Coelho	No 7 Sqn	Ground fire	Shot down by AAA, Sulaimanki area, pilot POW
8 Dec	Mystère IV		S/L Anukul	No 31 Sqn	Ground fire	Shot down by AAA, Fazilka area, pilot EOT and recovered
9 Dec	Su-7		F/L N Shankar	No 32 Sqn	Ground fire	Shot down by AAA, Amritsar area, pilot KIA
9 Dec	HF-24	BD859	S/L A V Kamat	No 10 Sqn	Ground fire	Shot down by AAA, Hyderabad area, pilot POW
10 Dec	Hunter	A938	S/L M K Jain	No 27 Sqn	Ground fire	Shot down by AAA, Chamb area, pilot KIA
10 Dec	Su-7	B798	F/L S K Chibber	No 108 Sqn	Ground fire	Shot down by AAA, Mandi Sadiqganj area, pilot KIA
10 Dec	Su-7		F/L Dilip Parulkar	No 26 Sqn	Ground fire	Shot down by AAA, Zafarwal area, pilot POW
10 Dec	Hunter		F/L L H Dixon	No 17 Sqn	Ground fire	Shot down by AAA, Lalmunirhat area, pilot ejected and escaped

Table 12: Indian Air Force Losses of the 1971 India-Pakistan War

Date	Aircraft	Tail No	Pilot	Unit	Cause	Notes
10 Dec	Hunter	BA275	S/L R C Sachdeva	No 14 Sqn	Ground fire	Shot down by AAA, Narayanganj area, pilot KIA
11 Dec	Su-7	B780	F/L K K Mohan	No 26 Sqn	Air combat	Shot down by W/C A I Bokhari while flying F-86E; Nainakot area, pilot KIA
11 Dec	HF-24	D1204	S/L M S Jatar	No 10 Sqn	Air raid	Destroyed on the ground at Uttarlai, by S/L Amanullah while flying F-104A; pilot survived
11 Dec	Canberra	F1024	F/L R D Naithani + F/L G Theophilus (N) + F/L Manohar Purhoit (N)	No 5 Sqn	Combat accident	Probably crashed due to disorientation, Bikaner area, crew KIA
11 Dec	MiG-21FL	C1107	F/L A B Dhavle	No 1 Sqn	Combat accident	Shot down by friendly MiG-21, pilot KIA
13 Dec	MiG-21FL	C705	W/C H S Gill	No 47 Sqn	Ground fire	Shot down by AAA, Badin area, pilot KIA
13 Dec	Mystère IV	IA1331	S/L J D Kumar	No 3 Sqn	Ground fire	Shot down by AAA, Sulaimanki area, pilot KIA
13 Dec	MiG-21FL		S/L P S Gill	No 28 Sqn	Ground fire	Shot down by air AAA, Tezgaon area, pilot ejected safely and escaped
14 Dec	Gnat		F/O N J S Sekhon	No 18 Sqn	Air combat	Shot down by F/L Salim Baig while flying F-86F; Srinagar area, pilot KIA
15 Dec	Canberra		F/O B R E Wilson + F/L R B Mehta (N)	No 16 Sqn	Ground fire	Shot down by AAA, Tezgaon area, crew KIA
16 Dec	Su-7	B889	F/L T S Dandass	No 26 Sqn	Ground fire	Shot down by AAA, Narowal area, pilot KIA
17 Dec	MiG-21FL	C716	F/L Tejwant Singh	No 29 Sqn	Air combat	Shot down by F/L Maqsood Amir while flying F-86E; Pasrur area, pilot POW
17 Dec	Mystère IV		F/L Tonkeshwar Das	No 3 Sqn	Combat accident	Engine flame-out, Haveli area, pilot ejected and recovered safely

Table 13: Pakistan Air Force Losses of the 1971 India-Pakistan War

Date	Aircraft	Tail No	Pilot	Unit	Cause	Notes
22 Nov	F-86E	-	F/L Parvaiz M Qureshi	No 14 Sqn	Air combat	Shot down by F/O Donald Lazarus while flying Gnat; Chuagacha area, pilot POW
22 Nov	F-86E	-	F/O Khalil Ahmed	No 14 Sqn	Air combat	Shot down by F/L M A Ganapthy while flying Gnat, Chuagacha area, pilot POW
4 Dec	F-86E	-	F/L Saeed Afzal	No 14 Sqn	Air combat	Shot down by F/O Harish Masand while flying Hunter; Kurmitola area, pilot KIA
4 Dec	F-86E	-	W/C S M Ahmed	Staff Ops Officer	Air combat	Shot down by W/C C N Chatrath while flying Hunter; Tezgaon area, pilot KIA
4 Dec	F-86E	-	F/L Sajjad Noor	No 14 Sqn	Air combat	Shot down by W/C C R Sunderesan while flying Hunter; Tezgaon area, pilot EOT
5 Dec	F-104A	56-804	S/L Amjad Hussain	No 9 Sqn	Ground fire	Shot down by AAA, Armritsar area, pilot POW
5 Dec	B-57C	53-3958	F/L Javed Iqbal + F/L G M Malik (N)	No 7 Sqn	Ground fire	Shot down by AAA, Amritsar area, crew KIA
5 Dec	B-57B	53-3943	S/L Ishfaq Hamid + S/L Zulfiqar Ahmed (N)	No 7 Sqn	Ground fire	Shot down by AAA, Bhuj area, crew KIA
6 Dec	B-57B	53-3939	S/L Khusro + S/L Peter Christy (N)	No 7 Sqn	Ground fire	Shot down by AAA, Jamnagar area, crew KIA
6 Dec	RB-57B	53-3934	-	No 7 Sqn	Air raid	Destroyed on the ground at Masroor by Canberra strike
7 Dec	F-86F	4030	F/O Hamid A Khawaja	No 15 Sqn	Accident	Flamed out during chase due fuel starvation, Khushalgharh area, pilot EOT
7 Dec	F-6	4110	F/L Wajid Ali Khan	No 11 Sqn	Ground fire	Shot down by AAA, Marala area, pilot POW
7 Dec	F-86E	1657	S/L Cecil Choudhry	No 18 Sqn	Ground fire	Shot down by friendly AAA, Zafarwal area, pilot EOT

Table 13: Pakistan Air Force Losses of the 1971 India-Pakistan War

Date	Aircraft	Tail No	Pilot	Unit	Cause	Notes
8 Dec	F-86F	1095	-	No. 15 Sqn	Air raid	Destroyed on the ground at Murid by Hunter strike (No 20 Sqn)
8 Dec	F-86F	3839	-	No. 15 Sqn	Air raid	Destroyed on the ground at Murid by Hunter strike (No 20 Sqn)
8 Dec	F-86F	3848	-	No. 15 Sqn	Air raid	Destroyed on the ground at Murid by Hunter strike (No 20 Sqn)
8 Dec	F-86F	3851	-	No. 15 Sqn	Air raid	Destroyed on the ground at Murid by Hunter strike (No 20 Sqn)
8 Dec	F-86F	4018	-	No. 15 Sqn	Air raid	Destroyed on the ground at Murid by Hunter strike (No 20 Sqn)
8 Dec	F-6	1508	F/L Afzal J Siddiqui	No. 23 Sqn	Combat accident	Shot down by own flight leader, Khalsapur area, pilot KIA
8 Dec	F-86F	4019	F/L Fazal Elahi	No 26 Sqn	Ground fire	Shot down by AAA, Chamb area, pilot KIA
10 Dec	F-86F	3856	S/L Aslam Choudhry	No 26 Sqn	Air combat	Shot down by S/L R N Bharadwaj while flying Hunter; Chamb area, pilot KIA
12 Dec	F-104A	56-773	W/C M L Middlecoat	No 9 Sqn	Air combat	Shot down by F/L Bharat B Soni while flying MiG-21; Jamnagar area, pilot KIA
12 Dec	F-6	1703	F/L Ejazuddin	No. 23 Sqn	Air combat	Shot down by F/L S S Malhotra while flying Su-7; Risalewala area, pilot EOT
13 Dec	F-86E	1718	F/O N N A Baig	No 19 Sqn	Air combat	Shot down by F/L Farokh J Mehta while flying Hunter; Talhar area, pilot KIA
16 Dec	11 F-86E	-	-	-	captured	captured intact after capitulation of East Pakistan
16 Dec	T-33A	-	-	-	captured	captured intact after capitulation of East Pakistan
16 Dec	RT-33A	-	-	-	captured	captured intact after capitulation of East Pakistan
17 Dec	F-104A	56-787 (ex-RJAF)	F/L Samad Changezi	No 9 Sqn	Air combat	Shot down by F/L Aruna K Datta while flying MiG-21, Naya Chor area, pilot KIA
17 Dec	F-6	4108	F/L Shahid Raza	No 25 Sqn	Ground fire	Shot down by AAA, Shakargarh area, pilot KIA

BIBLIOGRAPHY

Ahmed, Air Commodore Khaleel; *Legend of the Tail Choppers* (Islamabad: The Army Press, 2006)

Ahmed, Lieutenant Col (Retd) Habib; *The Battle of Hussainiwala and Qaiser-i-Hind* (Karachi: Oxford University Press, 2015)

Arif, General K M; *Khaki Shadows* (Karachi: Oxford University Press, 2001)

Azam, Major General Mohammad; Madni, Col Mushtaq; Cheema, Major Aamir Mushtaq; *History of Pakistan Army Aviation 1947-2007* (Islamabad: Army Press, 2008)

Aziz, K K; *The Making of Pakistan* (Lahore: Sang-e-Meel Publications, Lahore, 2005)

Bhutto, Z. A.; *Great Tragedy* (Pakistan People's Party, 1971)

Chopra, P.; *India's Second Liberation* (Cambridge: The MIT Press, 1974)

Cloughley, Brian; *A History of Pakistan Army* (3rd Edition) (Karachi: Oxford University Press, 2006)

Cohen, Stephen Philip; *The Pakistan Army* (Karachi: Oxford University Press, 1992)

Gill, John H; *An Atlas of the 1971 Indo-Pakistan War: The Creation of Bangladesh* (National Defense University, 2003)

Green, William; *The World's Fighting Planes* (London: Macdonald & Co Ltd, 1964)

Greene, Robert; *The 33 Strategies of War* (London: Profile Books, 2006)

Gunston, Bill; *The Encyclopaedia of World Air Power* (London: The Hamlyn Publishing Group, 1980)

Haider, Sajad; *Flight of the Falcon* (Lahore: Vanguard Books (Pvt) Ltd, 2009)

Haroon, Brig (Retd) Asif; *Roots of 1971 Tragedy* (Lahore: Sang-e-Meel Publications, 2005)

Husain, Major General Syed Wajahat; *1947: Before, During, After* (Lahore: Ferozsons (Pvt) Ltd, 2010)

Hussain, Syed Shabbir; Qureshi, Squadron Leader Tariq; *History of the Pakistan Air Force* (Peshawar: Air Headquarters, 1982)

Hussain, Syed Shahid; *What was Once East Pakistan* (Karachi: Oxford University Press, 2010)

Hussaini, S M A; *PAF Over the Years* (RAHQ Peshawar: PAF Book Club, 2002)

Khan, Arshad Sami; *Three President's and an Aide – Life Power and Politics* (New Delhi: Pentagon Press, 2008)

Khan, Lieutenant General Gul Hassan; *Memoirs* (Karachi: Oxford University Press, 1993)

Khan, Mohammad Asghar; *We've Learnt Nothing from History* (Karachi: Oxford University Press, 2005)

Khan, Brig (R) Z A; *The Way it Was* (Karachi: Dynavis (Pvt) Ltd, 1998)

Lal, Air Chief Marshal P C; *My Years with the IAF* (New Delhi: Lancer International, 1981)

Masud, Air Commodore M Z; *The Story of The Pakistan Air Force – A Saga of Courage and Honour* (Islamabad: Shaheen Foundation, 1988)

Milam, William B; *Bangladesh and Pakistan – Flirting with Failure in South Asia* (London: Hurst & Company, 2009)

Mitha, Major General A O; *Unlikely Beginnings* (Karachi: Oxford University Press, 2003)

Nawaz, Shuja; *Crossed Swords* (Karachi: Oxford University Press, 2008)

Niazi, Lieutenant General A A K; *The Betrayal of East Pakistan* (Karachi: Oxford University Press, 1998)

Nordeen Jr, Lon O; *Air Warfare in the Missile Age* (Washington: Smithsonian Institute Press, 1985)

Prasad, S N; *Official History of the 1971 India-Pakistan War*, (Delhi: 1992; released on Internet by 'Times of India' in 2000)

Qadri, Col Azam; Ali, Group Captain Muhammad; *Sentinels in the Sky* (Islamabad: PAF Book Club, Air Headquarters, 2014)

Qureshi, Major General Hakim Arshad; *The 1971 Indo-Pak War: A Soldier's Narrative* (Karachi: Oxford University Press, 2007)

Rafi, Air Commodore Rais A; *PAF Bomber Operations – 1965 & 1971 Wars* (Peshawar: PAF Book Club, Rear Air Headquarters, 2003)

Raja, Major General (R) Khadim Hussain; *A Stranger in My Own Country* (Karachi: Oxford University Press, 2012)

Salik, Siddiq; *Witness to Surrender* (Karachi: Oxford University Press, 1977)

Shah, Mansoor; *The Gold Bird* (Karachi: Oxford University Press, 2002)

Shamim, Air Chief Marshal Anwar; *Cutting Edge PAF* (Lahore: Vanguard Books (Pvt), 2010)

Shaw, Robert L; *Fighter Combat – Tactics and Manoeuvring* (Annapolis: Naval Institute Press, 1985)

Siddiqui, Brig A R; *East Pakistan: The End Game* (Karachi: Oxford University Press, 2004)

Singh, Pushpindar; Rikhye, Ravi; Steinmann, Peter; *Fiza'ya – Pysche of the Pakistan Air Force* (New Delhi: Society for Aerospace Studies, 1991)

Spick, Mike; *Jet Fighter Performance – Korea to Vietnam* (Surrey: Ian Allan Ltd, 1986)

NOTES

Chapter 1

1 "… resolved that it is the considered view of this session of the All-India Muslim League that no constitutional plan would be workable in this country or acceptable to the Muslims unless it is designed on the basic principle, viz that geographically contiguous units are demarcated into regions which would be so constituted, with such territorial adjustments as may be necessary, that the areas in which the Muslims are numerically in majority as in north-western and eastern zones of India, should be grouped to constitute independent states in which the constituent units shall be autonomous and sovereign."

2 William B Milam, *Bangladesh and Pakistan* (London: Hurst & Co, 2009), p. 18.

3 Ibid, p. 21.

4 Siddiq Salik, *Witness to Surrender*, p. 16.

5 Khawaja Nazimuddin was the second Prime Minister of Pakistan; he remained in the chair for 18 months. He belonged to the family of the Nawabs of Dacca, whose ancestral links to Kashmiri merchants date back to the early 18th century. Muhammad Ali Bogra, a Bengali of the Pakistan Muslim League, was the third Prime Minister of Pakistan; he remained in the chair for 28 months. Huseyn Shaheed Suhrawardy, a Bengali of the Awami League, was the fifth Prime Minister of Pakistan; he remained in the chair for just one year.

6 The four provinces, the federally administered tribal areas, and 10 of the 13 princely states of the western wing were merged into a single province of West Pakistan on 30 September 1955, although an official announcement had been made a year earlier. This arrangement, called the One Unit, lasted until it was rescinded by President Yahya Khan on 1 July 1970.

7 The Legal Framework Order was announced by President Yahya on 31 March 1970. It laid down the principles of the future constitution to guarantee the 'inviolability of national integrity' and the 'Islamic character of the Republic'.
8 The name Bangla Desh was originally written as two words, a convention that was discontinued after independence. The two-worded nomenclature is referred to as such because of mention in various books, before the name Bangladesh was adopted.
9 This statement is said to have been secretly recorded on tape by intelligence agents, and was played to President Yahya, as claimed by G W Chaudhry, *Last Days of United Pakistan* (London: Hurst and Company), p. 98. The statement has also been quoted by Salik.
10 *The Pakistan Observer*, Dacca, 10 December 1970.
11 Quote attributed to Vice Admiral Ahsan, Governor of East Pakistan, by Salik, p. 33.
12 Bhutto, *Great Tragedy*, p. 20.
13 'War till victory', *The Dawn*, 16 February 1971.
14 16 commandos were martyred in this action.
15 13 commandos were martyred in this action.
16 The symposium was organised by the Indian Council of World Affairs in New Delhi. Subrahmanyam's speech was reported by *The Hindustan Times*, New Delhi, 1 April 1971.
17 The Indo-Soviet Treaty of Peace, Friendship and Co-operation was signed on 9 August 1971.
18 Chopra, p. 155.
19 D R Manekar, *Pakistan Cut to Size*, Delhi; p. 133.
20 Lieutenant Gen Niazi, *The Betrayal of East Pakistan*, p. 237.
21 Salik, p. 116.
22 Ibid.
23 Col Carl Von Clausewitz, *On War*, p. 195.
24 Haider, *Flight of the Falcon*, p. 21.
25 Husain, p. 243.
26 At the outbreak of war, 23 Mirage III were available, one aircraft having crashed a few months before the war.
27 Twenty-three B-57Bs and two B-57Cs were inducted in 1959-60. Two of the B-57Bs were modified as reconnaissance and ELINT platforms (RB-57B) in 1962; of these, only one remained at the outbreak of the 1971 War.
28 Details of the PAF's inventory of combat aircraft are based on Official War Records.
29 The squadron was deployed to Masroor on 5 December, after completing its task of attacking Amritsar and Faridkot radars.
30 The base is now named Faisal after the late Saudi King.
31 Details of Utilisation Rate are based on an official post-war briefing delivered by the PAF's Director of Operations at the National Defence College, Rawalpindi, in 1972.

Chapter 2

1 Mansoor Shah, *The Gold Bird*.
2 Arshad Sami Khan, *Three President's and an Aide – Life Power and Politics*, (New Delhi: Pentagon Press, 2008).
3 *Official History of the 1971 India-Pakistan War*, p. 256.
4 Wing Commander Muhammad Yunis had the distinction of shooting down an IAF reconnaissance Canberra on a spying mission near Rawalpindi on 10 April 1959 while flying an F-86F; this was the PAF's first kill.
5 From retired Air Commodore J L Bhargava's website: http://marutfans.wordpress.com/2010/11/09/their-story-03-dec-71/
6 *Official History of the 1971 India-Pakistan War*, p. 249.
7 Ibid, p. 415.
8 Ibid, p. 271.
9 *Story of Pakistan Air Force – A Saga of Courage and Honour*, p. 451.
10 *Official History of the 1971 India-Pakistan War*, p. 424.
11 Ibid, p. 426.
12 The B-57 aircrew that flew the missions to Pathankot on the night of 6 December were: Mission at 00:13hrs – Squadron Leader Feroz Khan (P) and Squadron Leader Iftikhar Ghauri (N); Mission at 2317hrs – Squadron Leader Rais Rafi (P) and Flight Lieutenant Wasif Bokhari (N).
13 *The Times of India*, in a report (25 July 2010) on the reconstruction of Bhuj airfield after the major earthquake in Gujarat in 2001, recalls similar repair efforts following the destruction caused by PAF bombing three decades earlier. The newspaper quotes a 60-year old female labourer by the name of Hiru Bhudia of Madhapur village who had participated in the repair work during the war: "The airstrip in Bhuj was completely devastated by Pakistani bombers that dropped 14 napalm (?) bombs on the night of December 8, 1971. The airstrip needed to be reconstructed on a war footing, and for which, officials were not in a position to wait for long. They hurriedly took a decision to get the repair work done by locals. They contacted us and we responded to the crisis in an equally quick manner."
http://articles.timesofindia.indiatimes.com/2010-07-25/rajkot/28319257_1_bhuj-strip-bunkers
14 This fact was disclosed to the author by retired Air Marshal Denzil Keelor, whom he met in Delhi in May 2008, while on a private visit. Keelor stated that he was convalescing at a military hospital in Amritsar following his own ejection from a MiG-21, after he was shot down on the border by Pak Army AAA. On the morning of 6 December 1971, Keelor noted that extraordinary arrangements were being made in an adjacent ward under supervision of security personnel. Shortly afterwards, two injured PAF bomber aircrew were admitted to the ward. One of them died within a few hours, while the other, who was in a coma, survived for a couple of weeks before succumbing to his injuries. Both were buried in Nizam-ud-din Auliya graveyard in Delhi. Keelor disclosed that both had been badly beaten up by the mob which had rushed at them after their parachute landing at Amritsar. It may be mentioned that Squadron Leader Amjad Hussain, who had just become a POW after ejecting from an F-104, was given an opportunity to attend the funeral of one of the aircrew.
15 Squadron Leaders Ishfaq, Khusro and Christy were recently retired officers, recalled for duty from PIA.
16 *Official History of the 1971 India-Pakistan War*, p. 424.
17 PAF intelligence sources have noted the ejection of a certain Flight Lieutenant D R Natu over Amritsar, around the time of the F-104 raid, with suspicion. Indian sources claim that Natu ejected due to AAA damage that had occurred earlier during the mission.
18 *Official History of the 1971 India-Pakistan War*, p. 425.
19 Ibid, p. 426.
20 Ibid, p. 428.
21 Ibid, p. 429.
22 *"Plain Tails from the IAF: The Pathankot Raid of Dec 10,"* by Air Marshal K D K Lewis (Retd). It may be mentioned that the article centres on Lewis taking exception to the portrayal of Hunters being destroyed in a painting of the Pathankot raid by the PAF's official painter, S M A Hussaini.
23 *Official History of the 1971 India-Pakistan War*, p. 432.
24 Wing Commander Mervyn Middlecoat was shot down by Flight Lieutenant Bharat Bhushan Soni of No 47 Squadron.
25 The Gnat leader was briefly observed by Changazi at a higher altitude than the rest, and flying reciprocal to the direction of the engaged fighters. He was not seen again by anyone.
26 Contrary to the IAF's citation for Sekhon's award, none of the Sabres was hit during the dogfight.

Chapter 3

1 The pilot of this Su-7 was the OC of No 222 Squadron, Wing Commander Allan Albert da Costa.
2 A warhead's proximity detonation, unlike a direct hit, may not cause an explosion every time.
3 It was advisable (though not prohibited) to fire the centre gun and side guns separately, to prevent rattle and vibrations which could loosen or dislodge electrical connectors of radios, etc.
4 The semi-active radar-guided Matra-530 missile was rarely carried due to its bulk, as well as firing limitations.
5 The Canberra's 'Orange Putter' tail warning radar, an active transmitting device, was prone to picking up ground clutter, and was usually turned off by the pilots to avoid false alarms at lower altitudes. It is likely that Sasoon had also kept it off.
6 The pilot belonged to the Tactics & Air Combat Development Establishment based at Ambala.
7 Wreckage of Afzal's F-6 revealed Sidewinder warhead shrapnel embedded in the exhaust area, which quashed speculation that the F-6 may have flown through Kadam's exploding Su-7.
8 *Official History of the 1971 India-Pakistan War*, p. 427.
9 The IAF used Very High Frequency (VHF) while the PAF used Ultra High Frequency (UHF) for radio communications.
10 The IAF MiG-21s were usually configured with two K-13 missiles and a centreline drop tank each, the latter replacing the 23mm belly gun pack.
11 Flying Officers M Arshad Choudhry and Salim Baig were Tejwant's course-mates at Nellis AFB, USA. In a twist of fate, Baig was there to cheer up Tejwant when the latter was in custody as a POW in Rawalpindi. Maqsood Amir also briefly met his victim during the latter's transit to the POW camp.
12 The book's cover painting by Hussaini depicts this dogfight.
13 This attack was led by Lieutenant Arun Prakash (an IN pilot on deputation to the IAF), with Flying Officer B C Karumbaya as his wingman.
14 This attack was led by Squadron Leader R N Bharadwaj, with Flight Lieutenant Gahlaut as his wingman.

15 This attack was led by Squadron Leader A A D'Rozario, with Flying Officer S Balasubramaniam as his wingman. Two other formation members missed the target and exited.
16 This attack was led by Squadron Leader R N Bharadwaj; other formation members included Flight Lieutenant A L Deoskar, Flying Officer B C Karumbaya and Flying Officer Heble.
17 The aircrew of the downed Canberra included Flight Lieutenant S K Goswami (pilot) and Flight Lieutenant S C Mahajan (navigator) of Agra-based No 5 Squadron.
18 This attack was led by Squadron Leader V K Bhatia; other formation members included Flight Lieutenant A V Sathaye, Flight Lieutenant V V Tambay and Flight Lieutenant M S Grewal.
19 Tactics and Air Combat Development Establishment.
20 https://www.bharat-rakshak.com/IAF/history/1971war/1318-bhojwani-moss.html
21 This attack was led by Wing Commander C V Parker; other formation members included Squadron Leader K N Bajpai and Flying Officer De Monte.

Chapter 4

1 The F-104A supplied to the PAF and RJAF could carry either Sidewinder missiles or drop tanks on the wingtips. If both types of stores had to be carried, the drop tanks had to go under the wings with a threefold increase in drag. After the 1965 War, the PAF modified its F-104s to carry missiles on underwing pylons instead, so that the wingtips were available for carriage of drop tanks in the lower drag configuration. Considerable operational benefit was, thus, accrued as far as combat range and endurance were concerned. As the RJAF F-104s did not have provision for such a configuration, it was decided to use these aircraft for night air defence without missiles (i.e. gun only), with the drop tanks on the wingtips. The rationale posited that with the limited effort available, staying in the air for a longer duration was a better pay-off in terms of deterrence, rather than carrying out futile night interceptions in the absence of an effective low level GCI radar or a worthwhile AI radar.
2 The headquarters, which was earlier located at Badin, was moved to Korangi at the outbreak of war.
3 This radar was retrieved from Kurmitola near Dacca in October 1971, leaving East Pakistan with no high level radar cover.
4 The locations of all radars are believed to have been compromised by defecting Bengali personnel, long before the war started.
5 The F-86E was shot down by Flight Lieutenant Farokh Jahangir Mehta of the Jamnagar-based Hunter OCU.
6 It so happened that Bhatti's pair of RJAF F-104s, which had deployed at Drigh Road as a back-up to Masroor, was to return to its parent base as the war in the East had come to an abrupt end. Just before ferrying the aircraft back, the pair were asked to fly an ill-conceived 'show of presence' CAP between Mirpurkhas and Naya Chor without missiles, in a gun-only configuration. That is how an improperly armed pair ended up in a close dogfight that was not quite the F-104's forte.
7 The downed aircraft was RJAF F-104 serial number 56-787.
8 This raid was led by Wing Commander Donald Conquest, OC of the Hunter OCU at Jamnagar; Squadron Leader Farokh Mehta and Squadron Leader D H Nagi were the other formation members.
9 While other aircraft could operate from the undamaged portion, the fully laden B-57s needed a much longer runway for take-off.
10 The RB-57B was one of two standard B-57Bs specially modified in USA. These had a pair of 40" focal length cameras fitted in the bomb bay for oblique optical photography, in addition to a useful ELINT capability. One of the aircraft was lost in the 1965 War to friendly AAA. The RB-57B designation was unique to the PAF.
11 The raid was led by Wing Commander Donald Conquest.
12 Mr M Niaz, who was the Sales Development Engineer of ESSO in 1971, led the team that put out the fires. He states that out of the five tanks that were destroyed, three belonging to Dawood Petroleum Ltd contained gasoline fuel, one belonging to ESSO contained light diesel oil, and one belonging to Pakistan Refinery Ltd contained crude oil. A subsequent hit by a Styx missile fired by an IN Osa missile boat on the night of 8/9 December, destroyed one more tank containing crude oil.
13 This raid was led by Squadron Leader Tully of a Jaisalmer-based detachment of the Hunter OCU; other formation members were Squadron Leader Jasbir Singh, Flight Lieutenant Mukerjee and Flight Lieutenant Deepak Yadav.
14 AAA shot down a Canberra at Masroor, a MiG-21 at Badin and three HF-24s near Naya Chor and Hyderabad.

Chapter 5

1 *Official History of the 1971 India-Pakistan War*, p. 329.
2 Official PAF War Records.
3 Indian *Official History of the 1971 India-Pakistan War*, p. 357.
4 Ibid, p. 359.
5 Group Captain Sajad Haider, who was flying as an escort to Cecil's formation, recollects in his book *Flight of the Falcon*, (pp. 252-253) that he told Cecil to fly lower than 200 feet to avoid AAA fire. According to Haider, Cecil responded by explaining that he was not flying as low as instructed due to intense bird activity. Moments later Cecil called out that he had been hit by a bird and was ejecting.
6 More precisely, of the total 298 air support sorties, 289 were flown in Shakargarh Sector proper, while nine sorties were flown in the Marala area.
7 Official PAF War Records.
8 Territory lost in Shakargarh Salient was spread over a frontage of approximately 33 miles, with an average ingress of 7-8 miles.
9 17 Division's 66 Brigade was detached to 23 Division (Chamb Sector) while 88 Brigade was detached to 10 Division (Lahore Sector). The Divisional Artillery was detached to HQ 23 Division.
10 'Tank Busting in the Hunter', Air Commodore Narendra Gupta, *Take off* magazine, Issue 103.
11 The late Brig Zahir Alam, who commanded 38 Cavalry Regiment during the operation, confirms the loss of 20 tanks, all to air action. He gives a blow-by-blow account of the fiasco in his book *The Way it Was*, Dynavis (Pvt) Ltd, Karachi, 1998.
12 *Official History of the 1971 India-Pakistan War*, p. 395.
13 Ibid, p. 406.
14 Ibid, p. 427.
15 Of the total 175 sorties, 158 were flown in Chor Sector, 13 were flown in Ramgarh Sector and four sorties in Kutch Sector. Official PAF War Records.
16 *Official History of the 1971 India-Pakistan War*, p. 400.
17 *The Story of Pakistan Air Force – A Saga of Courage and Honour*, p. 464.
18 'Foxtrot Sector' was a large four-brigade sized division.
19 *Official History of the 1971 India-Pakistan War*, p. 386.
20 Indian counterattacks were launched on the nights of 3/4 December, 4/5 December, 5/6 December, 8/9 December and 13/14 December.
21 *Official History of the 1971 India-Pakistan War*, p. 387.
22 Brig Surjit Singh Chaudhry was replaced by Brig G S Reen who was, in turn, replaced by Brig Piara Singh.

Chapter 6

1 Space and Upper Atmospheric Research Committee.
2 Long ranges are possible under conditions of anomalous propagation of radio waves that is particularly prevalent in winter months in the Arabian Sea.
3 The one nearer to Karachi was the group of three missile boats, and the further one was the pair of frigates.
4 Contrary to some writings that PNS *Khaibar* was caught unawares, the *Official History of the 1971 India-Pakistan War* confirms that the first target that INS *Nirghat* engaged had been "zigzagging, revealing hostile intentions," before heading towards the task force. "This ship continued coming towards the task force and was quickly reducing distance." (p. 472.)
5 These additional aircraft included: one F-27 and two DHC-6 Twin Otters (PIA), a Cessna 310 (Governor Punjab), a DHC-2 Beaver (Dept of Plant Protection), two Cessna 150s (Karachi Aero Club), and an Aero Commander (PAF).
6 *Official History of the 1971 India-Pakistan War*, p. 474.
7 This was the group of vessels that was picked up by Flight Lieutenant Shabbir A Khan and Squadron Leader Ansar Ahmad on their B-57 radar while proceeding to attack Okha.
8 Only one tank containing crude oil caught fire during the attack on the night of 8/9 Dec.
9 *The New York Times* correspondent Henry Kamm reported in his despatch of 11 December that the wife and child of the Greek captain of *Gulf Star* were killed in the attack. He also reported that seven seamen were killed in the attack on *Harmatton*.
10 The PIA crew included Captain Mubashir Hameed, First Officer Syed Khalid Javed and Navigator B D Cheema. The PN observer on board was Lieutenant Commander A I Nagi. The loss of the F-27 was recorded by CAA and PIA as 'missing on flight from Karachi to Zahedan, Iran.'
11 The *Official History of the 1971 India-Pakistan War* confirms these three occasions:

"From evening of 3 Dec till 0200 hours on 4 Dec, the Main Fleet was shadowed by three maritime aircraft."

"On 6 Dec, several enemy aircraft were shadowing additional vessels (Saurashtra Group) that were to join the Main Fleet south west of Karachi. As a consequence, the group had to turn back without joining the Main Fleet."

"At 2040 hours on 8 Dec, two slow flying aircraft shadowed the Makran Group (INS *Mysore*, flagship of the Western Fleet)."

The number of aircraft reported to be shadowing the ships far exceeds their availability with Pak Navy, and the author is inclined to believe that some of these aircraft may have belonged to foreign forces, which may have entered the fray to keep a tab on what was going on.

12 *The Story of the Pakistan Air* Force, p. 466.

13 The aircraft belonged to Bombay-based No 310 Squadron of the Indian Navy. The crew included pilot Lieutenant Commander Ashok Roy and observers Lieutenant H S Sirohi and Aircraftman Vijayan, none of whom survived.

14 A B-57 strike on Bombay harbour, staged through Talhar, was planned but cancelled at the last moment later during the war. Wing Commander Mahmood Akhtar, the B-57 detachment commander at Masroor was to fly the mission. Some B-57s had been modified to carry four F-86 drop tanks under the wings to be able to fly a low level profile. Two similar long-range strikes had been flown earlier by Mianwali-based B-57s when they staged-through Rafiqui (Shorkot) to attack distant Agra.

Chapter 7

1 The IAF had deployed four Hunter squadrons, three each of MiG-21s and Gnats, and one each of Su-7s and Canberras.

2 *Saga of PAF in East Pakistan* by Air Marshal Inam-ul-Haque Khan, 'Defence Journal,' May 2009.

3 Ganapathy shot down Khalil and Lazarus shot down Mehdi.

4 Squadron Leader Brij Pal Singh Sikand, then a Flight Commander in the 1965 War, was able to redeem some honour in 1971, and eventually managed to rise to the rank of an Air Marshal.

5 Interview with author.

6 Ibid.

7 The first Hunter formation, with a TOT of 0735hrs, belonged to No 37 Squadron, and was led by its Squadron Commander, Wing Commander S P Kaul, with Flying Officer Harish Masand and Flight Lieutenant S K Sangar as his wingmen. This formation was escorted by two MiG-21s led by Wing Commander C V Gole of No 4 Squadron based at Gauhati. Closely in tow was the second Hunter formation belonging to No 17 Squadron, which included Squadron Leader Lele and Flying Officer Bains. The third formation of four MiG-21s, with a TOT of 0740 hours, belonged to No 28 Squadron, and was led by Wing Commander B K Bishnoi; it had two additional MiG-21s as escorts flown by Flight Lieutenant Manbir Singh and Flight Lieutenant D M Subiya. It was Subiya who kept Afzaal busy while the MiG-21 strike went through the attack on the airfield. (This information has been culled from the articles, *"Air Battle over Dacca"* by Polly Singh, and *"Thunder Over Dacca – No 28 Squadron in December 1971"* by Air Vice Marshal B K Bishnoi.)

8 Air Marshal Inam-ul-Haque mentions that an Army Subedar saw Ahmed ejecting out and landing safely; he then saw Ahmed being mobbed by locals and *Mukti Bahini*, who led him away.

9 Half an hour earlier, Flight Lieutenant Schames-ul-Haq and Flying Officer Mahmood Gul had been able to intercept two Su-7s attacking the airfield but could not shoot them down as the Su-7s accelerated away with afterburners blazing.

10 Limited by the number of wing stations (a total of four), the Su-7 could not carry air-to-air missiles, and the twin 30mm cannon were its only integral armament.

11 This account is largely based on an article titled, *"An Unmatched Feat in the Air"* by Flying Officer Shams-ul-Haq, which was published in the PAF's official 'Shaheen' magazine in 1972.

12 The fatal loss of two Hunter pilots of No 37 Squadron, Squadron Leader A R Samanta and Flying Officer S G Khonde over Dacca on 4 December is attributed to AAA hits in IAF citations. As per the PAF's standing instructions, the AAA guns held fire whenever a dogfight was in progress overhead, and this was doubly ensured by Killer Control. In this case too, there is no evidence to the contrary, and it is certain that one of the two pilots fell to Schames' guns. Samanta is the more likely victim as his mission time is closer to that of Schames' mission.

13 These two missions were successively led by Flight Lieutenant Ata-ur-Rahman and Squadron Leader Javed Afzaal.

14 *Thunder over Dacca*, by Air Vice Marshal B K Bishnoi, Vayu Aerospace, 1/1997.

15 One of the Twin Otters (registration AP-AWH) had been destroyed by a Su-7 in a strafing attack on 4 December, while the other one (registration AP-AWF) was flown out to Akyab the same night, with some PIA staff and a few families on board.

16 The Mi-8 helicopters were flown by new Pak Army crew to Bangkok, from where these were shipped to Karachi; the Beavers and the Twin Otter were flown to China for onward shipment to Karachi; the Alouette IIIs were airlifted by C-130 from Burma.

17 This figure is quoted by Lieutenant Gen Niazi in his book, *The Betrayal of East Pakistan*, p. 237.

Chapter 8

1 Until 1989, Anti-Aircraft Artillery was part of the artillery arm of the Pak Army.

2 The Taj Mahal is located three miles north-east of Agra runway.

3 A total of 258 rockets of the 2.75" FFAR variety were fired by the F-86s in various battle sectors. Since each LAU-32 rocket launcher had a capacity of seven rockets, it is reckoned that at least 18 sorties were flown with this weapon. Besides this, a total of 152 SNEB 68mm rockets were also fired by F-86s; up to 18 of these rockets could be carried in each SNEB-155 rocket launcher, which would work out to only four sorties with full load, though fewer rockets may have been actually carried per sortie.

4 A total of 188 S-5 57mm rockets were fired by the F-6s, all in Shakargarh Sector; since each ORO-57K rocket launcher had a capacity of eight rockets, at least 12 sorties are likely to have been flown with these rockets.

5 In other words, PAF shot down 18 IAF aircraft in air combat, against the loss of ten aircraft.

6 Utilisation rate = number of sorties/75 percent of available aircraft/number of days of war.

7 The table does not include T-6Gs and C-130s.

8 Includes 44 sorties flown in East Pakistan from 22 November until 6 December 1971.

9 Utilisation Rate is valid only for eight PAF F-104As: ten additional F-104As became available from 14 December onwards, but were flown sparingly.

10 The author of the *Official History of the 1971 India-Pakistan War* eventually brought himself to extend this compliment of sorts to the PAF in the concluding analysis, p. 449.

11 Note that these figures do not include aircraft captured on the ground in Dacca.

12 Mitha, p. 323.

13 Salik, p. 128.

14 Z.A. Khan, p. 326.

15 Ibid, p. 274.

16 Husain, p. 244.

17 Z.A. Khan, p. 328.

18 Husain, p. 244.

ACKNOWLEDGEMENTS AND INTERVIEWS

The author would like to extend his expressions of gratitude to the following veterans of the PAF, Pakistan Army and Pakistan Navy, who provided their recollections of the war, either through personal interviews, or in the form of electronic communication:

Air Chief Marshal M Anwar Shamim (Late)
Air Chief Marshal Jamal A Khan
Air Chief Marshal M Abbas Khattak
Air Marshal Zafar A Chaudhry (Late)
Air Marshal Inam-ul-Haque Khan (Late)
Air Marshal Sharbat Ali Changazi
Air Marshal Dilawar Hussain
Air Marshal Qazi Javed
Lieutenant General Israr Ghumman
Vice Admiral Asif Humayun
Air Vice Marshal Mian Sadruddin
Air Vice Marshal Mahmood Akhtar (Late)
Air Vice Marshal Ata-ur-Rahman
Rear Admiral M A K Lodhi
Major General Qasim Qureshi.
Air Commodore S Sajad Haider
Air Commodore Farooq Haider Khan
Air Commodore Rashid A Bhatti (Late)
Air Commodore Safdar Mahmood
Air Commodore Mahmood Gul
Group Captain Ali Imam Bukhari (Late)
Group Captain Maqsood Amir
Group Captain Naeem Atta
Wing Commander Salim Baig Mirza
Wing Commander Javed Afzaal
Wing Commander Javed Latif
Squadron Leader Tariq Qureshi
Flight Lieutenant Atiq Sufi (Late)
Flight Lieutenant Abdul Wahab (Late)
Flight Lieutenant Salman Rasheedi

ABOUT THE AUTHOR

Kaiser Tufail

Air Commodore Kaiser Tufail (retired) was commissioned in the Pakistan Air Force as a pilot in 1975. He went on to fly a variety of fighters including the quirky MiGs, the sleek Mirages and the much admired F-16s.

He held command of a fighter squadron, a wing and an air base. A graduate of the Air War College and the National Defence University, he earned his Master's degrees in Strategic Studies and War Studies. He retired in 2005, and since then has settled in Lahore.

He has been writing articles on defence matters in various local and international magazines. He has a special interest in military aviation, and Indo-Pak Wars. He is the author of a book, *Great Air Battles of Pakistan Air Force*, and this is his first book for Helion & Co.